Jorge Luis Borges: Conversa

Literary Conversation Series

Peggy Whitman Prenshaw
General Editor

Photo credit: Courtesy of Archive Photos

Jorge Luis Borges: Conversations

Edited by
Richard Burgin

University Press of Mississippi
Jackson

Books in English by Jorge Luis Borges

Ficciones. New York: Grove Press, 1962.
Labyrinths: Selected Stories and Other Writings. New York: New Directions, 1962.
Other Inquisitions 1937–52. Austin: University of Texas Press, 1964.
Dreamtigers. Austin: University of Texas Press, 1964.
A Personal Anthology. New York: Grove Press, 1967.
The Book of Imaginary Beings. With Margarita Guerrero. New York: Dutton, 1969.
The Aleph and Other Stories 1933–1969. New York: Dutton, 1970.
Doctor Brodie's Report. New York: Dutton, 1971.
An Introduction to American Literature. Lexington: University Press of Kentucky, 1971.
Extraordinary Tales. With A. Bioy Casares. New York: Herder and Herder, 1971.
A Universal History of Infamy. New York: Dutton, 1972.
Selected Poems 1923–1967. Boston: Delacorte Press/ A Seymour Lawrence Book, 1972.
In Praise of Darkness. New York: Dutton, 1974.
Chronicles of Bustos Domecq. With A. Bioy Casares. New York: Dutton, 1976.
The Book of Sand. New York: Dutton, 1977.
The Gold of the Tigers: Selected Later Poems. New York: Dutton, 1977.
Six Problems for Don Isidro Parodi. With A. Bioy Casares. New York: Dutton, 1981.
Borges: A Reader. New York: Dutton, 1981.
Evaristo Carriego. New York: Dutton, 1984.
Seven Nights. New York: New Directions, 1984.
Atlas. With Mariá Kodama. New York: Viking, 1986.

Copyright © 1998 by University Press of Mississippi
All rights reserved
Manufactured in the United States of America

01 00 99 98   4 3 2 1

The paper in this book meets the guidelines for permanence and durability of the Committee on Production Guidelines for Book Longevity of the Council on Library Resources.

Library of Congress Cataloging-in-Publication Data

Borges, Jorge Luis, 1899–
    Jorge Luis Borges : conversations / edited by Richard Burgin.
        p.   cm.—(Literary conversations series)
    Includes index.
    ISBN 1-57806-075-3 (cloth : alk. paper).—ISBN 1-57806-076-1
(pbk. : alk. paper)
    1. Borges, Jorge Luis. 1899– —Interviews.   2. Authors.
Argentine—20th century—Interviews.   I. Burgin, Richard.
II. Title.   III. Series.
PQ7797.B635Z472   1998
868—dc21
[B]   98-36711
                                                                CIP

British Library Cataloging-in-Publication Data available

Contents

v

Introduction

When Jorge Luis Borges first became known in the United States he was often described as a ghost-like character, albeit one of forbidding intelligence, a man so consumed by books that he somehow lacked normal human desires and personality traits. It was as if his commentators took Borges's literary themes of the fictive nature of identity and the dreamlike quality of existence and ascribed them to Borges himself. In the afterword to Borges's *Personal Anthology* (1970), for instance, there's an amusing exchange of letters between Borges's translators in which they openly (and perhaps only half-jokingly) speculate about whether there really is a single, actual "Jorge Luis Borges," writing of him somewhat as Borges wrote of Shakespeare in his famous parable, "Everyone and No One."

These speculations about Borges were not so unusual at the time and remind us just how powerfully convincing the Borgesian vision initially was for his mesmerized readers. But the people who first interviewed Jorge Luis Borges knew better. They met a very real man who was warm and candid, a modest old-world gentleman with an impish sense of humor: in short, a distinct personality with strong, often unfashionable convictions.

That his point of view was fixed and often passionate should not be surprising because by the time Borges began to be widely interviewed in English he was already in his sixties and a fully formed person. Indeed, the interviews in this anthology demonstrate that his views and attitudes remained remarkably consistent for the last twenty years of his life (1966–1986). Repeatedly Borges expresses his love of English and North American literature in general, and in particular for the writers Stevenson, Kipling, Shaw, Welles, Conrad, Chesterton, De Quincey, Poe, Emerson, Twain, Whitman, and Frost. Repeatedly Borges also emphasizes his love of clarity in writing, his preference for stories over novels, his strong aversion to overly analytical literary criticism, to Communism, Perón and anti-Semitism. There are also his beliefs that the differences among the story, poem, and essay are trivial, that enjoyment is the paramount purpose of literature, that he disbelieves in an afterlife, welcomes death and fears immortality, that time is the central philosophical problem, that the influence of his childhood reading in his father's library was primal, as is his enduring love for his family and for the friends of his youth and, in spite of his quarrels with it, for his country.

The picture that emerges is of a complicated but fully convincing human being, yet we can also understand the disbelieving awe of his early readers simply because Borges is such an imposing artistic and intellectual force. By acclamation Jorge Luis Borges is one of the century's seminal writers, but he is also more than that. He's a major innovator who has expanded forever the possibilities of both the story and the essay, and, though he would deny it, he's a thinker too (if not a philosopher with a capital P) who's introduced new themes into modern literature, such as the notion of infinity, and thereby altered the way his readers regard reality itself. No wonder people used to question his existence; Borges isn't, finally, a normal man, but he's not a demigod or ghost-like spirit either. I think the word genius is applicable, however, a gentle genius.

But if Borges is a genius with a consistent vision, that vision is also sufficiently rich that different interviewers at different times and occasions inevitably reveal new parts of it. Thus in Borges's 1966 interview with noted fiction writer Richard Stern (which appears here), Stern understandably asks about Borges's aesthetics of fiction, and Borges goes into unusual detail in answering him, expressing his desire to write more simple stories, "rather after the manner of Kipling's *Plain Tales from the Hills.*" In my own interviews with Borges, conducted during 1967 and '68 while I was a senior at Brandeis University and eventually published as *Conversations with Jorge Luis Borges* (the first book-length interview with Borges in English), I concentrate primarily on discussing the meanings and techniques he employed in his prose and poetry. The excerpt reprinted here focuses on his major stories, and Borges discusses them more closely than in any other interview in this collection simply because I asked him. Throughout this anthology, Borges rarely evades a question and virtually never refuses to answer one.

The interviews gathered here also belie the notion of Borges as exclusively an ivory tower dreamer. That was certainly a part of him, but he was also a cosmopolitan man who traveled extensively, spoke several languages fluently, was open and gregarious with people, and was keenly aware of the political and social situation of his country (though he repeatedly asserts that a writer shouldn't be judged by his political opinions). Consequently, the political and social events of the time sometimes directly influence the content of these conversations. In "Borges at NYU" edited by the Borges critic and scholar Ronald Christ (a colloquium reprinted from *TriQuarterly,* 1971), there are some pointed political questions posed by student radicals about Borges's moderate politics and lack of commitment to various leftist political causes. Oddly, this discussion also reveals an almost clownish side of Borges's humor as well as his prowess as a stand-up comedian as he rips off a series of fine one-liners. Besides reflecting the political preoccupations of the time, this discussion is notable for its extraordinary diversity of emotion. Similarly, Rita Guibert's fine, wide-ranging interview, conducted in 1968 but published in 1973, also reflects those frenetic times, as Borges is asked and talks at some length about hippies and drugs, conformism, materialism, and violence in American society. It was a measure of Borges's appeal, perhaps, that in the '60s and early '70s, a time marked by seemingly irreconcilable social conflicts, Borges was adopted by psychedelic experimenters and university professors alike.

Some of Borges's questioners knew him considerably better as a person than others. Seldon Rodman, for example, spent a good deal of time with Borges in his home city of Buenos Aires. The result is an exceptionally intimate narrative (with a generous amount of direct quotations from Borges) which gives us a good sense of Borges's everyday life. In Rodman's interviews (conducted over a three year period, 1969–72) we're given a description of Borges's apartment and his office at the National Library. We meet Borges's maid, some of his friends and collaborators, including his main translator, Norman Thomas Di Giovanni, who had moved to Buenos Aires at the time to work in direct collaboration with Borges. We also meet Borges's wife and then, two years later, learn of his reaction to his divorce from her in this excerpt:

> When I returned to Buenos Aires two years later, Borges hadn't changed but the circumstances of his life had. He was back with his mother, and he was not contesting his wife's demands for exorbitant alimony. I asked Di Giovanni why.
>
> "He's been living in constant fear that he *won't* have to pay alimony! He feels guilty as hell. He thinks he alone is responsible for the failure of the marriage and should pay for it. Also, don't forget that while Borges is kind, generous, humble, imaginative and noble, courage isn't part of his character. When his wife cursed him loudly at the airport once, with people all around listening in, he just stood there next to me with head bowed taking it without a word of rejoinder."

Like Rodman, Willis Barnstone (a Borges translator, in addition to being a poet and prolific author) had more than a professional relationship with

Borges. His interviews also show an unusually personal side of Borges. In
"With Borges in Buenos Aires" (originally published in *Denver Quarterly*,
1980), we follow Borges through a typical working day as he delivers a poem
to his newspaper editor's office at *La Nación.* "People came up to Borges
frequently and shook his hand. Borges said he hired all these pedestrians to
do this. . . . A man came up to us and rhetorically addressed Borges, seizing
his hand and shaking it furiously. 'Borges, you are immortal.'
    'Don't be a pessimist, sir,' Borges gently replied." The piece ends as
Borges boards a plane to America to begin a five-day lecture tour.
    In Barnstone's other interview published in this collection, "Thirteen
Questions: A Dialogue with Jorge Luis Borges" (*Chicago Review,* 1980),
Barnstone achieves a different kind of intimacy as he probes Borges about
the nature of consciousness, dreaming, death, and suicide. It is at once a
vaguely psychedelic, yet powerful record of Borges's metaphysics. Barnstone
is also responsible for translating a delightfully informal colloquium with
Borges at Indiana University in 1976 (originally published in *Boulevard* magazine, 1998) in which Borges answers questions from the panel of professors
present, as well as from the audience, on a variety of topics. Among other
things, Borges discusses the different impulses he feels in writing stories as
opposed to essays, his inability to create characters, the ethical function of
literature, how his identity has shifted in time ("I was unhappy during my
adolescence, but the truth is that I wanted to be unhappy."), and his attitude
toward God: "God is something we are always creating."
    Alastair Reid and Donald Yates are two other interlocutors in this volume
who had more than a professional interviewing relationship with Borges.
Reid, an eminent poet and man of letters, is one of Borges's translators. He
introduces Borges as a featured speaker in conjunction with the forum "Franz
Kafka and Modern World Literature: A Centennial Perspective" at the Modern Language Association in New York (1983). After Borges's relatively brief
opening statement, Reid serves as the main questioner as well as the moderator for questions from the audience. The forum is notable not only for Borges's insights into Kafka, whom he acknowledges to be a direct influence on
two of his stories, but also for what it shows us about a trait of Borges's
psychology one might call "people pleasing," for one can hardly help observing how Borges escalates his praise of Kafka as the proceedings go on,
seemingly to please the audience of Kafka devotees.
    There are two contributions from the Borges biographer Donald Yates in
this volume. "A Colloquy with Jorge Luis Borges" (held at the University of

Michigan in 1976) is noteworthy for Borges's observations on the form of
the novel and why he never wrote one, on Borges's insights into De Quincey
and Stevenson, and on the differences between Spanish and English. Yates's
"Simply a Man of Letters" is a reprint of a panel discussion held at a symposium on Borges at the University of Maine in 1982. Yates is the moderator
and principal interviewer. The discussion provides some important insights
into the conflict of Borges's public and private selves that he dramatized in
his celebrated parable "Borges and I." In response to Yates's question about
the parable, Borges says: "As for two Borges, I have been made keenly aware
that there are two, because when I think of myself, I think, let us say, of a
rather secret, a rather hesitant, groping man. Somehow, this can hardly be
reconciled to the fact that I seem to be giving lectures all the time and traveling all over the world."

While other interviewers in this anthology may not offer the types of inti-
macies that often emerge when the interviewer knows Borges well, they offer
instead the pleasures of a certain distance. L. S. Dembo's interview, first
published in *Contemporary Literature* (1970), features an arresting discussion on the limits of man's knowledge, the labyrinth as an image of perplexity, as well as the influence of dreams on Borges's work. In the interview
originally published in *Commonweal* (1968) Borges is questioned by Patricia
Marx, then a weekly interviewer for WNYC, and by the esteemed drama and
literary critic John Simon. The piece sparkles with intellectual energy, as
Borges comments on the difference between the real and fantastic, his personal religion, and the absence of sex in his work: "I suppose the reason is
that I think too much about it."

The last three interviews in this book were conducted when Borges was
over 80, but his candor and intellectual vigor are still completely intact. The
occasion for the interview by Jon Biguenet and Tom Whalen, editors of *The
New Orleans Review,* was Borges's 1982 trip to New Orleans, one of his
favorite cities, where he received various civic and academic honors. The
piece reveals Borges's deep modesty as he reflects on the influence of age,
loneliness, and blindness on his writing. There's a somewhat sad tone to the
interview, but it's relieved at times by Borges's characteristic humor. When
the inevitable question of identity arises and the editors ask him, "Which
Borges are we talking to?" he replies, "Well, you pays your money and you
takes your chances."

Clark M. Zlotchew traveled to Buenos Aires for this 1984 interview, originally published in *American Poetry Review,* that investigates a multiplicity of

topics such as Borges's writing habits and methods, his memory of seeing a man killed, the movie made of his life and another made of the story "The Intruder," his Jewish origin, Chess vs. Truco, and a clear-eyed description of the social ills of the Argentine.

Finally, there is Amelia Barili's interview "Borges on Life and Death." Barili, then the book review editor of the Buenos Aires newspaper *La Prensa,* befriended Borges (and began interviewing him) in 1981. Her last interview took place in November 1985, seven months before Borges died, and was published on the front page of *The New York Times Book Review* a month after Borges's death. The piece contains a sometimes searingly beautiful series of reflections by Borges on the Bible, the Kabalah, space, time, God, death, and immortality and makes a fitting conclusion to this volume.

Though Borges was deeply skeptical about chronological time, the pieces in this book (in keeping with the University Press of Mississippi Series) are presented in chronological order, uncut and edited only where there is a typographical or other obvious error. *Jorge Luis Borges: Conversations* is meant to have a mix of informality and lively scholarship. Reading it over in its entirety, I find several themes that emerge and reemerge with variations like themes in a piece of music. Is there a single overarching one? Perhaps the following quotation from Borges himself provides the answer: "Through the years a man peoples a space with images of provinces, kingdoms, mountains, bays, ships, islands, fishes, rooms, tools, stars, horses and people. Shortly before his death, he discovers that the patient labyrinth of lines traces the image of his own face."

I wish to thank Rebekah Grossman for her extraordinarily valuable research and Jeremy Countryman for his greatly appreciated assistance in a variety of areas. Willis Barnstone and Clark Zlotchew were generous in helping me locate some of the interviewers and in providing materials, as was Dan Shapiro of the Américas Society, and I owe much gratitude to Julia Hanna of Washington University for her help as well. I need to thank the distinguished Borges biographer Emir Rodriguez Monengal and Clark M. Zlotchew, as I relied heavily on their material in compiling my chronology for this book. Finally, I am grateful also to my wise and patient editor Seetha A-Srinivasan, and to my young beloved son Ricky, who inspires everything good that I attempt to do. I trust, to paraphrase Borges once again, that the most important names on this list have not been omitted.

Chronology

1899   Jorge Francisco Isidoro Luis Borges is born on August 24th to Jorge Guillermo Borges and Leonor Acevedo Suárez in Buenos Aires. His father is a lawyer, a psychology teacher, and sometime writer, with poor eyesight which Borges inherits. From his father's side he has mixed English and Portuguese blood, from his mother's close relatives in Uruguay. Borges's younger sister Norah is born in 1902. He is close with her, and she becomes a well-regarded painter. (A younger brother of Borges dies in infancy.) From his earliest recollections of childhood Borges is afraid of mirrors and carnival masks and loves tigers and the books in his father's library.

1906   Encouraged by his father to be a writer, Borges writes a composition on Greek mythology in English and "La Visera Fatal" in Spanish, a story which he borrows from *Don Quixote.*

1908   Borges translates Oscar Wilde's *The Happy Prince* into Spanish.

1912   Borges publishes his first short story, "King of the Jungle."

1914   Prior to the outbreak of World War I, Borges's father retires due to failing eyesight and the family moves to Europe. They visit London, Paris, and northern Italy before arriving in Geneva. The outbreak of war makes them stay there for four years. Already fluent in Spanish and English, Borges studies French and Latin at his Swiss school. He also studies German on his own, first by reading Heine, and eventually reads Nietzsche and Schopenhauer. In French, he reads Hugo and many of the French Symbolists. He continues reading English authors such as Carlyle and Chesterton and also discovers Whitman.

1919   The Borges family moves to Spain. In Madrid, Borges comes under the influence of the writer Rafael Cansinos-Asséns and also of the Ultraist poets. He immerses himself in Spanish literature and contributes poems, articles, and translations of the Expressionists to the Ultraist magazines. (His first poem, "Hymn to the Sea," is published in the magazine *Grecia.*) He also befriends Guillermo de Torre who helps promote Borges's literary theories and who eventually marries Norah Borges in 1928.

1921   The Borges family returns to Buenos Aires where Borges befriends a
        new literary/philosophical mentor, Macedonio Fernández, an old
        friend of his father's. Borges launches a little magazine that proclaims
        the Ultraist aesthetics called *Prism*—a poster-like sheet illustrated
        with Norah's woodcuts.

1922   With Macedonio Fernández, Borges and other friends found the little
        magazine *Proa* (*Prow*).

1923   Borges publishes his first book of poetry, *Passion for Buenos Aires*
        (featuring Norah's woodcuts). The family makes a second trip to Eu-
        rope.

1924   Borges returns to Buenos Aires and re-founds *Proa* (the original mag-
        azine had stopped production) with Ricardo Güiraldes and other writ-
        ers. (Güiraldes would publish *Don Segundo Sombra* in 1926, a
        gauchesque novel that became a classic of Argentine literature.)
        Borges collaborates in the influential avant-garde magazine *Martín
        Fierro*.

1925   Borges publishes his second book of poems, *Moon Across the Way,*
        and his first book of essays, *Inquisitions.* Borges eventually gathers
        and destroys all copies that he can of the latter and forbids its re-
        publication. Borges meets the essayist and literary patron Victorio
        Ocampo with whom he has a long literary relationship.

1926   Borges publishes his second book of essays, *The Extent of My Hope,*
        which is never reissued.

1928   Borges publishes his third book of essays, *The Language of the Ar-
        gentines.* He befriends the Mexican writer Alfonso Reyes whom
        Borges credits with helping him abandon his "avant-garde" and ba-
        roque style for his eventual classic style.

1929   Borges publishes his third book of poems, *San Martín Copybook,*
        which wins second prize in a municipal literary competition.

1930   Borges publishes a literary biography about the Argentine poet (and
        friend of his family) Evaristo Carriego. Through Victorio Ocampo he
        meets Adolfo Bioy Casares. They become lifelong friends and collab-
        orators.

1931   Victorio Ocampo founds *Sur,* which becomes Argentina's most im-
        portant literary journal. Borges frequently contributes to it.

1932   Borges publishes his fourth book of essays, *Discussión.*

1933   The magazine *Megaphone* devotes part of its August issue to a con-
        sideration of Borges's work. Borges is appointed literary editor of
        Crítica's Saturday supplement.

1935   Borges publishes *A Universal History of Infamy,* his first book of
        stories, containing many pieces he'd already published in *Crítica.*

1936   Borges publishes his fifth collection of essays, *History of Eternity.* He
        is appointed editor of the biweekly section "Foreign Books and Au-
        thors" for *El Hogar (Home)*, a position he holds until 1939. For *Sur*
        he translates Virginia Woolf's *A Room of One's Own.*

1937   The Kapelusz publishing house prints *Classical Anthology of Argen-
        tine Literature* which Borges edits with Pedro Henríquez Ureña.
        Borges claims Ureña did all the work. Borges translates Virginia
        Woolf's *Orlando* for *Sur.* Because of his father's declining health
        Borges secures a position as a first assistant at the Miguel Cané Mu-
        nicipal Library on the outskirts of Buenos Aires. He remains there
        (with one promotion) until 1946.

1938   An edition of Franz Kafka's *Metamorphosis* is published that Borges
        edits and prefaces. His father dies in February. Borges's poor eyesight
        contributes to a Christmas Eve accident that causes septicemia and
        almost costs him his life.

1939   While convalescing (to prove to himself that he's kept his sanity)
        Borges writes the short story "Pierre Menard, Author of the Qui-
        xote."

1940   With Bioy Casares and his new bride Silvinia Ocampo (Victorio's
        sister) Borges edits and publishes *Anthology of Fantastic Literature.*
        Borges also writes a prologue to Casares's science fiction novel, *The
        Invention of Morel,* which is a virtual manifesto for fantastic litera-
        ture.

1941   With the Sur publishing house Borges publishes his second book of
        stories, *The Garden of Forking Paths.* With Silvinia and Bioy Casares
        he edits *Anthology of Argentine Poetry.* Borges's translations for that
        year include Faulkner's *The Wild Palms* for *Sudamericana.*

1942   Using the pseudonym H. Bustos Domecq, Borges and Bioy Casares
        collaborate on a series of parodic detective stories, *Six Problems for
        Don Isidro Parodi* by Sur publishing house. The magazine *Sur* de-
        votes parts of the month's issue to a "Reparation for Borges" (for

The Garden of Forking Paths not receiving any literary prize) to which important writers from the Hispanic world contribute.

1943   Borges publishes his first collected poems, *Poemas,* in which he eliminates many earlier poems and rewrites others. With Casares he edits and publishes *The Best Detective Stories.*

1944   Borges publishes his most famous story collection, *Ficciones,* with Sur publishing house. The collection combines the stories of *The Garden of Forking Paths* with *Artifices.*

1945   Emecé publishes *El Compadrito,* an anthology of verse and prose about Buenos Aires hoodlums edited by Borges and Silvina Bullrich Palenque. The Argentine Society of Writers awards *Ficciones* its Grand Prix of d'Honneur.

1946   To punish Borges for having signed some political declarations against the Fascist Perón government, Borges is "promoted" from his position at the library to Inspector of Poultry. Borges resigns and begins a new career as a lecturer and public speaker. A government policeman is assigned to take notes at his lectures. *The Annals of Buenos Aires,* a new magazine, appoints Borges editor. Borges remains in this post until publication ceases in 1948. Among the new writers he introduces are Julio Cortázar. Under the pseudonym B. Suázez Lynch, Borges and Casares publish a detective novel, *A Model for Death.* With the pseudonym H. Bustos Domecq they also publish two fantastic stories entitled "Two Memorable Fantasies." Both books are privately published in limited editions and not reissued until 1970.

1947   In another private edition, Borges publishes his celebrated quasi-philosophical essay "New Refutation of Time."

1948   Borges's mother and sister are imprisoned for participating in a demonstration against Perón. His mother remains under house arrest for a month, while Norah spends time in the prostitute's section of the local prison.

1949   Losada publishes Borges's fourth book of stories, *The Aleph.*

1950   Borges is appointed Professor of English and American Literature of the Argentine Association of English Culture and President of the Argentine Society of Writers. He remains president of the society until 1953.

1951   Borges publishes an anthology of his own fiction, *Death and the*

Compass. He also publishes a scholarly book, *Ancient German Literature,* in Mexico (which he rewrites with María Esther Vázquez and re-publishes in 1965) and with Bioy Casares a second anthology of *The Best Detective Stories.*

1952   His sixth and most popular book of essays *Other Inquisitions* is published. *The Language of the Argentines* is reissued in a new edition.

1953   Borges publishes *Martin Fierro* (with Margarita Guerrero), a study of the Argentine poet. The Emecé publishing House begins publication of Borges's complete works. Borges and Leopoldo Torre Nilsson write the script for *Days of Wrath,* a film based on Borges's story "Emma Zunz."

1954   *Days of Wrath* appears. *Poems 1923–1953* and *Universal History of Infamy* are reissued as part of Borges's complete works.

1955   The military government that overthrows Perón appoints Borges Director of the National Library, a position he holds until 1973. With Bioy Casares, Borges publishes two rejected filmscripts, *The Hoodlums* and *The Believers' Paradise,* and two anthologies, *Extraordinary Tales* and *Gauchesque Poetry* (published in Mexico). With Luisa Mercedes Levinson, Borges publishes a collection of their stories, *Eloísa's Sister,* though only the title story was written in collaboration. With Betina Edelberg, Borges also publishes a study of the celebrated Argentine poet Leopoldo Lugones.

1956   The University of Cuyo in Argentina awards Borges his first of many honorary doctorates. Borges is appointed Professor of English Literature at the Faculty of Philosophy and Letters in Buenos Aires. With his eyesight failing Borges is advised to stop reading and writing, and his mother becomes, in effect, his private secretary.

1957   Borges publishes *Manual of Fantastic Zoology* (with Margarita Guerrero). Borges is awarded the National Prize for Literature.

1960   Borges publishes *El Hacedor* (translated into English as *Dreamtigers*), a collection of prose and verse, and edits *Book of Heaven and Hell* with Bioy Casares.

1961   Borges is awarded the Formentor International Publishers Prize (with Samuel Beckett), a key event in developing his international reputation. Borges teaches for a year at the University of Texas. An Argentine movie based on his story "Man from the Slums" is released.

1962   Borges is translated for the first time into English in book form with the publication of *Ficciones* and *Labyrinths*. Borges is awarded France's Commander of the Order of Arts and Letters and is elected a member of the Argentine Academy of Letters.

1963   Borges travels throughout Europe and wins the Prize of Argentina's National Endowment for the Arts.

1964   *The One, The Same,* Borges's fourth book of poetry, is published. In Paris *L'Herne* publishes the first large collection of testimonials and essays about Borges.

1965   Ana María Barrenechea publishes *Borges, the Labyrinth Maker,* the first book-length critical study of Borges in English. Borges publishes, with María Esther Vázquez, *Introduction to English Literature*. Borges is awarded the Order of the British Empire.

1966   Borges wins the 1965 Literary Prize of the Ingram Merrill Foundation of New York and is appointed Professor of English Literature at the Stella Maris Catholic University of Argentina.

1967   Borges marries Elsa Astete Millán, a childhood friend whom he meets again after she becomes a widow. They travel to Cambridge, Massachusetts, where Borges is Charles Elliot Norton Lecturer at Harvard. With Casares he publishes *Chronicles of Bustos Domecq,* and with Esther Zemborain de Torres he publishes *An Introduction to American Literature.*

1968   With Margarita Guerrero, Borges publishes *The Book of Imaginary Beings.*

1969   Borges's fifth book of poetry, *In Praise of Darkness,* is published. *Conversations with Jorge Luis Borges* by Richard Burgin (the first book-length series of interviews with Borges in English) is published by Holt Rinehart. E.P. Dutton begins publication of Borges's complete works in English. Several films based on Borges's stories are made in France, Italy, and Argentina.

1970   Borges publishes a new short story collection, *Dr. Brodie's Report.* Borges's "Autobiographical Essay" is published by *The New Yorker.* Bernardo Bertolucci adapts the Borges story "Theme of the Traitor and Hero" for Italian TV. Borges divorces Elsa Astete Millán.

1971   Columbia University awards Borges an honorary doctorate. Borges travels to England to receive an honorary doctorate from Oxford and to Israel to receive The Jerusalem Prize.

1972   Borges publishes *The Gold of the Tigers,* his sixth book of poetry, and receives an honorary doctorate from the University of Michigan.

1973   Borges receives "permission" to retire as Director of the National Library from the new Perón government. Borges wins the Alfonso Reyes International Prize in Mexico City.

1974   In one volume Emecé publishes *The Complete Works of Jorge Luis Borges.* It is 1,164 pages long. A new movie based on a script by Borges and Casares, *The Others,* is released in France.

1975   Borges's mother dies at 99. He publishes *The Unending Rose,* his seventh book of poems, *The Book of Sand,* his fifth book of stories, and *Prologues, with a Prologue of Prologues,* a selection of 38 prefaces he has written for different books. Two more of his stories are filmed in Argentina.

1976   Borges's eighth poetry collection, *The Iron Coin,* is published. The essay by Borges and Alicia Jurado "What Is Buddhism?" is published, as is *Book of Dreams,* a collection of his and other people's dreams. Lagos publishes *Borges in Song,* with twelve scores by various composers accompanying poems by Borges.

1977   Emecé publishes *History of Night,* his ninth book of poems. With Casares, Borges publishes *New Bustos Domecq Stories.* The Sorbonne awards Borges an honorary doctorate.

1978   With María Kodama, his secretary and friend, he edits *Short Anglo-Saxon Anthology.* A second movie version of *Emma Zunz,* directed by Leonard Katz, is released in the United States.

1979   Borges publishes *Oral Borges,* a collection of his most recent lectures, and *Complete Works in Collaboration,* which despite being 989 pages long only includes some of his collaborative works. Borges receives a Gold Medal from the French Academy, the Icelandic Falcon Cross, and the Order of Merit from the German Federal Republic. Borges travels to Japan with María Kodama.

1980   Borges wins the Cervantes Prize and is received by the King and Queen of Spain. *The Intruder,* a film by Carlos Hugo Christensen, based on Borges's story of the same name, appears.

1981   Alianza Editorial publishes Borges's tenth poetry collection, *The Compendium.* Éspasa-Calpe publishes *Nine Dantesque Essays* by Borges. Harvard University awards him an honorary doctorate.

1982   The anthology, *Pages of Jorge Luis Borges,* is published by Celtia, with a preliminary study by Alica Jurado.

1983   The President of France, Francois Mitterand, bestows the Legion of Honor on Borges.

1984   Borges publishes *Atlas,* with photographs taken by María Kodama.

1985   Mondadari publishes the complete works of Borges translated into Italian. *Borges, Self-Portrait of the World,* a play by Carlo Rapetti based on Borgesian texts, debuts.

1986   Borges marries María Kodama. Jorge Luis Borges dies on June 14 in Geneva.

Jorge Luis Borges: Conversations

Borges on Borges

Richard Stern / 1966

From *The Invention of the Real,* The University of Georgia Press, Athens, 1982, pp. 27–45. Reprinted by permission.

This 1966 interview with Jorge Luis Borges became a calling card during a South American trip in march 1979. (It had been distributed by my sponsors.) Borges is the closest thing to a hero on the immense continent, respected to the point of worship even by those who don't read him or who detest his politics. (He defined democracy as "forty million imbeciles who elect another who strips them bare." The definition had some authority coming from a man who'd resigned his job the day after the elected Juan Perón took power.) In March 1979, eighty years old, he looked but did not feel well. ("I cannot hold out much longer," he told a Montevideo newspaper.) But we talked nonstop for two hours, literature, history, politics, jokes. Two days later, back from lectures in Rosario and Cordoba, I returned to the little apartment on Maipú to read Browning and Rossetti to him. He directed my friend Alane Rollings and me to the shelves where his eyes functioned. (When I mentioned a poem of Jonson's, he said, "I have it, but don't know where.") The reading excited us immensely. He called out lines, said, "You see, you see, it's the Devil," or gripped my arm and cried, "*Qué lindo, Qué lindo.*" The poem that rocked us was "Childe Roland to the Dark Tower Came." "Though I've never understood it."

> As when a sick man very near to death
> Seems dead indeed, and feels begin and end
> The tears and takes the farewell of each friend . . .

Sitting next to the blind old fellow in the bare sitting room, Roland's quest did not seem so mysterious, only exciting beyond other expression.

When an old lady walked into the room, I did not, would not stop. We were within that poem and couldn't break out. Together Borges and I chanted the last line: "*Childe Roland to the Dark Tower came.*"

Then silence and drift back to the small room, the yellow sofa, the white bookshelves. "There's some one here," I said. The white-haired lady came to the risen Borges. "Georgy," she said. "It's Esther." "*Mi prima,*" he told us. "Just back from Europe." It was time to go. "You have given me a wonderful morning."

A year later, delicate and strong as ever, he was back in the States, lecturing, or rather participating in endless question-and-answer sessions, tossing his large-toothed, blind smile toward the most intimate interrogators, answering everything as if all would be known anyway. At a party he recited German and Anglo-Saxon, asked what people

1

had read, what they thought. The Chicago host, René da Costa, helped
him to the bathroom, where, said René, he recited, with the same
scholarly exuberance, the contents of toilet walls remembered from
Paris, Rome, the old days in Buenos Aires.

The Foolish Cement Pavilion on Chicago's Midway is the Center for Continuing Education. (What most continually educates is the industrial conference.) Off the low-browed, submarine-dim corridors of the bottom level is
the University of Chicago's Radio and Television Office. Here came Borges,
slender, frail, his walk a bit askew, arm on that of a guide. His face is thin
and long, the length emphasized by vertical grooves in the cheek flesh. A
physically unforceful person, but with a gift for gesture and pose. Shaking
hands, he draws close, his popped, muddled, gray-blue eyes inches from the
shaker's face. "I make out lights and shadows." A gentle man who quickly
touches the heart.

As Proust says of kings that they are *always* remarkable for simplicity, so
fine writers who have been long praised are *always* egalitarian with younger
colleagues. And when they are physically fragile, they develop Chaplinesque
ways of charming the sting from that belligerence all noted men encounter.
(Those who've seen the tiny Sartre scurrying about to offer and light cigarettes, pay for drinks, and sit smilingly alert while gallons of stupidity and
vituperation inundate him will have seen a master example.)

The night before, Borges talked to a delighted audience about Whitman.
A kindly speech, apparently recollected instead of read or improvised, somewhat soft and overextended, effulgent of Hispanic charm. The best of it was
his memory of reading Whitman as a student in Geneva, "taking him like a
cure." That remembered Whitman, the personality of *Leaves of Grass,* was
"divine," a permanent presence like Quixote and Hamlet, a totally different
being from the seedy Brooklyn newspaperman shuttling to Manhattan on the
ferry.

Borges and I sit facing each other at a table in the little recording studio,
microphone dangled above our noses. I apologize for my ignorance of Spanish, South America, the literature and customs of Hispanic culture. He replies
that he will outdo me in ignorance. The control man signals, and here is
much of what was recorded.

Stern: Last night you were talking of a multiplicity of Whitmans. Looking
through your poems and stories, one sees at least a number of Borgeses.
Sometimes, as in the charming *Borges and I,* you have written about this.

Borges: I suppose we all are in a sense Dr. Jekylls and Mr. Hydes, any amount of Jekylls and any amount of Hydes, and a lot of others thrown in between.

Stern: For some years now, you have become a man-to-be-interviewed, a man who comments on Borges, or what Borges has done. Have you discovered a new Borges, a Borges created out of responses to attention?

Borges: I hope I have, because when I was a young man I expected no one to read my stuff. So of course I could be as baroque as I liked. I used to write in a very far-fetched and stilted style. But now I've got to think of my readers and so, of course, that makes for good literary manners. All sorts of writers act in a different way. They try to be obscure and they generally succeed. Well, I have done my best to be clear and understandable and I think—so it is said—I have succeeded. Now I'm going to begin writing as soon as I get back to Buenos Aires, my home town, a book of straightforward short stories rather after the manner of Kipling's *Plain Tales from the Hills*. Not the last stories he wrote, those are very complex, very involved, and very sad also. I shall try to tell in a very straightforward way, plain stories. So I will try to get away from mazes, mirrors, from daggers, from tigers, because all those things now have become a bit of a bore to me. I will try to write a book so good that nobody will think I've written it. That's my aim.

Stern: Will the hills these tales come from be as they were for Kipling, remembered ones? With remembered people?

Borges: Yes, they will be. I intend to go back to my childhood, because I think a writer should avoid contemporary subjects. If I set out to describe a particular café in a particular quarter of Buenos Aires, then people will find that I'm making all sorts of mistakes, while if I write about what happened in a northern or southern slum of Buenos Aires some sixty years ago, nobody will care or remember. And that leaves me a little literary elbow room. I can dream at my ease, I can imagine things. I don't have to go into details. I don't have to become a historian or a newspaperman. I can just dream away. If the fact are essentially true, I don't have to worry about the circumstances. So my intention is to publish a book of some ten or fifteen short stories—let's say stories seven or eight pages long. And all of them will be quite clear. I've written one already.

Stern: At some time in your life perhaps the notion came to you that these tales, stories and poems were not only worked-out reveries but something committed to paper by an act. Though you say you expected no one to read your stuff.

Borges: There were both these facts. Of course what was important was the fact that they were reveries or they were daydreams. Of course the fight of putting them onto paper gave me some trouble and lots of fun also. I remember when I was writing a rather grim story . . . I felt quite happy, because a writer should feel happy when he writes.

Stern: When he writes well, or thinks so.

Borges: I wonder if one can speak about writing well. But at my age I know my possibilities. I know I can't write things that are far better or far worse than the things I've already written. So I let myself go. I mean, at my age—I'm sixty-eight—I suppose I've really found my own voice, my own stand.

Stern: Yet you talk of writing in another way.

Borges: Yes. I mean I want to write simple things, but at the same time, of course, I'm a writer. I can't get away from myself; I wish I could. Of course I'm tied down to my past.

Stern: You don't like the notion of art as an expression of personality.

Borges: I wrote a story once, a kind of parable about a man who began a very large picture, and therein was a kind of map, for example, hills, horses, streams, fishes, and woods and towers and men and all sorts of things. And then when the last moment came, when the day of his death came, he found that he had been making a picture of himself. That is the case with most writers. We are supposed to be writing about different things. But really what is left at the end is our memory. I mean, what the reader finds at the end is our face, our features, though we are quite unaware of it. So this means that we can't run away from ourselves. But we don't have to try to—a search goes on in ourselves all the time.

Stern: You remember the James story of the figure in the carpet. You have another version of this somewhere. In a footnote, I think. You talk about the divine mind which adds up every gesture a man makes in his life and discerns its form with the same ease that lets us see three lines as a triangle. From sixty-eight years, fifty of writing stories and poems, what do you see in the relation between the writer's figure in the carpet and this life figure?

Borges: One can hardly speak about those things. Every time I write I try to forget myself and to concentrate on the subject. Then I also think of the reader. I try to make the thing clear for him. What I've found out is that really I've been writing the same stuff over and over again. For example, I wrote a poem to a Saxon poet. I was thinking of the author of *The Wanderer.* Then a year afterwards I wrote a sonnet on the same subject without knowing it. And, thinking of stories of mine, I thought of two stories as quite different. And then a critic found out that though the setting was different, though it happened in different countries, the story was essentially the same.

Stern: Is that what may be meant by a Borges created by a critic's awareness?

Borges: I think that in my case what I really know are my own limitations. I mean, I know that there are certain things that I cannot attempt. For example, I thought I had evolved a new plot. I told it to one of my friends who said, "Yes, that would be a fine plot but after all it's the same plot you already used," and then he mentioned a few stories I had written.

Stern: Do you think that the impulse to say "this is the same" or "I must try something new" is something which a writer living before, say, the Renaissance would have thought about?

Borges: No, I suppose he wouldn't have thought about that because in those days they had a limited number of subjects. I don't think any knowledge was expected from a writer. And perhaps it was also good, because if you write a story whose plot is known to a reader then that saves you a lot of trouble because the reader knows all about the plot and you can concentrate on the details. In the case of Browning, for example, once he had told the plot in the first book, then he could go on to follow all the interrelations. All the many painters, for example, who have painted the Crucifixion have done the same thing.

Stern: Longinus says that much "modern"—first-century—literature was the deformed outgrowth of a search for novelty.

Borges: What do you think of that? Longinus. Of course, Homer is the primitive writer. But, for example, I have known people who knew the Red Indians in my country, and they had no historic consciousness whatever. I remember one of our generals spoke to an Indian chief, and he said to him, "How awful it must be for you, how sorrowful to think that once you were the lords of the pampas, and then the white men came and now you are being driven out." And the Indian chief looked at him in amazement and said, "No. Ever since I was a boy I've seen white men." Then I remember that my grandmother told me they had slaves at home, and the slaves were staying with the family that owned them, of course. And I asked her if the slaves had any consciousness, if the slaves knew that their fathers had come from Africa and had been sold in the marketplace. She told me they had no knowledge of it whatever. Historic memory went back to their childhood, they had no notion about their grandfathers and so on, so they never knew they had come from Africa.

Stern: You spoke of your limitations. What are they, as you see them?

Borges: For example, I would never think of attempting a novel, because I know I would get sick and tired of it before I had written the first chapter. Then I know that I can't attempt descriptions, and I think that psychological analysis is something I should avoid, because I can't do it. But if I can imagine a person, I think I would try to show what is going on in his mind through his acts. That's what happens in the Norse sagas. You're never told anything about what the character is thinking, but you find it out by his sayings or, still better, by his acts.

Stern: You've not felt an impulse to keep going, to keep on with characters, to show them in relationship to other characters?

Borges: I had no special interest in that kind of novel. And my friends tell me that there's something very childish about me because I'm very interested in plots and an intelligent man is supposed to have no use for plots. Of course, once you really enjoy novels where very little happens, where the characters are being idolized all the time, that's the kind of book I would hardly read.

Stern: Stravinsky was asked last year [1967] what new thing had come into literature in recent years. He said he never would have guessed that people could make so much of so little. He was praising Beckett and—

Borges: But was it real praise?

Stern: My version sounds ironic, but his wasn't.

Borges: I had a different experience, but still it's very enchanting. Let me tell it to you. I remember reading the *History of Argentine Literature* by Ricardo Rojas. When I looked over that book, eight volumes and perhaps utter nothingness behind the volumes, I thought how intelligent this man must be in order to have written this book and gotten away with it. He's written this book and in spite of this, he's famous, he's respected.

Stern: The elephant mustn't let the ant write his epitaph. Shall we talk about brevity as a determinant of other artistic elements? We seldom talk of

the consequences of such things as brevity. Your tales and poems, as I know
them, are brief.

Borges: This is caused, of course, by laziness.

Stern: That may be its source, though I doubt it, since forty or fifty volumes testify at least to some form of energy.

Borges: When I say laziness, I mean the task of taking a pen and writing.
Of course, I don't think I'm lazy at thinking or dreaming. Writing's the kind
of activity between thinking and dreaming. You have a dream at the outset
and then somehow you have to pin it down.

Stern: Is there perhaps a kind of symmetry or absolutism that comes with
brevity? I've noticed, looking through your pages, this kind of thing. You
say, "Everybody made such and such a choice," or "No one dissented."

Borges: Well, if I understand you, you mean that brevity makes for fair-
ness.

Stern: No, I think not. Brevity makes for a kind of—
Borges: Sweeping statements.

Stern: Yes.
Borges: Yes, because if you're writing in a brief way and you interlard
that with "so I think," or "perhaps," or "maybe," or "it is not impossible,"
it waters down and weakens what you're saying. So all that kind of thing is
left to the reader. You simply give him a possible explanation of things or a
statement that seems just possible to you and the reader of course has to turn
it over in his mind.

Stern: One of the beauties of your stories and poems seems to be a clash
between this—let's say—absoluteness and the enigmatic essence.
Borges: I'll allow myself a confession. The confession is this: whenever I
write a story I know that I have to work in some details, because people
expect to be told, for example, what kind of flowers will be found, for example, in that particular kind of ground. Those details are required not by the
naturalists but by the realists. Now when I've written a story, I generally ask
my mother, "Now this happens in a tenement house. What kind of flowers
would we have?" Or, "This happens in a *quinta* near Buenos Aires fifty years
ago, what kind of flowers did they have?" And then my mother gives me full
realistic details and I work them in. And then I go to somebody else, because
I'm very absentminded and hardly notice such things. So when I write my

stories there are practically no details and everything happens in the abstract. Well, if I know the reader may feel put out or perhaps he feels that he's floating about, then I give him a few details, but those are supplied by my family.

Stern: Well, one feels confidence in barely furnished stores; one isn't being swindled by decor. But then your stories are full of this odd tension or whatever it is, between the peculiar surety and the irreducible strangeness. Perhaps that is the Borges one wants to disinter from the various Borgeses.

Borges: Well, you see, I'm not really a thinker. I'm a literary man and I have done my best to use the literary possibilities of philosophy. I'm not a philosopher myself, except in the sense of being very much puzzled with the world and with my own life. When people ask me, for example, if I really believe that the cosmic process will go on and will repeat itself, I feel that I have nothing at all to do with that. I have tried to apply the aesthetic possibilities, let's say, of the transmutation of souls or the fourth dimension, to literature to see what could be evolved from them. But really I would not think of myself as a thinker or philosopher, and I follow no particular school.

Stern: Yet certain philosophic filings are drawn to your magnet and not others.

Borges: Well, that merely means I have my limits. I can be interested in certain subjects and not in others. For example, I've spent most of my life puzzling over time, the problem of time and of course my own identity. At least, they go together, because I feel that time is the stuff that I'm made of. But really, I have no particular theory about time. I have only felt it.

Stern: I read that one of your favorite Borges stories is "The South."

Borges: I think it's the best story because, in any case, it's the most complex. It can be read in two ways. You may read it in a straightforward way and you may think that those things happen to a hero. Then, you may think there's a kind of moral behind it—the idea that he loved the south and in the end the south destroyed him. But there's another possibility, the possibility of the second half of the story which is hallucination. When the man is killed, he's not really killed. He died in the hospital, and though that was a dream, a kind of wishful thinking, that was the kind of death he would have liked to have—in the pampas with a knife in his hand being stabbed to death. That was what he was looking forward to all the time. So I've written that story in order that it would be read both ways. Of course, I was thinking of Henry James.

Stern: I know a bit of your relationship to Argentinian ancestors who figured with San Martin and others, and, that in you home there were swords on the walls.

Borges: I've always felt a kind of wistfulness for epic. I think, for example, that my grandfather was killed in a battle, that my great-grandfather fought the Spaniards, that another of my great-grandfathers fought the Brazilians, another fought the Red Indians. I think they had a fine destiny, but at the same time, perhaps they were not as aware of their destiny as I am, because they just went throught it. But I am more aware of the epic significance of those destinies than they were, because they wanted to do their job and one of their jobs was to fight and be killed. That was all in a day's work.

Stern: So many of us praise what we feel we aren't.

Borges: Even if we think of the things we lack—I mean if you're a healthy man you don't think about health. If a woman loves you, you think of something else. You're happy, but you don't have to worry about it. At the same time, when you write about any particular unhappiness that has come to you, you're in a sense liberating yourself. Even if it is a confession. For example, if I tell you something in confidence, at the moment I'm telling you the things, I am not there as the actual person, because in the very act of telling it, I'm somebody else. I'm somebody who can look at things from a distance, who can put it into words, who can tell it to somebody else.

Stern: But here, in "The South" there's this praise of a kind of honor which—

Borges: Some sixty years ago in my country it was very important for a man to be brave or to be considered brave. I mean for a man to be a coward was a shame. I have known that feeling even, for example, among hoodlums, among very poor people. They were very ignorant, very limited men, and yet they all felt that to be a coward was the one unforgivable sin, the sin against the Holy Ghost. I have known, for example, the case of men defying a man that they had never seen before simply because they were sure that he was a brave man that was very handy with his knife. They wanted to find out who was a better man, so they would seek him out and sometimes get killed for their pains simply because of—what? "I'm as good a man as he is. If he's better than I am then let him prove it." Nowadays, of course, all that has completely vanished in my country. Nobody cares about being brave. People care about being rich or about being notorious, what people are talking about, and that sort of thing.

I have thought of writing a story about a man who is defied, who refuses a challenge, but he can do that because he knows he's not afraid. I thought of writing a story about a man who is just a common hoodlum, and then suddenly he sees through the utter vanity of being brave, trying to live up to a reputation. Then he's a coward, people mock at him. Well, if he knows in his heart that he's not afraid, he can take it. Of course, that's a very difficult story to write because the whole thing has to happen in his mind, unless, of course, there were two stories, unless you were told the facts at first and then in the end you might find out that the coward was really a brave man, because he knew that he wasn't afraid.

Stern: I suppose the writers who count for us most offer us the pleasures of realistic choices.

Borges: I always get rather angry at those who speak of reality on one side and of literature on the other as though literature were not a part of reality. If you read a book, it's as much of an experience as if you had traveled, or if you were jilted. As for my stories, I have tried to be loyal to them. I never write anything until I can fully imagine it as possible. I'm not out for novelty or for astounding people. When I write something, it's because I know that I can really think about it. For example, if any of my characters say anything, then it's because I feel that those are the words they might have said. I try not to work in any other matter. I've been an enemy of the Communists, of the Nazis, of our dictator, when we had him, but I never let those opinions interfere with my work. When I'm writing a story or a poem, I'm not thinking of my opinions but of the possible implications of what I write, I try to be loyal, try to draw the thing as I see it, that's all. I don't think of a writer's opinions as really very valuable. For example, in the case of Kipling. I greatly admire Kipling. I don't think we have to worry about his political opinions.

Stern: The stories frequently contradict his directly expressed opinions.

Borges: Yes, in the case of Kipling it's really remarkable. For example, in *Kim,* the finest characters are natives and he was quite unaware of that, because he was all the time speaking of the white man's burden and so on and yet the English characters are not very good.

Stern: They tear themselves apart in those hills where they don't belong.

Borges: I wonder if Kipling knew that? He must have felt it. I wonder if we see him as he was. I think of Kipling as a really great writer.

Stern: Joyce said that the three great talents of the nineteenth century were Tolstoy, Kipling and—can you guess?

Borges: No.

Stern: D'Annunzio.
Borges: That's a comedown.

Stern: I haven't read enough to say.
Borges: I've read very little D'Annunzio, and the very fact that I've read very little of him is my judgment of him. Tolstoy, Kipling and D'Annunzio. I wonder how you can admire all three. He had a very catholic mind.

Stern: Well, they all had immense energy, all were mad for straight stories. Once again, it's praising what one isn't.
Borges: Well, I admire Tolstoy, of course, but D'Annunzio, I find him so bombastic. I think if a man has moral defects, they always find their way into his work. So I think if we write in purple patches all the time, I think it's a sin of vanity and that sin should hardly be forgiven. I think a writer should be able to write in a plain way, because if he's trying to impress a reader all the time, the reader, of course, finds it out and then he refuses to be impressed.

Stern: Do you think there is any good writing that comes from personal defect? Rage? Meanness?
Borges: I wonder. Rage, of course. Now in the case of Oscar Wilde, for example—after all, he was writing purple patches all the time—but, at the same time, you feel that this was fun. That he wasn't taking them too seriously. There was also an Oscar Wilde who wrote *The Portrait of Dorian Grey.*

Stern: I suppose a life like Wilde's in which one must always disguise and then always make something of one's disguises—
Borges: Yes, but through the disguises, I think, a very level character.

Stern: And brave. You feel a man who disguises himself all the time must be a coward, but in Wilde's case you feel, "Ah, there's real bravery."
Borges: You remember what Chesterton wrote about Oscar Wilde. He had to sum him up in a page in one of the University Library books. Then he wrote a very fine book on *The Victorian Age in Literature.* And the book is full of epigrams, but they all make good points, and when he comes to Oscar Wilde he sums him up with these words, "Wilde was an Irish fighter." A thing that nobody ever thought of saying about Wilde. He says that he showed that in his trial and that all during his life he had been fighting really, fighting

public opinion and at the same time getting hold of it. But the case of
D'Annunzio I think is different because the purple patches one feels have
been written without a smile, where in the case of Wilde you feel that he was
smiling all the time and maybe laughing at what he was doing. It was a kind
of joke.

Stern: You think D'Annunzio was emotionally simple or emotionally cor-
rupt?

Borges: I suppose both, but emotionally simple, I should say. I think Italians are clearer, but I don't think they're very subtle. I don't speak of all of
them, but in my time I have found Italians practical men, all very cocksure
of themselves and, of course, theatrical.

Stern: After the last World War, there's been a great deal of marvelously
direct Italian art in movies and books. Mussolini may have used up an extra
decade's quota of bombast.

Borges: Well, I will make a last confession. I don't like Italian films.
Whereas *Psycho* was a very fine film. I had a discussion with an Argentine
critic. He told me the whole thing was a parody, that the whole thing was
meant as a joke. I said, "Well, all love is a joke." But it's not being taken as
a joke. It's a nightmare really. I suppose that comes from Jekyll and Hyde
because they're the same essentially.

The tape ran out here. We continued talking at the table for half an hour or
so. "It's not something for the machine," said Borges, "but conversation,
une tranche de vie." We drank coffee from paper cups and he spoke of the
screenplay he was writing with Bioy Casares and someone else. *Invasion,*
about six lazy men who succeed in repelling one. He'd written a couple of
others over the years but nothing had come of them.

We put on overcoats and went out. A gray day, halfway to snow. He wanted
to walk back to the Quadrangle Club, where his wife was waiting. He talked
of the difficulties of life in Argentina, the tiny salary he made as director of
the National Library and professor of English and American literature ("You
have to do it all in a semester"). "Less than a streetcleaner." Argentinians
didn't think of themselves as South Americans. "Brazil is South America.
You know, exotic, Indian, Negro."

"And Argentina?"

A laugh, the long, soft head scooping up towards mine. "A sort of Paris.
Yes, where everything is derived, the Teatro Colon from the Opéra, the sky-

scrapers from, from Chicago. Everything imitation." He'd had troubles there under Perón. His mother was put under house arrest, his sister in prison, "a jail for prostitutes to increase the humiliation. It was a way of getting at me. She wrote that she was fine. That made me worry." He had the boyish direct- ness that is the New World charm, gentler and more melancholy in its south- ern version. On the other hand, there was a strength of bravery and good heart in it.

At the club he did not want to be helped up the stairs. He'd found ways of getting his bearings, and said goodby with that intimate courtesy which makes some farewells oddly sweet and painful.

The Living Labyrinth of Literature; Some Major Work; Nazis; Detective Stories; Ethics, Violence, and the Problem of Time . . .

Richard Burgin / 1967

From *Conversations with Jorge Luis Borges,* Henry Holt and Company, 1969, pp. 19–65. Reprinted by permission.

Burgin: Your writing always, from the first, had its source in other books?

Borges: Yes, that's true. Well, because I think of reading a book as no less an experience than traveling or falling in love. I think that reading Berkeley or Shaw or Emerson, those are quite as real experiences to me as seeing London, for example. Of course, I saw London through Dickens and through Chesterton and through Stevenson, no? Many people are apt to think of real life on the one side, that means toothache, headache, traveling and so on, and then you have on the other side, you have imaginary life and fancy and that means the arts. But I don't think that that distinction holds water. I think that everything is a part of life. For example, today I was telling my wife, I have traveled, well, I won't say all over the world, but all over the west, no? And yet I find that I have written poems about out-of-the-way slums of Buenos Aires, I have written poems on rather drab street corners. And I have never written poems on a great subject, I mean on a famous subject. For example, I greatly enjoy New York, but I don't think I would write about New York. Maybe I'll write about some street corner, because after all so many people have done that other kind of thing.

Burgin: You wrote a poem about Emerson, though, and Jonathan Edwards and Spinoza.

Borges: That's true, yes. But in my country writing about Emerson and Jonathan Edwards is writing perhaps about rather secret characters.

Burgin: Because they're occult, almost.

Borges: Yes, more or less. I wrote a poem about Sarmiento because I had to and because I love him, but really I prefer minor characters or if not, if I write about Spinoza and Emerson or about Shakespeare and Cervantes, they

14

are major characters, but I write about them in a way that makes them like characters out of books, rather than famous men.

Burgin: The last time I was here we were talking about your latest book in English, *A Personal Anthology*. Those pieces you decided not to include in it you relegated to a kind of mortality, for yourself anyway. Do you feel you're your own best critic?

Borges: No, but I believe that some of my pieces have been overrated. Or, perhaps, I may think that I can let them go their way because people are already fond of them, no? So, I don't have to help them along.

Burgin: For example, "The Theologians." You didn't want to include that?

Borges: Did I include that?

Burgin: No, you didn't.

Borges: Yes, but there the reason was different. The reason was that although I liked the story, I thought that not too many people would like it.

Burgin: A concession to popular taste.

Borges: No, but I thought that since these stories are going to be read by people who may or may not read the other books, I'll try—and besides, people are always saying that I'm priggish and hard and that there is something that is very mazy about me—I'll do my best not to discourage them, no? Instead, I'll help them along. But if I offer them a story like "The Theologians," then they'll feel rather baffled, taken aback, and that may scare them away.

Burgin: Was that how you felt about "Pierre Menard"—was that why you also excluded it from *A Personal Anthology?*

Borges: You know, that was the first story I wrote. But it's not wholly a story . . . it's a kind of essay, and then I think that in that story you get a feeling of tiredness and skepticism, no? Because you think of Menard as coming at the end of a very long literary period, and he comes to the moment when he finds that he doesn't want to encumber the world with any more books. And that, although his fate is to be a literary man, he's not out for fame. He's writing for himself and he decides to do something very, very unobtrusive, he'll rewrite a book that is already there, and very much there, *Don Quixote*. And then, of course, that story has the idea, what I said in my first lecture here, that every time a book is read or reread, then something happens to the book.

Burgin: It becomes modified.

Borges: Yes, modified, and every time you read it, it's really a new experience.

Burgin: Since you see the world's literature as constantly changing, as continuously being modified by time, does this make you feel a sense of futility about creating so-called original works of literature?

Borges: But not only futility. I see it as something living and growing. I think of the world's literature as a kind of forest, I mean it's tangled and it entangles us but it's growing. Well, to come back to my inevitable image of a labyrinth, well it's a living labyrinth, no? A living maze. Perhaps the word labyrinth is more mysterious than the word maze.

Burgin: Maze is almost too mechanical a word.

Borges: Yes, and you feel the "amazement" in the word. With labyrinth you think of Crete and you think of the Greeks. While in maze you may think of Hampton Court, well, not very much of a labyrinth, a kind of toy labyrinth.

Burgin: What about "Emma Zunz," that's a story of a living labyrinth.

Borges: It's very strange, because in a story like "The Immortal" I did my best to be magnificent, while the story "Emma Zunz" is a very drab story, a very gray story, and even the name Emma was chosen because I thought it particularly ugly, but not strikingly ugly, no? And the name Zunz is a very poor name, no? I remember I had a great friend named Emma and she said to me, "But why did you give that awful girl my name?" And then, of course, I couldn't say the truth, but the truth was that when I wrote down the name Emma with the two *m*'s and Zunz with the two *z*'s, I was trying to get an ugly and at the same time a colorless name, and I had quite forgotten that one of my best friends was called Emma. The name seems so meaningless, so insignificant, doesn't it sound that way to you?

Burgin: But one still feels compassion for her. I mean, she is a kind of tool of destiny.

Borges: Yes, she's a tool of destiny, but I think there's something very mean about revenge, even a just revenge, no? Something futile about it. I dislike revenge. I think that the only possible revenge is forgetfulness, oblivion. That's the only revenge. But, of course, oblivion makes for forgiving, no?

Burgin: Well, I know you don't like revenge, and I don't think you lose your temper much either, do you?

Borges: I've been angry perhaps, well, I'm almost seventy, I feel I've been angry four or five times in my life, not more than that.

Burgin: That's remarkable. You were angry at Perón certainly.
Borges: Yes. That was different.

Burgin: Of course.
Borges: One day when I was speaking about Coleridge I remember four students walked into my class and told me that a decision had been taken by an assembly for a strike and they asked me to stop my lecturing. And then I was taken aback and suddenly I found that without knowing it I had walked from this side of the room to the other, that I was facing those four young men, telling them that a man may make a decision for himself but not for other people, and that were they crazy enough to think that I would stand that kind of nonsense. And then they stared at me because they were astounded at my taking it in that way. Of course, I realized that I was an elderly man, half blind, and they were four hefty, four husky young men, but I was so angry that I said to them, "Well as there are many ladies here, if you have anything more to say to me, let's go out on the street and have it out."

Burgin: You said that?
Borges: Yes, and then, well, they walked away and then I said, "Well, after this interlude, I think we may go on." And I was rather ashamed of having shouted, and of having felt so angry. That was one of the few times in my life that thing has happened to me.

Burgin: How long ago was this?
Borges: This must have been some five years ago. And then the same sort of thing happened twice again, and I reacted much in the same way, but afterwards I felt very, very much ashamed of it.

Burgin: This was a strike against the university?
Borges: Yes.

Burgin: What were they striking for?
Borges: They were striking because there was a strike among the laborers in the port and they thought the students had to join them. But I always think of strikes as a kind of blackmail, no? I wonder what you think about it?

Burgin: Students are often striking in this country.
Borges: In my country also. That they should do it is right, but that they

should prevent other people from going to classes, I don't understand. That they should try to bully me? And then I said, well if they knock me down, that doesn't matter, because after all the issue of a fight is of no importance whatever. What is important is that a man should not let himself be bullied, don't you think so? After all, what happens to him is not important because nobody thinks that I'm a prizefighter or that I'm any good at fighting. What is important is that I should not let myself be bullied before my students, because if I do, they won't respect me, and I won't respect myself.

Burgin: Sometimes values, then, are even more important than one's well-being?

Borges: Oh yes, of course. After all, one's well-being is physical. As I don't think physical things are very real—of course they are real, if you fall off a cliff. That's quite real, no? But in that case I felt that whatever happened to me was quite trifling, utterly trifling. Of course, they were trying to bluff me, because I don't think they had any idea of being violent. But that was one of the few times in my life I've been really angry. And then I was very much ashamed of the fact. I felt that, after all, as a professor, as a man of letters, I shouldn't have been angry, I should have tried to reason with them, instead of saying to them "well, come on and have it out," because after all I was behaving in much the same way as they were.

Burgin: This reminds me a little bit of "The South."
Borges: Yes.

Burgin: I think that's one of your most personal stories.
Borges: Yes, it is.

Burgin: The idea of bravery means a lot to you, doesn't it?
Borges: I think it does because I'm not brave myself. I think if I were really brave it wouldn't mean anything to me. For example, I've been ducking a dentist for a year or so. I'm not personally brave and as my father and my grandfather and my great grandfather were personally brave men, I mean some of them fell in action. . . .

Burgin: You don't think writing is a kind of bravery?
Borges: It could be, yes. But perhaps if I were personally brave I wouldn't care so much about bravery. Because, of course, what one cares for is what one hasn't got, no? I mean if a person loves you, you take it for granted, and you may even get tired of her. But if you are jilted, you feel that the bottom

is out of the universe, no? But those things are bound to happen. What you really value is what you miss, not what you have.

Burgin: You say people should be ashamed of anger, but you don't think people should be ashamed of this; of "what to make of a diminished thing?"

Borges: I don't think one can help it.

Burgin: Can you help anger?

Borges: Yes, yes, I think that many people encourage anger or think it a very fine thing.

Burgin: They think it's manly to fight.

Borges: Yes, and it isn't, eh?

Burgin: No. It isn't.

Borges: I don't think there's anything praiseworthy in anger. It's a kind of weakness. Because, really, I think that you should allow very few people to be able to hurt you unless, of course, they bludgeon you or shoot you. For example, I can't understand anybody being angry because a waiter keeps him waiting too long, or because a porter is uncivil to him, or because somebody behind a counter doesn't take him into account because, after all, those people are like shapes in a dream, no? While the only people who can really hurt you, except in a physical way, by stabbing you or shooting you, are the people you care for. A friend was saying to me, "but you haven't forgiven so and so and yet you have forgiven somebody who has behaved far worse." I said, "Yes, but so and so was, or I thought he was, a personal friend and so it's rather difficult to forgive him, while the other is an utter stranger so whatever he does, he can't hurt me because he's not that near to me." I mean if you care for people they can hurt you very much, they can hurt you by being indifferent to you, or by slighting you.

Burgin: You said the highest form of revenge is oblivion.

Borges: Oblivion, yes, quite right, but, for example, if I were insulted by a stranger in the street, I don't think I would give the matter a second thought. I would just pretend I hadn't heard him and go on, because, after all, I don't exist for him, so why should he exist for me? Of course, in the case of the students walking into my room, walking into my classroom, they knew me, they knew that I was teaching English Literature, it was quite different. But if they had been strangers, if they had been, well, brawlers in the street, or drunkards, I suppose I would have taken anything from them and forgotten all about it.

Burgin: You never got into any fights in childhood?

Borges: Yes, I did. But that was a code. I had to do it. Well, my eyesight was bad; it was very weak and I was generally defeated. But it had to be done. Because there was a code and, in fact, when I was a boy, there was even a code of dueling. But I think dueling is a very stupid custom, no? After all, it's quite irrelevant. If you quarrel with me and I quarrel with you, what has our swordsmanship or our marksmanship to do with it? Nothing—unless you have the mystical idea that God will punish the wrong. I don't think anybody has that kind of idea, no? Well, suppose we get back to more . . . because, I don't know why, I seem to be rambling on.

Burgin: But this is probably better than anything because it really enables me to know you.

Borges: Yes, but it will not be very surprising or very interesting.

Burgin: I mean people that write about you all write the same things.

Borges: Yes, yes, and they all make things too self-conscious and too intricate at the same time, no? Don't you think so?

Burgin: Well, of course it's hard to write about a writer you like; it's hard to write anyway. You wrote a poem roughly about that, didn't you? "The Other Tiger."

Borges: Ah yes, that one is about the futility of art, no? Or rather not of art but of art as conveying reality or life. Because, of course, the poem is supposed to be endless, because the moment I write about the tiger, the tiger isn't the tiger, he becomes a set of words in the poem. *"El otro tigre, el que no esta en el verso."* I was walking up and down the library, and then I wrote that poem in a day or so. I think it's quite a good poem, no? It's a parable also, and yet the parable is not too obvious, the reader doesn't have to be worried by it, or even understand it. And then I think I have three tigers, but the reader should be made to feel that the poem is endless.

Burgin: You'll always be trying to capture the tiger.

Borges: Yes, because the tiger will always be . . .

Burgin: Outside of art.

Borges: Outside of art, yes. So it's a kind of hopeless poem, no? The same idea that you get in "A Yellow Rose." In fact, I never thought of it, but when I wrote "The Other Tiger," I was rewriting "A Yellow Rose."

Burgin: You often speak of your stories as echoing other stories you've written before. Was that the case also with "Deutsches Requiem?"

Borges: Ah yes. The idea there was that I had met some Nazis, or rather Argentine Nazis. And then I thought that something might be said for them. That if they really held that code of cruelty, of bravery, then they might be, well, of course, lunatics, but there was something epic about them, no? Now I said, I'll try and imagine a Nazi, not Nazis as they actually are, but I'll try and imagine a man who really thinks that violence and fighting are better than making up things, and peacefulness. I'll do that. And then, I'll make him feel like a Nazi, or the Platonic idea of a Nazi. I wrote that after the Second World War because I thought that, after all, nobody had a word to say for the tragedy of Germany. I mean such an important nation. A nation that had produced Schopenhauer and Brahms and so many poets and so many philosophers, and yet it fell a victim to a very clumsy idea. I thought, well, I will try and imagine a real Nazi, not a Nazi who is fond of self-pity, as they are, but a Nazi who feels that a violent world is a better world than a peaceful world, and who doesn't care for victory, who is mainly concerned for the *fact* of fighting. Then that Nazi wouldn't mind Germany's being defeated because, after all, if they were defeated, then the others were better fighters. The important thing is that violence should *be*. And then I imagined that Nazi, and I wrote the story. Because there were so many people in Buenos Aires who were on the side of Hitler.

Burgin: How horrible.

Borges: It's awful. They were very mean people. But after all, Germany fought splendidly at the beginning of the war. I mean, if you admire Napoleon or if you admire Cromwell, or if you admire any violent manifestation, why not admire Hitler, who did what the others did?

Burgin: On a much larger scale.

Borges: On a much larger scale and in a much shorter time. Because he achieved in a few years what Napoleon failed to do in a longer period. And then I realized that those people who were on the side of Germany, that they never thought of the German victories or the German glory. What they really liked was the idea of the blitzkrieg, of London being on fire, of the country being destroyed. As to the German fighters, they took no stock in them. Then I thought, well, now Germany has lost, now America has saved us from this nightmare, but since nobody can doubt on which side I stood, I'll see what can be done from a literary point of view in favor of the Nazis. And then I created that ideal Nazi. Of course, no Nazi was ever like that, because they were full of self-pity; when they were on trial no one thought of saying, "Yes,

I'm guilty, I ought to be shot; why not, this is as it should be and I would shoot you if I could." Nobody said that. They were all apologizing and crying because there is something very weak and sentimental about the Germans, something I thoroughly disliked about them. I felt it before, but when I went to Germany I was feeling it all the time. I suppose I told you a conversation I had with a German professor, no?

Burgin: No, you didn't.

Borges: Well, I was being shown all over Berlin, one of the ugliest cities in the world, no? Very showy.

Burgin: I've never been to Germany.

Borges: Well, you shouldn't, especially if you love Germany, because once you get there you'll begin to hate it. Then I was being shown over Berlin. Of course, there were any number of vacant lots, large patches of empty ground where houses had stood and they had been bombed very thoroughly by the American airmen, and then, you have some German, no?

Burgin: No, I'm sorry.

Borges: Well, I'll translate. He said to me, "What have you to say about these ruins?" Then I thought, Germany has started this kind of warfare, the Allies did it because they had to, because the Germans began it. So why should I be pitying this country because of what had happened to it, because *they* started the bombing, and in a very cowardly way. I think Goering told his people that they would be destroying England and that they had nothing whatever to fear from the English airmen. That wasn't a noble thing to say, no? In fact, as a politician he should have said, "We are doing our best to destroy England, maybe we'll get hurt in the process, but it's a risk we have to run"—even if he thought it wasn't that way. So when the professor said to me "What have you to say about these ruins?"—well, my German is not too good, but I had to make my answer very curt, so I said, "I've seen London." And then, of course, he dried up, no? He changed the subject because he had wanted me to pity him.

Burgin: He wanted a quote from Borges.

Borges: Well, I gave him a quotation, no?

Burgin: But not the one he wanted.

Borges: Not the one he wanted. Then I said, to myself, what a pity that I have English blood, because it would have been better if I had been a straight South American. But, after all, I don't think he knew it.

Burgin: He should have read "The Warrior and the Captive" and then he would have found out.

Borges: Yes, he would have found out—yes.

Burgin: That's a good story, don't you think? It's very concise.

Borges: Yes.

Burgin: You're able to work in . . .

Borges: No! I worked in nothing; my grandmother told me the whole thing. Yes, because she was on the frontier and this happened way back in the 1800s.

Burgin: But you linked it with something that happened in history.

Borges: With something told by Croce, yes.

Burgin: And that's what makes it effective.

Borges: Yes. I thought that the two stories, the two characters, might be essentially the same. A barbarian being wooed to Rome, to civilization, and then an English girl turning to witchcraft, to barbarians, to living in the pampas. In fact, it's the same story as "The Theologians," now that I come to think of it. In "The Theologians" you have two enemies and one of them sends the other to the stake. And then they find out somehow they're the same man. But I think "The Warrior and the Captive" is a better story, no?

Burgin: I wouldn't say so, no.

Borges: No? Why?

Burgin: There's something almost tragic about "The Theologians." It's a very moving story.

Borges: Yes, "The Theologians" is more of a tale; the other is merely the quotation, or the telling, of two parables.

Burgin: I mean "The Theologians" are pathetic and yet there's something noble about them; their earnestness, their self-importance.

Borges: Yes, and it's more of a tale. While in the other I think that the tale is spoiled, by the fact of, well, you think of the writer as thinking himself clever, no? In taking two different instances and bringing them together. But "The Warrior and the Captive" makes for easier reading, while most people have been utterly baffled and bored by "The Theologians."

Burgin: No, I love that story.

Borges: Well, I love it also, but I'm speaking of my friends, or some of my friends. They all thought that the whole thing was quite pointless.

Burgin: But I also love "The Garden of Forking Paths," and you don't like that one.

Borges: I think it's quite good as a detective story, yes.

Burgin: I think it's more than a detective story, though.

Borges: Well, it should be. Because, after all, I had Chesterton behind me and Chesterton knew how to make the most of a detective story. Far more than Ellery Queen or Erle Stanley Gardner. Well, *Ellery Queen's* quite a good story.

Burgin: You once edited some anthologies of detective stories, didn't you?

Borges: I was a director of a series called *The Seventh Circle,* and we published some hundred and fifty detective novels. We began with Nicholas Blake; we went on to Michael Innis, then to Wilkie Collins, then to Dickens' *Mystery of Edwin Drood,* then to different American and English writers, and it had a huge success, because the idea that a detective story could also be literary was a new idea in the Argentine. Because people thought of them, as they must have thought of Westerns, as being merely amusing. I think that those books did a lot of good, because they reminded writers that plots were important. If you read detective novels, and if you take up other novels afterwards, the first thing that strikes you—it's unjust, of course, but it happens—is to think of the other books as being shapeless. While in a detective novel everything is very nicely worked in. In fact, it's so nicely worked in that it becomes mechanical, as Stevenson pointed out.

Burgin: I know you've always tried to avoid seeming mechanical in your fiction and also from seeming too spectacular. But I was surprised to hear you say that "The Immortal" was overwritten.

Borges: Yes, I think I told you that it was too finely written. I feel that you may read the story and miss the point because of the labored writing.

Burgin: Was the story perhaps inspired by Swift's immortals in *Gulliver's Travels?*

Borges: No, because his immortals were very different. They were doddering old things, no? No, I never thought of that. No, I began thinking of the injustice or rather how illogical it was for Christians, let's say, to believe in the immortal soul, and at the same time to believe that what we did during that very brief span of life was important, because even if we lived to be a hundred years old, that's nothing compared to everlastingness, to eternity. I thought, well, even if we live to a hundred, anything we do is unimportant if we go on living, and then I also worked in that mathematical idea that if time is endless, all things are bound to happen to all men, and in that case, after some thousand years everyone of us would be a saint, a murderer, a traitor, an adulterer, a fool, a wise man.

Burgin: The word, or concept, of destiny would have no meaning.

Borges: No, it would have no meaning. Consequently, in order to make that idea more impressive I thought of Homer forgetting his Greek, forgetting that he had composed the *Iliad,* admiring a not too faithful translation of it by Pope. And then in the end, as the reader had to be made aware that the teller was Homer, I made him tell a confused story where Homer appears not as himself but as a friend. Because, of course, after all that time he was ignorant. And I gave him the name of the wandering Jew Cartaphilus. I thought that helped the tale.

Burgin: We seem to be talking about violence and also about the problem of time, but that's not unusual, really, since you've often linked these problems, for instance, in a story like "The Secret Miracle."

Borges: Yes, I think I wrote that during the Second World War. What chiefly interested me—or rather, I was interested in two things. First, in an unassuming miracle, no? For the miracle is wrought for one man only. And then in the idea, this is, I suppose, a religious idea, of a man justifying himself to God by something known only to God, no? God giving him his chance.

Burgin: A very personal pact between the two.

Borges: Yes. A personal pact between God and the man. And also, of course, the idea of, well, this is a common idea among the mystics, the idea of something lasting a very short while on earth and a long time in heaven, or in a man's mind, no? I suppose those ideas were behind the tale. Now maybe there are others. And then, as I had also thought out the idea of a drama in two acts, and in the first act you would have something very noble and rather pompous, and then in the second act you would find that the real thing was rather tawdry, I thought, "Well, I'll never write that play, but I'll work that idea of the play into a tale of mine." Of course, I couldn't say that Hládik had thought out a drama or a work of art and say nothing whatever about it. Because then, of course, that would fall flat, I had to make it convincing. So, I wove, I interwove those two ideas. . . . Now that story has been one of my lucky ones. I'm not especially fond of it, but many people are. And it has even been published in popular magazines in Buenos Aires.

Burgin: Maybe they think of it as a more optimistic story of yours, in a way. . . . It ties in with your ideas on time, your "New Refutation of Time."

Borges: Yes, yes, and the idea of different times, no? Of different time schemes. Psychological time.

Burgin: Another story that I would think of in relation to "The Secret Miracle" is "The Other Death"—I mean in the sense that in both tales the hero tries to extend the properties of time, in one by increasing the amount of experience given to man within a unit of time and in the other by reversing time or a man's life in time.

Borges: Ah! That's one of my best stories, I think. But first I thought of it as a kind of trick story. I felt that I had read about a theologian called Damian, or some such name, and that he thought that all things were possible to God except to undo the past, and then Oscar Wilde said that Christianity made that possible because if a man forgave another he *was* undoing the past. I mean, if you have acted wrongly and that act is forgiven you, then the deed is undone. But I thought I had read a story about a past thing being undone.

My first idea was very trivial. I thought of having chessmen inside a box, or pebbles, and of their position being changed by a man thinking about it. Then I thought this is too arid, I don't think anybody could be convinced by it, and then I thought, well, I'll take a cue from Conrad and the idea of *Lord Jim,* Lord Jim who had been a coward and who wanted to be a brave man, but I'll do it in a magic way.

In my story, you have an Argentine gaucho, among Uruguayan gauchos, who's a coward and feels he should redeem himself, and then he goes back to the Argentine, he lives in a lonely way and he becomes a brave man to himself. And in the end he has undone the past. Instead of running away from that earlier battle in one of the civil wars in Uruguay, he undoes the past, and the people who knew him after the battle, after he had been a coward, forget all about his cowardice, and the teller of the story meets a colonel who had fought in that war and remembers him dying as a brave man should. And the colonel also remembers an unreal detail that is worked in on purpose—he remembers that the man got a bullet wound through the chest. Now, of course, if he had been wounded and fallen off his horse, the other wouldn't have seen where he was wounded.

Burgin: This feeling of wanting to undo something or to change something in the past also gets into "The Waiting."

Borges: Well, that happened. No, because the story, well, of course, I can't remember what the man felt at the end, but the idea of a man who went into hiding and was found out after a long time, this happened. It happened, I think it was a Turk and his enemies were also Turks. But I thought that if I worked in Turks, the reader would feel, after all, that I knew little about them. So I turned him into an Italian, because in Buenos Aires everybody is more or less Italian, or is supposed to know a lot about them. Besides, as there are Italian secret societies, the story was essentially the same. But if I'd given it the real Turkish-Egyptian setting, then the reader would have been rather suspicious of me, no? He would have said, "Here is Borges writing about Turks, and he knows little or nothing about them." But if I write about Italians, I'm talking about my next-door neighbors. Yes, as everybody in Buenos Aires is more or less Italian, it makes me feel I'm not really Argentine because I have no Italian blood. That makes me a bit of a foreigner.

Burgin: But what I meant was this idea of regret, which is essentially a metaphysical regret that we feel against an inevitable destiny. I mean, that feeling is in a lot of your stories. For example, "The South" or "The House of Asterion." Speaking of "The House of Asterion," I understand you wrote that in a single day.

Borges: Yes. I wrote that in a single day. Because I was editor of a magazine, and there were three blank pages to be filled, there was no time. So I told the illustrator, I want you to work a picture more or less on these lines, and then I wrote the story. I wrote far into the night. And I thought that the whole point lay in the fact of the story being told by, in a sense, the same scheme as "The Form of the Sword," but instead of a man you had a monster telling the story. And also I felt there might be something true in the idea of a monster wanting to be killed, needing to be killed, no? Knowing itself masterless. I mean, he knew all the time there was something awful about him, so he must have felt thankful to the hero who killed him.

Now during the Second World War, I wrote many articles on the war, and in one of them I said that Hitler would be defeated because in his heart of hearts he really wanted defeat. He knew that the whole scheme of Nazism and world empire, all that was preposterous, or perhaps he might have felt that the tragic ending was a better ending than the other, because I don't think that Hitler could have believed in all that stuff about the Germanic race and so on.

**III   Favorite Stories; Insomnia; a Changing Picture; *Alice in
        Wonderland; Ulysses;* Robert Browning; Henry James and Kafka;
        Melville. . . .**

Burgin: You seem to disapprove of or criticize so much of your writing.
Which of your stories, say, are you fond of?

Borges: "The South" and that new story I told you about, called "The
Intruder." I think that's my best story. And then "Funes the Memorious"
isn't too bad. Yes, I think that's quite a good story. And perhaps "Death and
the Mariner's Compass" is a good story.

Burgin: "The Aleph" isn's one of your favorite stories?

Borges: "The Aleph" yes, and "The Zahir." "The Zahir" is about . . . an
unforgettable twenty-cent coin. I wonder if you remember it.

Burgin: Of course. I remember.

Borges: And I wrote that out of the word unforgettable, *"inolvidable";*
because I read somewhere, "You should hear so-and-so act or sing, he or
she's unforgettable." And I thought, well what if there were really something
unforgettable. Because I'm interested in words, as you may have noticed. I
said, well, let's suppose something really unforgettable, something that you
couldn't forget even for a split second. And then, after that, I invented the
whole story. But it all came out of the word unforgetable, *"inolvidable."*

Burgin: In a sense, that's a kind of variation on "Funes the Memorious"
and even "The Immortal."

Borges: Yes, but in this case it had to be one thing. And then, of course,
that thing had to be something very plain, because if I speak of an unforgettable sphinx or an unforgettable sunset, that's too easy. So I thought, well, I'll
take a coin because, I suppose, from the mint you get millions and millions
of coins all alike, but let's suppose that one of them is, in some hidden way,
unforgettable, and the man sees that coin. He's unable to forget it and then
he goes mad. That will give the impression that the man was mad and that
was why he thought the coin was unforgettable, no? So the story could be
read in two slightly different ways. And then I said, "Well, we have to make
the reader believe the story, or at least suspend his disbelief, as Coleridge
said. So if something had happened to him before he saw the coin, for example, if a woman he loved had died, that might make it easier for the reader
and for myself. Because I can't have the teller of the story buying a package

of cigarettes and getting an unforgettable coin. I have to give him some circumstances, to justify what happened to him.

Burgin: And so you did.

Borges: Yes. But those stories go together. "Zahir" is one of the names of God, I think. I got it out of Lang's *Modern Egyptians,* I think, or perhaps out of Burton.

Burgin: The story "Funes the Memorious" is, among other things, about insomnia.

Borges: About insomnia, yes. A kind of metaphor.

Burgin: I take it, then, you've had insomnia.

Borges: Oh yes.

Burgin: I have also.

Borges: Do you?

Burgin: I don't any more, but I have had it. It's a terrible thing, isn't it?

Borges: Yes. I think there's something awful about sleeplessness.

Burgin: Because you think it will never end.

Borges: Yes, but one also thinks, or rather one feels, that it's not merely a case of being sleepless, but that somebody's *doing* that to you.

Burgin: A kind of cosmic paranoia.

Borges: Cosmic paranoia, or some fiendish foe, no? You don't feel it's an accident. You feel that somebody is trying to kill you in a sense, or to hurt you, no?

Burgin: How long did you have it?

Borges: Oh, about a year. In Buenos Aires, of course, it's worse than having it here. Because it goes with the long summer nights, with the mosquitoes, with the fact of tossing about in your bed, having to turn your pillow over and over again. In a cold country I think it's easier, no?

Burgin: No sleeping pills there?

Borges: Oh yes, I had sleeping pills also, but after a time they did me no good. And then there was a clock. It worried me very much. Because without a clock you may doze off, and then you may try to humbug yourself into thinking that you've slept a long time. If you have a clock, then it will give you, the time in the face every quarter of the hour, and then you say, "Well, now it's two o'clock, now it's a quarter past, now half past two, now quarter to three, now the three strokes, and then you go on and on . . . it's awful. Because you know you haven't missed any of the strokes.

Burgin: What finally got you over the insomnia?

Borges: I can hardly remember it, because I had sleeping pills and I also went to another house where there were no clocks, and then I could humbug myself into the belief that I had slept. And finally, I did sleep. But then I saw a doctor, he was very intelligent about it. He told me, "You don't have to worry about sleeplessness because even if you are not sleeping you are resting, because the mere fact of resting, of being in bed, of the darkness, all those things are good for you. So that even if you can't sleep, you don't have to worry." I wonder if it's a true argument, but, of course, that's hardly to the point; the fact is that I did my best to believe in it, and then, once I got over that, that after all a sleepless night meant nothing, I went to sleep quite easily. After a time, of course, as one tends to forget one's painful experiences, I can't tell you what the details were of that period. Is there another tale or poem you want to talk about?

Burgin: What about the story "The South"? Now you've said that story is your personal favorite. Do you still feel that way?

Borges: But I think I've written a better story called "La Intrusa" and you'll find that story in the last edition of *El Aleph* or of *A Personal Anthology*. I think that's better than the other. I think that's the best story I ever wrote. There's nothing personal about it, it's the story of two hoodlums. The intruder is the woman who comes into the lives of two brothers who are hoodlums. It isn't a trick story. Because if you read it as a trick story, then, of course, you'll find that you know what's going to happen at the end of a page or so, but it isn't meant to be a trick story. On the contrary. What I was trying to do was to tell an inevitable story so that the end shouldn't come as a surprise.

Burgin: That's sort of like "The South," though. The sense of inevitability in that story.

Borges: Yes, yes. But, I think that "La Intrusa" is better, because it's simpler.

Burgin: When did you write it?

Borges: I wrote it about a year or so ago, and I dedicated it to my mother. She thought that the story was a very unpleasant one. She thought it awful.

But when it came to the end there was a moment when one of the characters had to say something, then my mother found the words. And if you read the story, there's a fact I would like you to notice. There are three characters and there is only one character who speaks. The others, well, the others say things and we're told about them. But only one of the characters speaks directly, and he's the one who's the leader of the story. I mean, he's behind all the facts of the story. He makes the final decision, he works out the whole thing, and in order to make that plainer, he's the only character whose voice we hear, throughout the story.

Burgin: Is it a very short story?

Borges: Yes, five pages. I think it's the best thing I've done. Because, for example, in "Hombre de la Esquina Rosada," I rather overdid the local color and I spoiled it. But here I think you find, well, I won't say local color, but you feel that the whole thing happened in the slums around Buenos Aires, and that the whole thing happened some fifty or sixty years ago. And yet, there's nothing picturesque about it. There are, of course, a few Argentine words, but they are not used because they are picturesque but because they are the exact words, no? I mean if I used any other, I would make the whole thing phony.

Burgin: What about "Death and the Compass"? Do you like the way you treat the local color in that story?

Borges: Yes, but in "Death and the Compass," the story is a kind of nightmare, no? It's not a real story. While in "La Intrusa" things are awful, but I think that they are somehow real, and very sad also.

Burgin: You've quoted Conrad as saying that the real world is so fantastic that it, in a sense, *is* fantastic, there's no difference.

Borges: Ah, that's wonderful, eh? Yes, it's almost an insult to the mysteries of the world to think that we could invent anything or that we needed to invent anything. And the fact that a writer who wrote fantastic stories had no feeling for the complexity of the world. Perhaps in the foreword to a story called "The Shadow Line," a very fine story in Everyman's Library—I think he wrote a foreword to that story—there you'll find the quote. Because, you see, people asked him whether "The Shadow Line" was a fantastic story or a realistic story, and he answered that he did not know the difference. And that he would never try to write a "fantastic" story because that would mean he was very insensitive, no?

Burgin: I'm curious also about the story "Tlön, Uqbar, Orbis Tertius."
Borges: One of the best stories I ever wrote, eh?

Burgin: You didn't include it in your *Personal Anthology.*
Borges: No, because a friend of mine told me that many people thought of me as writing cramped and involved tales and she thought that since the real aim of the book was to bring readers nearer to me, it might on the whole be wiser if that story was left out. Because though she liked the story, she thought that it conveyed the wrong idea about me. That it would scare people away from reading the other stories. She said, "For this *Personal Anthology,* you want to make things easier for the reader. While if you give him, well, such a mouthful, you may scare him away and he won't read any of the others." Perhaps the only way to make people read "Tlön, Uqbar, Orbis Tertius" is to make them read other stories first. In Buenos Aires, I mean there are many people who write well, but most of them are trying their hand at realistic stories, no? So this kind of story, of course, falls outside the common expected. That's why I left it out; but it's one of my best stories, perhaps.

Burgin: You work in your friend Casares again.
Borges: Yes, well, yes, that's a kind of stock joke we have of working in imaginary and real people in the same story. For example, if I quote an apocryphal book, then the next book to be quoted is a real one, or perhaps an imaginary one, by a real writer, no? When a man writes he feels rather lonely, and then he has to keep his spirits up, no?

Burgin: Of course, it must be much more difficult for you to write now because of your blindness.
Borges: It's not difficult, it's impossible. I have to limit myself to short pieces. Yes, because I like to go over what I write, I'm very shaky about what I write. So before I used to write any amount of rough drafts, but now, as I can't do them, I have to imagine drafts. So then, walking up and down the streets or walking up and down the National Library, I think what I want to write, but, of course, they have to be short pieces because otherwise, if I want to see them all at once—that can't be done with long texts. I try to shorten them as much as I can, so I write sonnets, stories maybe one or two pages long. The last thing I wrote, rather a long short story, well, it was six pages.

Burgin: "La Intrusa."
Borges: "La Intrusa," yes. I don't think I'll ever go any farther than that.

No, I don't think I'll be able to do it. I want to see at once glance what I've done . . . that's why I don't believe in the novel because I believe a novel is as hazy to the writer as to the reader. I mean a writer writes maybe a chapter, then another, then another one, and in the end he has a kind of bird's eye view of the whole thing, but he may not be very accurate.

Burgin: Have you written anything since you've been in America?

Borges: I wrote some quite short pieces; I've written two sonnets, not too good ones, and then a poem about a friend who had promised us a picture. He died. He's a well-known Argentine painter, Larco, and then I thought of the picture he had promised us, promised my wife and me—I met him in the street—and then I thought that in a sense he had given us a picture because he had intended to do so, and so the picture was in some mystic way or other with us, except that the picture was perhaps a richer picture because it was a picture that kept growing and changing with time and we could imagine it in many different ways, and then in the end I thanked him for that unceasing, shifting picture, saying that, of course, he wouldn't find any place on the four walls of a room, but still he'd be there with us. That was more or less the plot of the poem. I wrote that in a kind of prose poem.

Burgin: That's very nice.

Borges: Well, I wonder. Now, when I was in New York, I began writing a poem and then I realized it was the same poem I had written to my friend all over again, yes, because it was snowing and we were on the, I don't know, sixteenth floor of one of those New York towers, and then I lay there, it was snowing very hard, we were practically snowed in, snow-bound, because we couldn't walk, and then I felt that somehow the mere fact of being in the heart of New York and of knowing that all those complex and beautiful buildings were around us, that mere fact made us see them and possess them better than if we had been gaping at shop windows or other sights, no? It's the same idea, of course. And suddenly I realized that I'd been going over the same ground, the idea of having something because you don't have it or because you have it in a more abstract way.

Burgin: This seems to be the type of feeling one gets from a story like "The Circular Ruins." Can you tell me what the pattern was behind that story?

Borges: No. I can't say much about the conception, but I can tell you that when I wrote that story the writing took me a week. I went to my regular business. I went to—I was working at a very small and rather shabby public library in Buenos Aires, in a very gray and featureless street. I had to go there every day and work six hours, and then sometimes I would meet my friends, we would go and see a film, or I would have dinner with somebody, but all the time I felt that life was unreal. What was really near to me was that story I was writing. That's the only time in my life I've had that feeling, so that story must have meant something—to me.

Burgin: Have you ever read any poetry by Wallace Stevens?

Borges: I seem to recall the name in some anthology. Why? Is there something akin to it?

Burgin: I think he believes a lot in the integrity of the dreamer, in the integrity of the life of the imagination as opposed to the physical universe.

Borges: Yes, well, but I don't think that feeling got into the story, it was merely a kind of intensity I had. That story came from the sentence "And I left off dreaming about you"—in *Alice in Wonderland.*

Burgin: You like *Alice in Wonderland,* don't you?

Borges: Oh, it's a wonderful book! But when I read it, I don't think I was quite as conscious of its being a nightmare book and I wonder if Lewis Carroll was. Maybe the nightmare touch is stronger because he wasn't aware of it, no? And it came to him from something inner.

I remember as a child I, of course, I greatly enjoyed the book, but I felt that there was—of course, I never put this feeling into words—but I felt something eerie, something uncanny about it. But now when I reread it, I think the nightmare touches are pretty clear. And perhaps, perhaps Lewis Carroll disliked Sir John Tenniel's pictures, well, they're pen-and-ink drawings in the Victorian manner, very solid, and perhaps he thought, or he felt rather, that Sir John Tenniel had missed the nightmare touch and that he would have preferred something simpler.

Burgin: I don't know if I believe in pictures with a book. Do you?

Borges: Henry James didn't. Henry James didn't because he said that pictures were taken in at a glance and so, of course, as the visual element is stronger, well, a picture makes an impact on you, that is, if you see, for example, a picture of a man, you see him all at once, while if you read an accouant of him or a description of him, then the description is successive. The illustration is entire, it is, in a certain sense, in eternity, or rather in the present. Then he said what was the use of his describing a person in forty or fifty lines when that description was blotted by the illustration. I think some editor or other proposed to Henry James an illustrated edition and first he wouldn't accept the idea, and then he accepted it on condition that there would be no pictures of scenes, or of characters. For the pictures should be, let's say, around the text, no?—they should never overlap the text. So he felt much the same way as you do, no?

Burgin: Would you dislike an edition of your works with illustrations?

Borges: No, I wouldn't, because in my books I don't think the visual element is very important. I would like it because I don't think it would do the text any harm, and it might enrich the text. But perhaps Henry James *had* a definite idea of what his characters were like, though one doesn't get that idea. When one reads his books, one doesnt' feel that he, that he could have known the people if he met them in the street. Perhaps I think of Henry James as being a finer storyteller than he was a novelist. I think his novels are very burdensome to read, no? Don't you think so? I think Henry James was a great master of situations, in a sense, of his *plot,* but his characters hardly exist outside the story. I think of his characters as being unreal. I think that the characters are made—well, perhaps, in a detective story, for example, the characters are made for the plot, for the sake of the plot, and that all his long analysis is perhaps a kind of fake, or maybe he was deceiving himself.

Burgin: What novelists do you think could create characters?

Borges: Conrad, and Dickens. Conrad certainly, because in Conrad you feel that everything is real and at the same time very poetical, no? I should put Conrad as a novelist far above Henry James. When I was a young man I thought Dostoevski was the greatest novelist. And then after ten years or so, when I reread him, I felt greatly disappointed. I felt that the characters were unreal and that also the characters were part of a plot. Because in real life, even in a difficult situation, even when you are worrying very much about something, even when you feel anguish or when you feel hatred—well, I've never felt hatred—or love or fury maybe, you also live along other lines, no? I mean, a man is in love, but at the same time he is interested in the cinema, or he is thinking about mathematics or poetry or politics, while in novels, in most novels, the characters are simply living through what's happening to them. No, that might be the case with very simple people, but I don't see, I don't think that happens.

Burgin: Do you think a book like *Ulysses,* for example, was, among other things, an attempt to show the full spectrum of thought?

Borges: Yes, but I think that *Ulysses* is a failure, really. Well, by the time it's read through, you know thousands and thousands of circumstances about the characters, but you don't know them. And if you think of the characters in Joyce, you don't think of them as you think of the characters in Stevenson or in Dickens, because in the case of a character, let's say in a book by Stevenson, a man may appear, may last a page, but you feel that you know him or that there's more in him to be known, but in the case of *Ulysses* you are told thousands of circumstances about the characters. You know, for example, well, you know that they went twice to the men's room, you know all the books they read, you know their exact positions when they are sitting down or standing up, but you don't really know them. It's as if Joyce had gone over them with a microscope or a magnifying glass.

Burgin: I imagine you've revealed a lot about English literature to your students.

Borges: Nobody knows a lot about English literature, it's so rich . . . But I believe, for example, that I have revealed Robert Browning to many young men in Buenos Aires who knew nothing whatever about him. Now I'm wondering if Browning, instead of writing poetry—of course, he should have written poetry—but I think that many of Browning's pieces would have fared better, at least as far as the reader goes, had they been written as short stories. For example, I think that he wrote some very fine verses in *The Ring and the Book*. We find it burdensome because I suppose we've grown out of the habit of reading long poems in blank verse. But had he written it in prose, had *The Ring and the Book* been written as a novel, and the same story told over and over again by different characters, he might have been more amusing, no? Though he would have lost many fine passages of verse. Then I should think of Robert Browning as the forerunner of all modern literature. But nowadays we don't, because we're put off by the . . .

Burgin: Poetic technicalities.

Borges: Yes, the poetic technicalities, by the blank verse, by the rather artificial style. But had he been, let's say, well, yes, had he been a good prose writer, then I think that we should think of Browning as being the forerunner of what is called modern literature.

Burgin: Why do you say that?

Borges: Because when I told the plots of his poems to my students, they were wild about them. And then, when they read them, they found them, well, a task. But if you tell somebody the framework of *The Ring and the Book,* it's very interesting. The idea of having the same story told by different characters from different angles, that seems to be, well, more or less, what Henry James would have liked you to do—a long time before Henry James. I mean that you should think of Browning as having been the forerunner, quite as good as the forerunner, of Henry James or of Kafka. While today we don't think of him in that way; and nobody seems to be reading him, except out of duty, but I think people should enjoy reading him.

Burgin: You've linked Henry James and Kafka before—you seem to associate them in your mind for some reason.

Borges: I think that there is a likeness between them. I think that the sense of things being ambiguous, of things being meaningless, of living in a meaningless universe, of things being many-sided and finally unexplained; well, Henry James wrote to his brother that he thought of the world as being a diamond museum, a museum of monsters. I think that he must have felt life in much the same way.

Burgin: And yet the characters in James or in Kafka are always striving for something definite. They always have definite goals.

Borges: They have definite goals, but they never attain them. I mean, when you've read the first page of *The Trial* you know that he'll never know why he's being judged, why he's being tried, I mean, in the case of Henry James, the same thing happens. The moment you know that the man is after the Aspern papers, you know, well, either that he'll never find the papers, or that if he does find them, they'll be worthless. You may feel that.

Burgin: But then it's more a sense of impotence than it is an ambiguity.

Borges: Of course, but it's also an ambiguity. For example, "The Turn of the Screw." That's a stock example. One might find others. "The Abasement of the Northmores"—the whole story is told as a tale of revenge. And, in the end, you don't know whether the revenge will work out or not. Because, after all, the letters of the widow's husband, they may be published and nothing may come of them. So that in the end, the whole story is about revenge, and when you reach the last page, you do not know whether the woman will accomplish her purpose or not. A very strange story. . . . I suppose that you prefer Kafka to Henry James?

Burgin: No, they stand for different things for me.

Borges: But do they?

Burgin: You don't seem to think so. But I think that Henry James believed in society, he never really questioned the social order.

Borges: I don't think so.

Burgin: I think he accepted society. I think that he couldn't conceive of a world without society and he believed in man and, moreover, in certain conventions. He was a student of man's behavior.

Borges: Yes, I know, but he believed in them in a desperate way, because it was the only thing he could grasp.

Burgin: It was an order, a sense of order.

Borges: But I don't think he felt happy.

Burgin: But Kafka's imagination is far more metaphorical.

Borges: Yes, but I think that you get many things in James that you don't get in Kafka. For example, in Henry James you are made to feel that there *is* a meaning behind experience, perhaps too many meanings. While in Kafka, you know that he knew no more about the castle or about the judges and the trial than you do. Because the castle and the judges are symbols of the universe, and nobody is expected to know anything about the universe. But in the case of Henry James, you think that he might have had his personal theories or you feel that he knows more of what he's talking about. I mean that though his stories may be parables of the subject, still they're not written by him to be parables. I think he was really very interested in the solution, maybe he had two or three solutions and so in a sense I think of Henry James as being far more complex than Kafka, but that may be a weakness. Perhaps the strength of Kafka may lie in his lack of complexity.

Burgin: I think of James as being able to create characters; whereas Kafka has no characters, Kafka is closer to poetry really. He works with metaphors and types as opposed to characters.

Borges: No, there are no characters.

Burgin: But James could create characters.

Borges: Are you sure of that?

Burgin: You don't seem to think so.

Borges: No, I think that what is interesting in James are the situations more than the characters. Let's take a very obvious example. If I think of Dickens, I'm thinking of Sir Pickwick, Pip, David Copperfield. I think of people, well, I might go on and on. While if I think of James, I'm thinking about a situation and a plot. I'm not thinking about people, I'm thinking about what happened to them. If I think about *What Maisy Knew*, I think of the framework of a hideous story of adultery being told by a child who cannot understand. I think of that and not of Maisy herself and not of her parents or of her mother's lover and so on.

Burgin: You also said that you don't think *Ulysses* has any real characters either.

Borges: No.

Burgin: What do you think of when you think of that book? The language perhaps?

Borges: Yes, I think of it as being verbal. I think I said that we know thousands of things about Daedalus or about Bloom, but I don't think we know them. At least I don't. But I think I know quite a lot about the characters in Shakespeare or in Dickens. Now—I'll qualify this, I suppose you can help me out—in the case of *Moby Dick*, I think that I believe in the story rather than in the characters, because the whole story is a symbol, the white whale stands for evil, and Captain Ahab stands, I suppose, for the wrong way of doing battle against evil, but I cannot believe in him personally. Can you?

Burgin: To think only in terms of an allegory or a symbol seems reductive of the text, it reduces the story to one of its elements.

Borges: Yes, of course it does. That's why Melville said that the book was not an allegory, no?

Burgin: But I don't think it's so specific that you can say the whale stands for evil, maybe the whale stands for many things—you feel many things, but you can't perhaps verbalize the exact thing that the whale stands for. I mean I don't like to think of it in terms of algebra, where one thing equals another.

Borges: No, no, of course the idea of the whale is richer than the idea of evil.

Burgin: Yes.

Borges: Of course, I'm not allowed to see the work in Melville's mind, but you think of Captain Ahab as being more complex than any abstract statement.

Burgin: Yes. Ahab has presence, he has real presence on the page, but I don't really think of him as a real man.

Borges: I think of Billy Budd as being a real man.

Burgin: Yes.

Borges: And Benito Cereno—but in the case of *Moby Dick,* the whole thing is so overloaded with gorgeous language, no?

Burgin: Shakespearean, almost.

Borges: Shakespearean and Carlylean also, no? Because you feel that Carlyle is in Melville.

Burgin: What about "Bartleby the Scrivener"—did you like that story?

Borges: Yes, I remember an anthology that came out in Buenos Aires, well, about six months ago. Six Argentine writers could choose the best story they knew. And one of those writers took that story "Bartleby."

Burgin: The best story by Melville or the best story by anybody?

Borges: I mean by anybody.

Burgin: One story from all of world literature, that's very difficult.

Borges: Yes, but I don't think the aim was really to find out the best stories in the world by any means, I think what they wanted was to get an anthology that people might want us to buy, no? That people might be interested in. Then one took "Bartleby," and one took, I don't know why, a very disagreeable and rather bogus story by Lovecraft. Have you read Lovecraft?

Burgin: No, I haven't.

Borges: Well, no reason why you should. And somebody had a story about a mermaid by Hans Andersen, I suppose you know it. Well, it's not a very good story.

Burgin: Strange choices.

Borges: Then somebody had a short Chinese story, quite a good story—three pages long. And then, I wonder what you will make of my choice? I took Hawthorne's "Wakefield," about the man who stays away from home all those years. Well, strangely enough, there were six stories and three by American authors, Melville, Lovecraft and Hawthorne.

Burgin: Did you have a hard time picking the Hawthorne from the others or did you know it right away?

Borges: No. Well, of course, I really wasn't thinking of all the stories I know. And it had to be a story already translated into Spanish. That limited my choice. Besides, as I didn't want to astonish people, because I think that to take a story by Lovecraft and to say it's the best story in the world, that's done in order to amaze people. Because I don't think that anybody would think that Lovecraft wrote the finest story in the world, if the phrase the finest story in the world can have any meaning. I hesitated between that story and some story by Kipling. And then I thought that that story was a very fine story to be written ever so long ago. The book came out and now there is going to be a second series, by different writers, of course. It was a book that sold very well.

Burgin: Have you had occasion to go to Salem since you've been here?

Borges: Yes, I went several times to Salem and then I went to Walden also. And I should say that the whole American adventure began here, no? That the history of America began here, in fact, I should say that the West was invented by New Englanders, no?

Jorge Luis Borges

Rita Guibert / 1968

Reprinted from *Seven Voices: Seven Latin American Writers Talk to Rita Guibert,* by Rita Guibert, Alfred A. Knopf, Inc., 1973, pp. 77–117. Copyright © 1973 by Rita Guibert. Reprinted by permission.

When Borges was a guest lecturer at Harvard I called him asking for an interview. A week later I met him in his Cambridge apartment where he was living with his wife. He had married—at sixty-nine for the first time, a marriage that ended in divorce shortly thereafter.

Borges comes from an intellectual, upper middle class Argentine family and he looks the part, dressing in a conservative fashion, behaving with old-fashioned politesse. While he looks pale and fragile, his voice is deep and vibrant like a much younger man's. In spite of his busy schedule he used to take long walks through the Cambridge streets he loves so much; the cold and snow didn't stop him from walking every day to his office and returning to his apartment for lunch. When I accompanied him on some of these daily strolls he would reminisce about his daily walks through the streets of Buenos Aires, or comment on the old brick houses in Boston, or recite old English sagas in the original Anglo-Saxon.

Near-blind, he has an excellent memory and an acute sense of direction. Sometimes he insited on walking me to my hotel, a block away from his apartment, never hesitating to return by himself; he could point out the exact spot in the bookcase where one of his books could be located, or would swiftly cross the room to answer the phone or a knock at the door. He was invited to appear on a Boston TV show, and when he was leaving his apartment the taxi driver who was waiting for him at the door said, "I'm here to pick up a blind man." Borges, undisturbed, responded, "I'm the blind man. One moment, please."

He can be as warm and charming as he can be elusive and ironic. When a visitor told him, "Poetry is my hobby," he replied, "It's mine too, but in a South American way." During my week-long interview his moods changed from serenity to cheerfulness to an extreme childlike impatience. When the *Life* photographer didn't arrive the day he was expected, Borges became very restless; when we met a year later it was the first thing he joked about. He listened to my tapes with a boyish enjoyment after I had recorded his casual poetry readings.

At a dinner with his Harvard and Radcliffe students he was cheerful and friendly. According to them, Borges got them so interested in Latin America that they didn't care if they could not discuss contemporary politics with him. As one student summarized his feeling: "He is a present-day figure, much more avantguard than many of his contemporaries. Because he is not faddish, he continues to be fresh and new."

Borges's writing *does* reflect his lack of interest in the contemporary world, for he lives in another world, a world of fantasies, mirrors, daggers, labyrinths, imaginary things. But he did speak to me in his beautiful Spanish, with ease and nostalgia, about his life, his work, his dearest friends. To highlight his comment he recited *coplas* and *milongas* or asked me to read some of his long poems that he had not memorized.

Reticent about his private life, he alludes to "two Borges"—one the man, the other the writer—and he describes them in his essay "Borges and I." ("The other one, the one called Borges, is the one things happen to.") But the two, the person and "the other one," sometimes become fused. Borges, the man, was moved to tears when in 1971 Columbia University gave him an honorary degree. And, as he confessed in "Borges and I": "It should be an exaggeration to say that ours is a hostile relationship; I live, let myself go on living, so that Borges may contrive his literature, and this literature justifies me."

What effect has the loss of your sight had on your life and work?

On my father's side I belong to the fifth, or possibly sixth generation that included many who lost their sight. I watched my father and my grandmother go blind. My own sight was never good, and I knew what fate had in store for me. I was also able to admire the combination of submissiveness and irony with which my father endured his blindness for more than a year. Perhaps this forbearance is as typical of the blind as irritability is typical of the deaf; maybe a blind man senses the friendliness of the people around him. One proof of this is that there are lots of comic stories about deaf people and none about the blind. It would be too cruel to joke about the blind. I've quite lost count of the operations they have performed on me, and by 1955, when the revolutionary government appointed me director of the National Library, I was no longer able to read. That was when I wrote my "Poem of Gifts," in which I said that God "with magnificent irony, gave me books and darkness at the same time." The books were the 800,000 volumes of the National Library, and I have been getting closer to total darkness ever since that time. But it has hardly been a painful process, because dusk came so very slowly. There was a moment when I could only read books with large print, and then another when I could only read the title page or the words on the spine, and then another when I could read nothing at all. A slow dusk, which wasn't especially painful to me. And now I can still see, but very little; I can't see your face at this moment, but there is an immeasurable difference between seeing very little and not seeing at all. A person who can't see at all is like a prisoner, whereas I can see enough to go about the town—whether it's Cambridge or Buenos Aires—with a certain illusion of liberty. Of course, I can't cross a street without help, and as people are very polite in New England and in Buenos Aires, they generally offer to help of their own accord when they see me hesitating on the edge of the sidewalk.

My blindness has certainly had an effect on my "work," in quotes. I've never written a novel because I think that as a novel has a consecutive existence for the reader it may also have a purely consecutive existence for the writer. On the other hand, a story is something that you take in at a single reading. As Poe used to say: "There's no such thing as a long poem." Poe wrote a number of short poems. The fact that I like to take great trouble over my writing has made me abandon story writing and return to classical poetic forms, because rhyme has mnemonic value. If I know the first line it gives me the fourth where the rhyme recurs. So I've returned to regular verse forms, because a sonnet is a portable thing, as it were. I can go on walking all over the town while I carry a sonnet in my head, polishing and altering as I go. You can't do that with a long piece of prose. I also write verses for *milongas* and other short compositions—such as fables and parables—taking up about a page or a page and a half; these too can be carried in the head, and dictated and corrected later.

There's another thing I would like to mention, and that is that time passes differently when one has lost one's sight. Formerly, if I took a train journey of half an hour or so it used to seem interminable, and I had to read or do something to pass the time. Whereas now that there are inevitable hours of solitude in my life, I've got used to being alone and thinking about something, or else I simply don't think and am merely content to exist. I let time flow past me, and it seems to pass differently. I'm not sure whether it goes faster, but it certainly contains a sort of serenity and much more concentration. Also I have a better memory than I did before; that may be because I used to read superficially, knowing that I could always come back to the book. But if I ask someone to read to me nowadays, I can't keep on pestering him. When someone reads aloud to me I listen more attentively than before. My memory was naturally visual, but now I've had to learn the art of auditory memory. When I could see a little, I used to open a book and know instinctively that what I had read was, let us say, at the bottom of one of the odd pages, and its general whereabouts in the book. Now I have to manage differently. I've got quite a good memory and I began learning Old English in

1955, when I could no longer read. Since then I've held a seminar in Old English for a small group of students. Once I got them to draw on the blackboard in the National Library the two runic letters representing the sound *th* in Anglo-Saxon. I know hundreds of lines of Anglo-Saxon verse by heart, but I couldn't clearly imagine the page they were written on. The students drew them very large, in chalk, and now I have some idea what those unseen pages look like.

From some of your poems, such as "Another Poem of Gifts," and "New England 1967," in which you say "And America is waiting for me at every corner," I gather that you feel affection for the United States.

Ever since the days of my childhood, when I read Mark Twain, Bret Harte, Hawthorn, Jack London, and Edgar Allan Poe, I've been very much attached to the United States. I still am. Perhaps I'm influenced by the fact that I had an English grandmother, and English and Spanish were spoken indiscriminately in our house when I was a boy, so much so that I wasn't even aware that they were separate languages. When I was talking to my paternal grandmother I had to speak in a manner that I afterwards discovered was called English, and when I was talking to my mother or her parents I had to talk a language that afterwards turned out to be Spanish. My affection for the United States makes me deplore the fact that many Latin Americans, and very likely many North Americans as well, admire the United States for the wrong things. For instance, when I think of the United States I visualize those New England houses, houses built of red brick, or else the sort of wooden Parthenons one sees in the South; I think of a way of life, and also of writers who have meant a lot to me. First of all I think of Whitman, Thoreau, Melville, Henry James, and Emerson. But I notice that most people admire this country for its gadgets, its supermarkets and things like paper bags—even garbage bags—and plastics. All these things are perishable, however, and are made for use, not for worship. It seems to me that we should praise or condemn the United States for quite different things. You live here, and I don't suppose you spend all your time thinking about gadgets. And perhaps the streets of New England are more typically American than the skyscrapers, or anyhow people love them more. What I'm trying to say is that it's important to see this side of America too. Although I prefer New England, when I was in New York I felt enormously proud of it, and thought to myself: "Good Lord, how well the city has turned out," just as if I'd built it myself. In my poem "Another Poem of Gifts," I praise God for many things, and among others:

> For the hard riders who, on the plains,
> Drive on the cattle and the dawn,
> For mornings in Montevideo . . .
> For the high towers of San Francisco and Manhattan Island . . .

And also for mornings in Texas, for Emerson's poetry, for the events of my life, for music, for English poetry; for my grandmother, my English grandmother, who when she was dying called us all to her side and said: "Nothing in particular is happening. I'm only an old woman who is dying very, very slowly; there's no reason for the whole house to worry about it. I have to apologize to you all." What a beautiful thing!

> For Frances Haslam, who begged her children's pardon
> For dying so slowly,
> For the minutes that precede sleep,
> For sleep and death,
> Those two hidden treasures,
> For the intimate gifts I do not mention
> For music, that mysterious form of time.

My grandmother was the wife of Colonel Borges, who was killed in action in the revolution of 1874. She had seen life on the frontier among the Indians, and had talked to their chief, Pincén. That was at Junín.

Why do you think the American way of life is being copied everywhere?

I think it's part of a general trend. When I was born—in 1899—the world, or Argentina and Buenos Aires at least looked toward France. That is to say, although we were Argentines we were Frenchmen at heart, or playing at being French. But now the trend is to look toward the United States. This is reflected in everything: in sports, in people's way of life, in the fact that they used to get drunk on absinthe and now prefer to do it on whiskey, and even when the whiskey is Scotch they think of it as American. It makes no difference. Politics has become so important that at present two countries stand out from the rest, quite apart from our preferences or dislikes. Those two countries are the United States and the Soviet Union. Of course, I personally love England very much and I would like it if people also looked toward England, but I realize that's not happening. In the world of today, those two countries stand for history, and are in conflict. We have reached a state of war between the two trends and one or the other will prevail—democracy or communism, or rather what is called democracy and what is called communism.

With which country do you feel most identified—with France, where your talent was first recognized, or with the United States?

With the United States. I am not against France. How could I suggest that we forget the country that produced Voltaire, Verlaine, and Hugo? Without French culture we should not have had the literary renewal called Modernism, we should have had no Rubén Darío, no Lugones. I can never disown the culture of any country. I was educated in Switzerland, and got my baccalaureate in Geneva during the First World War. Although I am very fond of Switzerland, I don't feel identified with that country. Nor, of course, do I want to say a single word against France, yet I wouldn't care to live there either . . . oh well, the fact is I wouldn't like to live anywhere except the Argentine Republic. If I couldn't live in Buenos Aires, my second choice would be Montevideo, which is much the same. Here in the States, I feel homesick for Buenos Aires—that's only too obvious in everything I've written recently. This doesn't mean that Buenos Aires seems to me a particularly beautiful town; on the contrary, I think it's really rather drab. That has nothing to do with it; one doesn't love a town for its architecture.

When did you first come to the United States?

Six years ago. I came with my mother; we spent five months in Texas and I taught Argentine literature there. But I was a student as well as a professor, and attended Dr. Willard's classes in Old English. After that we went to New Mexico, Arizona, and San Francisco—one of the most beautiful cities in the world—and Los Angeles, which is one of the most horrible.

Is this your first visit to Harvard?

I gave a lecture at Harvard a few years ago, but I can't remember much about it; it was just something that turned up. This is my first official visit. I am the Charles Eliot Norton Professor of Poetry, and some of my distinguished forerunners have been e. e. cummings and the great Spanish poet Jorge Guillén. I was invited to lecture on poetry. I've taken a line from Yeats as my theme and the title of my lectures—"This Craft of Verse." I also gave a course on Argentine poetry here at Harvard.

What can you tell me about your months at Harvard?

I've met with a hospitality, a warmth here that has really amazed me; it has almost frightened me. I've heard applause such as I've never before heard in my life. I have been cheered in Buenos Aires, but partly out of amiability. Here the applause has been so warm-hearted that it has astonished me. I don't know what the reason for this is and I've been trying to think of an explanation. To a certain extent, my being blind may have helped me, although I'm not really entitled to the description because I can still see your face, even if only as a hazy shape. Then there's the fact that I'm a foreigner. Perhaps a foreigner always gets a warmer reception, because he can't be anyone's rival, he's someone who appears and will disappear again. Then I think there may be another reason. Usually when a Latin American or a Spaniard comes here he keeps on emphasizing the exceptional merit of what is being done in his own country, whereas when I give lectures on poetry I take my examples from English poets, Scandinavian poets, Latin, Spanish, and American poets, so they don't feel that I'm "selling anything" as you say here, but am someone who is genuinely interested in poetry. All this may have helped me.

Is there much interest in Argentine literature?

Yes, a great deal. However, I've discovered that very little is known about it, because the teachers are generally Spaniards, who are naturally more inclined to tell them about what is being written on the other side of the Atlantic. Or else, if they are Cubans or Mexicans, of course they teach what is nearer at hand and what they themselves like best. Whereas we Argentines are such a long way off that naturally very little is known about us. So very little that when I mention a name like Lugones, for instance, I notice that the students stare at me rather strangely. They have never heard of him.

Which writers did you teach?

I thought that what always interested foreigners most was local color. So, as we have a quite striking literature of this type, I began by talking about the gauchesco poets. I talked about Bartolomé Hidalgo, Hilario Ascasubi, Estanislao del Campo, and José Hernández. I devoted more than one class to *Martín Fierro,* and another to the gaucho novels of Eduardo Gutiérrez; I also talked about *Don Segundo Sombra,* whose author, Ricardo Güiraldes, was a great friend of mine. Then I told them about Sarmiento, Almafuerte, Lugones, Martínez Estrada, Enrique Banchs, and something about Bioy Casares, Carlos Mastronardi, and Manuel Peyrou. You will think that I was unfair to many people, but I preferred the study of a few writers to the listing of many after the manner of a telephone directory. It would be pointless to say that there was a famous poet called Rafael Obligado, give his dates, say that he wrote *Santos Vega,* and pass on to the next. That's no use to anyone. Instead, we read the first part of *Martín Fierro,* many things by Ascasubi, and as for Lugones, I succeeded in interesting my students a great deal in him. I reminded them that in 1907 Lugones had published a book of tales, called *Las fuerzas extrañas* (Strange Forces), and that two of these stories, written under the influence of Wells and Poe, approached what is called science fiction today and, what's more, were very good. One striking story, *Yzur,* is about a monkey, who learns to speak and goes mad in the process. It's a very tragic tale. This sort of science fiction was not being written in Spanish in the year 1907. I've also been delighted to find that many students take an interest in writers who are Argentines but not professionally so. This morning a girl told me she was working on a thesis on Enrique Banchs. He's a great Argentine poet who doesn't try to be particularly Argentine. He writes admirable sonnets with an unconscious Argentine flavor. Other students have brought me theses about the *Lunario sentimental* by Leopoldo Lugones and Banchs's *La urna.* It's clear that these students don't read Argentine books as documents about a far-off and picturesque country; they are in search of literature.

This morning, in the coffee shop, you were very pleased when one of your students told you about the work he was doing on Carlos Mastronardi.

Carlos Mastronardi means a lot to me, and I was very much moved to think that this great poet and friend should be the subject of a New England student's thoughts. He was going to write about the poem "Luz de provincia" (Light of the Province), dedicated to the province of Entre Rios, and almost the only work by Mastronardi. It's a poem I've read with love all through the years, and a line occurs in it which I always remember with pleasure: "the beloved, the gentle, the beloved province"; the word "beloved" returns as if the poet felt it to be the last word, as if he was tired of searching for adjectives and returned to his own love for his province.

In what language did you teach Argentine literature?

In Spanish, and I would say the students' Spanish was good. Of course, my own is less Mexican, less Cuban, and less Spanish than theirs. That's only to be expected, isn't it? But they can follow the classes, and what is more important still, they can tell if a poem is good or bad. I don't think a professor ought to praise everything he teaches, or his students may begin to be a little suspicious. When we were reading the poems of Lugones and I came across a line I didn't like, I either said so or left it to them to find out. I think I succeeded in creating an atmosphere of give-and-take between us, and not just telling them that So-and-So was a great poet and that they must accept him as such. I also achieved my main object: I got them to enjoy Almafuerte, to enjoy Hernández, Lugones, and Banchs. I think this is more important than anything else. When one of my students enjoys these writers, I feel I have achieved something.

If there a good understanding between you and your students?

I've found the atmosphere very welcoming. Something very strange happens. When I'm talking to the students here at Harvard I forget that I'm speaking English and that I'm at Harvard, and I feel just as if I were talking to my friends in Buenos Aires. They seem to me so alike! I have the same impression of conversation, of discussion, that I remember so well in Buenos Aires. When I'm talking to my students I refuse to be so pedantic as to think of them as students and myself as their professor; we begin to discuss some literary topic and then we become two human beings talking about what interests us. I don't even feel tempted to talk didactically, or give them advice; its a conversation in which we are both really collaborating. I very much enjoy talking to young people. And I realize from their questions that I am in very intelligent company, and that the students here seem less interested in examinations and degrees than in what they are studying. That's terrific. I've met some people who know my work much better than I do myself, because I only wrote the words once and they have read them several times and tried to analyze them, whereas when I write something I publish it in order to forget about it. They have asked me quite difficult questions showing their interest in the subject, though sometimes I find them puzzling. Often it's because I've forgotten the details of what I've written, and when I'm aksed "Why did So-and-So remain silent for a while and then begin to talk?" I say: "Who?" I don't remember the character, and I don't remember why he was doing what he did at that moment. I've also been asked some very intelligent questions. Students found hidden affinities in texts that I thought were very far removed from one another. For instance, they made me see that a story I wrote about the labyrinth had links with a certain detective story, something I hadn't realized myself.

Do you find great differences between American and Argentine students?

On the whole I think that one of the diseases of our time consists in exaggerating the differences between one country and another. I believe young people are much the same everywhere. Possibly Argentine students are more timid than Americans. Here a student can interrupt one and ask a question, but that may be because it's understood here that a student who questions his professor is not doing it out of impertinence but because the subject interests him. In Buenos Aires maybe they think a student asks questions so as to make a nuisance of himself.

Isn't this the result of the attitude of professors in Argentina?
Perhaps. Although I've maintained that it wasn't so, I have found it very difficult to get a classroom discussion going back home. Of course, I prefer discussing with my students rather than laying down the law. I have the impression that they work harder here. At home, as a result of university reform, there were some very idle people who only worked for their examinations. For instance, I was present at an examination when the professor asked one of the students what subject he had chosen. What sort of way is that to conduct an examination? And I remember one girl taking an essay she had brought with her out of her case, and reading it. I interrupted her and said: "Young lady, this is the Faculty of Philosophy and Letters; there's no need for you to prove to us that you can read and write. You chose your subject yourself, why don't you speak about it?" And some of the professors said: "Oh well, we shouldn't expect so much."

What do you think about the hippies and drug-taking?
I don't think either hippies or drugs deserve any encouragement. They seem to me to represent something typical of the United States. In spite of all his good qualities, an American has a tendency to solitude, or rather he's a victim of solitude. I'm reminded of a book by David Riesman, called *The Lonely Crowd*. One of the advantages we Latin Americans have over North Americans is that we can communicate more easily, whereas I've noticed that North Americans experience a difficulty in communication which they try to conceal by means of all their celebrations, like Christmas, and by forming a lot of societies and holding congresses where people wear a little label with their name written on it. All this seems to me a rather pathetic pretense of friendship, or of being among other people, perhaps every one of whom is really very lonely. You notice the same thing in the English, except that an Englishman doesn't mind being alone; he's comfortable when he's alone. I've known of intimate friends in England who have never once confided in each other, yet feel they are friends. Anything I say about hippies, however, is quite valueless, because I've never talked to one in my life. People have drawn my attention to a rather exotically dressed young man in the street, and told me, "That's a hippie"; I pretend to see him but I don't, and afterwards they tell me he has long hair and a beard, and takes drugs. I don't think any of that is much good, nor that it will lead them very far. It's always

the same: if someone is against a convention his only way of attacking it is by creating another convention, so that when most people are clean-shaven he grows a beard, and when beards are worn he shaves his off. He's merely changing from one convention to another. I remember that the first night I went out after my arrival, I was told that there were groups of young people dressed with careful extravagance, and that they were hippies. Generalizing as usual, I wondered how I was going to teach Argentine literature to these young people who had resolved to disagree with everything; but when I held my first class I realized that this wasn't so, that not a single one was a hippie.

They disagree with the establishment and the consumers' society.

Yes, and they want to connect this with Thoreau, don't they? I've read Veblen's book, *The Theory of the Leisure Class,* in which he says that one of the characteristics of modern society is that people have to spend money conspicuously, and thus impose a number of obligations on themselves. They have to live in a certain part of town, they must spend their holidays at a certain beach. Veblen says that a tailor in London or Paris receives an exaggerated sum because what people want of him is precisely that his goods should be very expensive. Or, for instance, a painter may paint a contemptible picture, but as he's a famous artist he sells it for an enormously high figure, because the purpose of buying it is that the buyer can say, "I've got a Picasso." Naturally I believe this sort of thing should be opposed, and if the hippies think they can fight it, more power to them. Meanwhile I myself don't hold any of these superstitions. I don't believe one must live in a certain district or dress in a certain fashion.

The hippies also rebel against violence. Do you agree with them about that?

That seems to me an excellent thing. It's rather the same as what Lanza del Vasto used to preach. He gave a lecture in the National Library and spoke in favor of passive resistance. I was foolish enough to ask him: "Tell me, do you believe passive resistance is infallible?" The reply he made was very reasonable. "No,"he said, "passive resistance is just as fallible as active resistance. I believe one should attempt it, but it's not a panacea." "Do you believe that passive resistance would have had any effect against the Soviet dictatorship, or Hitler, or Perón?" "Probably not; all the same you take the risk." It's a means to an end which can't be guaranteed, and the hippies seem to think likewise.

Toynbee has said that hippies are the product of technology and science. Do you agree?

It's easier to say that they are the product of technology and science after

they've appeared on the scene. The interesting thing would have been to say
so before.

*Would you say that an Argentine has a distinct identity, just as a modern
Frenchman, a Mexican, or American has, for instance?*
   People often confuse the difficulty of definition with the difficulty of the
problems themselves. In this case it would be very hard to define an Argentine, just as it is hard to define the color red, the taste of coffee, or the quality
of epic poetry. All the same, we Argentines know, or rather feel what it
means to be Argentines, and that's much more important than any definition.
We feel without needing to define it that an Argentine is different from a
Spaniard, a Colombian, or a Chilean, and that he differs very little from a
Uruguayan. I think that ought to satisfy us, because one doesn't generally
conduct one's life by means of definitions so much as by direct intuitions.
Although it's hard to define the Argentine way of talking, no sooner does a
person start speaking than one knows if he's an Argentine or not, and which
region he comes from. I believe we recognize the Argentine flavor, not only
in gaucho poetry or the novels of Gutiérrez or Güiraldes, which have deliberately aimed at it, but also in poets who don't set out to be Argentine, who are
not professionally and incessantly Argentine. Everyone feels that a poem by
Fernández Moreno is an Argentine poem, and I hope that my own pages give
a feeling that I'm an Argentine, especially those pages devoid of local color.
If I write an article on some abstract problem, or if I discuss some metaphysical theme, my way of doing it is different from what a Spaniard's would be,
my syntax is different—one might almost say my tone of voice is different.
This is why I believe that although there is such a thing as being Argentine,
there's no point in trying to define it. If we did, we should afterwards be
pinned to the definition, and no longer be spontaneous Argentines. It's just
the same with the language. When I began writing I wanted to write classical
seventeenth-century Spanish; afterwards I bought a dictionary of Argentine
expressions and became studiously Argentine. Later on I wrote a story like
"Hombre de la esquina rosada." (Streetcorner Man), in which I tried to be
picturesque and exaggerated the local color. Now I think I've caught the
Argentine accent; there's no need to search for it when writing or speaking,
because I've got it.

Would you call yourself a typical Argentine?
   The fact is that I don't know whether a *typical* Argentine exists; I don't
know if there is an Argentine archetype. To say I identify myself with a

country is a bit of a fraud; in Buenos Aires I identify myself with six or seven people whom I see all the time. Above all with certain habits: mornings walking down Calle Florida, afternoons walking to the Southside to the National Library.

Have you ever thought of leaving Buenos Aires?

I couldn't live anywhere but Buenos Aires. I'm used to it, just as I'm used to my own voice, to my body, to being Borges, to that series of habits that's known as Borges—and one part of these habits is Buenos Aires. My real life is in Buenos Aires; and besides I'm nearly seventy, it would be absurd for me to want to start a new life elsewhere. Nor have I any reason to do so. My mother lives in Buenos Aires; my sister, my nephews, my friends are all in Buenos Aires, and my life is there. I'm a director of the National Library, occupy the chair of English and American literature at the University, and I also hold a seminar in Old English. A proof that there's still some of the right spirit left in Argentina is that this seminar is attended by a small group, nearly all girls, some of whom have office jobs. They are studying something which will be of no practical use to them.

If an intellectual shuts himself up in an ivory tower, and sometimes even ignores reality, can he contribute to solving the problems of his society?

Possibly shutting oneself in an ivory tower and thinking about other things may be one way of modifying reality. I live in an ivory tower—as you call it—creating a poem, or a book, and that can be just as real as anything else. People are generally wrong when they take reality as meaning daily life, and think of the rest as unreal. In the long run, emotions, ideas, and speculations are just as real as everyday events, and can also cause everyday events. I believe that all the dreamers and philosophers in the world are having an influence on our present-day life.

You've written several milongas *lately. Why* milongas *rather than tangos?*

Unlike most Argentines, I believe the tango began to decline with Gardel and the sentimental tangos of the type of *"La comparsita."* The earlier ones were far better, those we call the tangos of the old guard: I'm thinking of *"El cuzquito," "El pollito," "La morocha," "Rodríguez Peña," "El choclo," "Una noche de garufa,"* and *"El apache argentino."* All these tangos had the same spirit of dash and bravery as the *milonga,* which was a much older form. The tango dates from the 1880's, and had its origins in bawdyhouses. The *milonga* was already there. When I was asked to write the lyrics for a tango, I thought to myself: "No, I'd rather write words for *milongas*," and I wrote them all about real persons, using the names of actual hoodlums I had known personally, or whose story or legend I had heard as a boy. My best is one of the first I wrote, the "Milonga of Jacinto Chiclana," which refers to a man who was stabbed to death in a crowd near the Plaza del Once in Buenos Aires.

You've also written about the city of Buenos Aires.
    Yes, quite a lot. When I returned from Europe in 1921 I wanted to write a book of memories of the Palermo district. I knew the caudillo Nicolás Paredes at that time. Later I dedicated a *milonga* to him, but in it I called him Nicanor, because relations of his were still living and I didn't know whether they would like what I said about his having killed two men. I made this slight alteration in his name, firstly for reasons of personal security and also because it made for easier rhyming. No one who has lived in Palermo could be unaware that I was really referring to Nicolás Paredes, nor fail to recognize him under my very thin disguise.

When you returned to Buenos Aires in the twenties, why were you so attracted by the compadrito, *or hoodlum?*
    Well, that actually came a little later. I felt the attraction because there was something about the old-time hoodlum that struck me as new—the idea of disinterested courage for its own sake. He wasn't defending a position, say, or ready to fight for the money; he fought disinterestedly. I remember a friend of mine, Ernesto Poncio, author of one of the earliest and best tangos, *"Don Juan,"* saying to me: "I've been in prison lots of times, Borges, but always for manslaughter." What he meant by this boast was that he hadn't been a thief or a pimp, but that he'd simply killed a man. He'd gained a reputation as a brave man and he had to live up to it. To me there's something pathetic about such poor men as these hoodlums were—wagon drivers or slaughterhouse workers—clinging to one luxury: that of being brave and quick to kill or be killed at any moment, maybe by someone they didn't know. It's what I tried to convey in my poem "El Tango."
    I've talked to lots of people about the early days of the tango, and they all tell me the same thing—that it did not come from the people. It began in brothels, in about 1880, so I was told by one of my uncles, who had been a bit of a rake in his day. I think the proof is that if the tango had been popular its instrument would have been the guitar, as in the case of the *milonga*. Instead, it was played by piano, flute, and violin—instruments belonging to

a higher economic level. Where could people living in tenement houses get
money to buy pianos? This is confirmed by what contemporaries say, and
also by a poem by Marcelo del Mazo, describing a dance at the beginning of
the century.

And the bandoneón?

That came much later. And even if it had been earlier, it was never a
popular instrument. The guitar is the instrument of the people of Buenos
Aires; the *bandoneón* may possibly have been played by the Genoese in the
Boca.

Are there any of these old-time hoodlums left today?

I don't think so, nor does the word have the same meaning. In the old days
a hoodlum only used to kill once in a blue moon. Today we have gangsters,
and now murderous attacks and crimes are frequent in Buenos Aires. It's like
your gangsters here; what they do is a matter of economics.

Is there a cult of gauchos and the pampa?

The cult of the gaucho is even more vigorous in Uruguay than among us
Argentines. I know this from the experience of an uncle of mine, the Uruguayan writer Luis Melián Lafinur, who went so far as declaring that there
was nothing special about the gaucho except, of course, for incest.

The cult of the pampa is perhaps less in evidence. The word is little used
in the country; it belongs to literary circles in Buenos Aires. I think one of
the false notes in *Don Segundo Sombra* is that the characters talk about the
pampa. They say, "We were men of the pampa," for instance. Ascasubi and
Hernández used the word, but in a different sense, referring to the territory
occupied by Indians. That's why I've done my best to avoid it. On the other
hand, "plains," although it's not used in the country, is a less pretentious
word. Bioy Casares told me that when he was a boy one very rarely saw a
proper gaucho complete with poncho, baggy trousers, and blanket; some
wore a poncho, others baggy trousers and blanket, but only today do you see
people rigged up from head to foot as gauchos. Strangely enough—so he
says—country people don't dress like people of the province of Buenos Aires
any more, but like gauchos from Salta. This is because a lot of films have
been made about them, and also because gauchos buy whatever they find in
the shops. He told me that in the province of Buenos Aires you see gauchos
with wide-brimmed hats—a thing that would have amazed any gaucho fifty
years ago. The country is full of gauchos nowadays, something that never
happened before when the country was more creole.

And what about the cult of mate?

Yes, it is still an Argentine habit. I think they see it as a way of passing time, like cards. It's a form of idleness, not of nourishment. I've not tasted mate for forty years. At one time I used to drink it and was proud of my addiction, but I was very bad at it. There were always a lot of dismal little bits floating in it. After the death of my grandfather, who was a mate drinker, we gave it up.

To return to your work: which writers have inspired you?

I've been inspired by all the books I've ever read and those I've not read as well—all literature before my time. I owe a lot to people whose names I don't know. You see, I write in one language, Spanish, and am influenced by English literature; that means that thousands of persons are influencing me. A language is in itself a literary tradition.

I've spent many years of my life studying Chinese philosophy, for instance, especially Taoism, which interests me very much, but I've also studied Buddhism and am interested in Sufism. Therefore, all this has influenced me, but I don't know to what extent. I'm not sure whether I've studied these religions and Oriental philosophies because of their effect on my thoughts and actions, or from an imaginative point of view, for literary reasons. But I think this may happen with every philosophy. Except for Schopenhauer or Berkeley, no philosopher has ever given me the sensation that I was reading a true or even probable description of the world. I've looked at metaphysics rather more as a branch of fantastic literature. For instance, I'm not sure whether I'm a Christian, but I've read a great many books on theology for the sake of their theological problems—free will, punishment, and eternal happiness. All these problems have interested me as food for my imagination.

Of course, if I may mention some names, it gives me pleasure to acknowledge my gratitude to Whitman, Chesterton, Shaw, and others to whom I often return, like Emerson. I would include some who may not be very famous as writers. For instance, of all the people I've known, the one who impressed me most as a person was Macedonio Fernández, an Argentine writer whose conversation was far above anything he wrote. He was a man who had read little, but thought for himself. He impressed me enormously. I've talked with famous people from other countries, like Waldo Frank and Ortega y Gasset, and I hardly recall those conversations. On the other hand, if I was told it was possible to talk with Macedonio Fernández, quite apart from the miracle of talking to someone who is dead, I'd be so greatly interested in what he said that I'd forget I was conversing with a ghost. A writer called Rafael Cansinos-Assens, an Andalusian Jew, also had a great influence on me; he seemed to belong to every century. I met him in Spain. Of the people I've mentioned, apart from my father, whom I can't judge because I was too close to him, those who have impressed me most were Macedonio Fernández and Cansinos-Assens. I've got very pleasant memories of Lugones, but perhaps I should omit them. What Lugones wrote is more important than my conversations with him. It would seem to me both unjust and illogical not to mention here someone of essential importance to me, one of the few people who have been essential to me, and that is my mother—my mother who is now living in Buenos Aires, who was honorably imprisoned at the time of Perón's dictatorship along with my sister and one of my nephews, my mother, who in spite of having just had her ninety-first birthday is far younger than I am or than most of the women I know. I feel that she has in a sense collaborated in what I have written. And I repeat, it would be absurd to talk about myself and not mention Leonor Acevedo de Borges.

Would you like to say something about the work of the writers you admire so much: Whitman, Chesterton, and Shaw?

Whitman is one of the poets who has most impressed me in the whole of my life. I think there's a tendency to confuse Mr. Walter Whitman, the author of *Leaves of Grass* with Walt Whitman, the protagonist of *Leaves of Grass,* and that Walt Whitman does not provide us with an image so much as a sort of magnification of the poet. In *Leaves of Grass,* Walter Whitman wrote a species of epic whose portagonist was Walt Whitman—not the Whitman who was writing but the man he would like to have been. Of course, I'm not saying this in criticism of Whitman; his work should not be read as the confessions of a man of the nineteenth century, but rather as an epic about an imaginary figure, a utopian figure, who is to some extent a magnification and projection of the writer as well as of the reader. You will remember that in *Leaves of Grass* the author often merges himself with the reader, and of course this expresses his theory of democracy, the idea that a single unique protagonist can represent a whole epoch. The importance of Whitman cannot be overstated. Even taking into account the versicles of the Bible or of Blake, Whitman can be said to be the inventor of free verse. He can be looked at in two ways: there is his civic side—the fact that one is aware of crowds, great cities, and America—and there is also an intimate element, though we can't be sure whether it is genuine or not. The character Whitman has created is one of the most lovable and memorable in all literature. He is a character like Don Quixote or Hamlet, but someone no less complex and possibly more lovable than either of them.

Bernard Shaw is an author to whom I keep returning. I think he too is a writer who is often only read in part. One tends to think particularly of his early work, books in which he fought against the social order of his day. But beyond this, Shaw has epic significance, and is the only writer of our time who has imagined and presented heroes to his readers. On the whole, modern writers tend to reveal men's weaknesses, and seem to delight in their unhappiness; in Shaw's case, however, we have characters like Major Barbara or Caesar, who are heroic and whom one can admire. Contemporary literature since Dostoevski—and even earlier, since Byron—seems to delight in man's guilt and weaknesses. In Shaw's work the greatest human virtues are extolled. For example, that a man can forget his own fate, that a man may not value his own happiness, that he may say like our Almafuerte: "I'm not interested in my own life," because he is interested in something beyond personal circumstances. If one had to point out the best English prose, one would look for it in Shaw's prefaces and in many speeches of his characters. He is one of the writers I love best.

I also have a great affection for Chesterton. Chesterton's imagination was of a different sort from Shaw's, but I think Shaw will last longer than Chesterton. Chesterton's works are full of surprises, and I have come to the conclusion that the element that wears least well in a book is surprise. Shaw has a classical inspiration that we don't find in Chesterton. It's a pity that Chesterton's flavor should fade, but I think it likely that in a hundred or two hundred years' time Chesterton will only figure in histories of literature, and Shaw in literature itself.

When did you publish your first book?

In 1923. My father had told me that when I wrote a book I thought worth printing, he would give me the money to publish it. I had written two books before this, and had the good sense to destroy them. One called *Los ritmos rojos* (Red Rhythms) was as bad as its title, and consisted of poems on the Russian Revolution. At that time, communism stood for an idea of universal brotherhood. Next, I wrote a book called *Los naipes del tahur* (The Sharper's Cards), in which I tried to write like Pío Baroja. I realized these two books were bad, and I have expunged them from my memory; I remember their titles but nothing more. I did publish my third book, *Fervor de Buenos Aires,* because I was going to Europe for a year and wouldn't be present when the book came out, giving me a certain impunity. Alfredo Bianchi and Roberto Giusti were joint editors of the magazine *Nosotros*. I had the book printed, and went to the office of *Nosotros* taking fifty some copies. Bianchi stared at me in horror and said: "But do you want me to sell this book?" "No; I'm not mad," I replied. "What I want is something that the book's format makes possible—for you to slip a copy into the pocket of every overcoat that passes through your office." And in fact, when I returned after a year, not a single copy was left, and laudatory articles had been published about that book. I met young men who had read it and found something in it. That delighted me.

In *Fervor de Buenos Aires,* I wanted to write in a somewhat Latinized Spanish; afterwards, under the influence of Macedonio Fernández, I tried to discover a metaphysical form of poetry, dealing with those perplexities we call philosophy, and later still I wanted to write about Buenos Aires—about my rediscovery of Buenos Aires after so many years in Europe. All this was present in *Fervor de Buenos Aires* in a somewhat incoherent and therefore awkward form. But I think I am in that book, and that everything I have done since is to be found between its lines. I recognize myself in it more than I do in my other books, although I don't suppose the reader would recognize me. It seems to me that in it I was on the point of writing what I was to write thirty or forty years later.

If you read my collected poems you'll see that I have very few themes. I've written three or four poems, I'm not sure which, about the death of my grandfather, Colonel Borges, who was killed in action in 1874; there's a poem about my grandfather in *Fervor de Buenos Aires,* and I see that I've returned to the subject in other books. I think I gave final expression to it in a poem to Junín in my last book. It's as if I had spent my whole life writing seven or eight poems and trying out different variations, as if each book expunged the one before. But I'm not ashamed of this; it's proof that I write sincerely, since it wouldn't be very difficult to find other themes. If I return to the same ones it is because I feel them to be essential, and also because I feel I've not done with them, that I still owe them something. In other cases, I have also written the same poem twice over—for example, "Odyssey, Book 23" and "Alexander Selkirk." When I wrote "Alexander Selkirk" I had no idea that I had already written the same poem about a different character.

Will there be a change of style in your future works?

I began writing in a very self-conscious, baroque style. It was probably due to youthful timidity. The young often suspect that their plots and poems aren't very interesting, so they try to conceal them or elaborate on them by other means. When I began to write I tried to adopt the style of classical Spanish seventeenth-century writers, such as Quevedo or Saavedra Fajardo. Then I reflected that it was my duty as an Argintine to write like an Argentine. I bought a dictionary of Argentinisms, and managed to become so Argentine in my style and vocabulary that people couldn't understand me and I couldn't even remember very well myself what the words meant. Words passed directly from the dictionary to my manuscript without corresponding to any experience. Now, after a great many years, I believe that it's best to write with a very simple vocabulary, and concentrate on the person whom certain modern poets are apt to forget entirely: the reader. Faulkner was a writer of genius, yet he had a perverse, a dreadfully bad influence on other writers. His idea of telling a story by juggling with time, and sometimes having recourse to two characters both with the same name amounts to a way of creating and perfecting chaos. We shouldn't aim at confusion, however easy it is to slip into it. So I try to limit my vocabulary; I don't try to be Argentine, any more than I fatally and necessarily am, and I always try to smooth over the reader's difficulties, which doesn't mean that I always write lucidly. A writer often gives way to clumsiness, either because he is tired, or because he assumes that what he understands will be comprehensible to everyone else.

Don't you think words and quotations in a foreign language may sometimes confuse the reader?

Certainly, but I'm used to thinking in English, and I also believe some English words are untranslatable, so I occasionally use them for the sake of precision. I'm not "showing off." Since I've done most of my reading in English, it's natural that the first word that comes to mind is often an English one. I usually try to reject it in case it might bewilder the reader. Stevenson used to say that on a well-written page the words should all look in the same direction, and perhaps a word in another language looks the other way and may confuse the reader; but there are some words one can't resign oneself to doing without because they express exactly what one wants to say.

Will you go on writing about imaginary things or about real things?

I want to write about real things, but I believe that realism is difficult, particularly if one wants to make it contemporary. If I write a story about some actual street or district of Buenos Aires, someone will immediately point out that people there don't talk like that. Therefore, I think it is more suitable for a writer to look for a subject that is rather further off either in time or space. I'm thinking of setting my stories in a somewhat remote period, say about fifty years ago, and perhaps in somewhat unknown or forgotten quarters of Buenos Aires, so that no one will know exactly how people used to talk and behave there. It seems to me this gives the author's imagination more freedom. I believe the reader is happier when he's reading about something that happened some time ago, because he's not confronted by reality, he's not having to carry out a sort of comparison or inspection of what the author is saying. I think the mistake made in *Don Segundo Sombra* was to aim at very faithful realism in a book which, after all, was an elegy of pastoral life.

Why did you use the pseudonym H. Bustos Domecq in your book Seis problemas para Don Isidro Parodi *(Six Problems for Don Isidro Parodi)?*

That's quite simple. I wrote the book in collaboration with Adolfo Bioy Casares. We knew that books written in collaboration are read as puzzles, with the reader trying to figure out who wrote this and who wrote that. So, as the book was written more or less as a joke, we decided to create a third man: "H.," because it seemed quite likely that he would have a name no one knew; "Bustos" because that was my great-grandfather's name, and "Domecq" from a great-grandfather of Bioy's. The odd thing is that this third person really exists, because what we write isn't like Bioy's work nor like mine. It has a different style, different idiosyncrasies, even the syntax is different. But in order that this third person should exist we had to forget that there were two of us. As we write, we become Bustos Domecq. If anyone asked me whether the plot was Bioy's or mine, who had invented some metaphor, and if this or that joke came from his side of the table or mine, I wouldn't know. The first time we began writing together, we immediately forgot there were two of us, and sometimes one of us would anticipate what the other was going to say. Actually, we allowed ourselves every possible freedom; we were as free as a single person alone with his thoughts. We got a lot of amusement out of writing. It's very difficult to write in collaboration; I've tried to do it with other friends but we got nowhere. My collaborator either wanted all his suggestions to be adopted or else was so polite that he approved of anything I said. One of the pleasures I promise myself when I return to Argentina is to go on collaborating with Bioy Casares.

Always as Bustos Domecq?

We have another name, Suárez Lynch—"Suárez" was one of my great-grandfathers and "Lynch" one of Bioy's—used when Bustos Domecq was recognized as our joint pen name. Last year we published the *Chronicles of Bustos Domecq,* a series of accounts of imaginary painters, sculptors, architects, cooks, and others. It is a sort of satire. We've got another book in reserve for future publication under the name of Suárez Lynch.

And as Jorge Luis Borges what are you writing at present?

I'm writing a story which will apparently deal with the dictatorship and the 1955 revolution. But that won't be its only subject. There will be another, a very Argentine one—friendship. I think it has a quite good plot, but the importance of it lies behind the events. I began dictating this story to my mother two or three years ago in Buenos Aires, but after two pages I realized that I was making a mistake, and that I had begun in a way that couldn't turn out well. Now, here in New England, I've suddenly seen how I must begin it. Sometimes it's a good thing to be far away from one's manuscript, because if I had been in Buenos Aires I might well have got onto the wrong track again. Now I have the advantage of having forgotten it and of starting from scratch. I think it may be one of my successful stories.

Does it have a title yet?

I think it will be called "Los amigos" (The Friends), but I'm not sure yet. It sounds like the name of a bar.

Have you any other work on hand?

At the moment, I'm working on some sonnets, which come to me slowly. I'm also thinking of writing a book on medieval Anglo-Saxon and Scandinavian literature. I've already done some work on it, but I shall go on with it in Buenos Aires, where I have my library. Later, I want to publish a book of psychological tales. I shall try to do without magic, labyrinths, mirrors, daggers, and all my other manias; there won't be any deaths, and the important thing will be the characters themselves. I want plots too, of course, for the reader's sake. And I continue to add to my collected poems. Every edition gives me a chance to cut out a few poems and add others. Every edition is a little larger than the last. And now the writer Norman Thomas di Giovanni, who has already published an anthology of Jorge Guillén, is working with me on an edition of my poems in English, which will be published in 1972, and contain some hundred poems translated by outstanding American and English poets.

You've also written some film scripts, haven't you?

Hugo Santiago, Adolfo Bioy Casares, and I have written the script of a film called *Invasion.* The setting is Buenos Aires, but a Buenos Aires of dreams or nightmare. The plot is Santiago's, and he will direct it.

Another story of mine, "El muerto" (The Dead Man) may possibly be
screened in the United States. The story takes place on the frontier between
Brazil and Uruguay, but I think they'll shoot it in the United States; the
important thing is the plot rather than local color, and I suggested that they
should change the location to the Far West. I think they're already working
on the script.

I have written two other film scripts with Adolfo Bioy Casares, but they
were turned down by Argentine producers and have appeared only in book
form. They are called *Los orilleros* (River Bank Dwellers) and *El paraíso de
los creyentes* (The Paradise of Believers).

What sort of films do you like?

I have to look for films where the dialogue is important, like *A Man for All
Seasons,* or else musicals like *West Side Story* or *My Fair Lady.* But Italian
and Swedish films are forbidden me, because I understand neither of these
languages and cannot see them. I like westerns very much, and also Hitchcock's films. One of the films that has impressed me most was *High Noon.*
It's a classic western, one of the best that has been made. Everyone likes
westerns, because they stand for the epic in an age whose writers have forgotten that it's the oldest form of poetry, or indeed of literature, since poetry
came before prose. Hollywood, with its westerns, has salvaged the epic for
the world. What humanity is looking for in westerns is the zest and spirit of
the epic, enjoyment of courage and adventure. On the whole I prefer American films to any other. French films seem to me a glorification of boredom.
When I was in Paris talking to French writers, I told them, with the innocent
aim of shocking them but also without departing from the truth, that I liked
American films best. They all agreed with me that if one went to the cinema
in search of sheer enjoyment, one would find it in American pictures. They
said that films like *Last Year in Marienbad* and *Hiroshima Mon Amour* were
seen out of a sense of duty, and very few people really enjoyed them.

What about the Argentine cinema?

René Mujica made a film of *"Hombre de la esquina rosada";* he did a
good job with the possibilities provided by the plot. I liked it. But on the
whole Argentine films aren't popular in Buenos Aires; people go to them out
of a sense of duty, because they think of them as experimental. There are no
directors, and their plots are very simple. In a country as economically re-
stricted as ours one should aim at films where the dialogue is important. For
instance, there's no reason why one shouldn't make a film like *The Collector,*

in which there were only three characters, a lot of dialogue, and no need for
great financial outlay.

And the Argentine theater?

There's considerable interest in the theater in Buenos Aires, particularly
in the companies of amateur actors who now go by the name of "vocational";
they may well be saving our theater. I've seen performances by them of
Shakespeare, Ibsen, and O'Neill. I think the public enjoys good things, and
if you give them good films and plays they appreciate them.

Are you interested in detective stories?

Yes. Bioy Casares and I suggested to an Argentine firm that they publish a
series of detective stories. At first they said that such novels suited the United
States and England, but that no one in the Argentine Republic was going to
buy them. In the end we convinced them, but only after a year's persuasion,
and now the series called *El séptimo círculo* (The Seventh Circle), edited by
Bioy Casares and myself, has published about two hundred titles, and some
have gone into three or four editions. I also tried to persuade the same publishers to do a science fiction series and they said that no one would buy
them. Another firm is publishing them and I approved the first, Bradbury's
Martian Chronicles.

In your literary career, what do you remember with most pleasure?

People have been very good to me, and my work has gained a recognition
that has been the creation of my admirers rather than the result of its own
merit. The strange thing is that all this has been a very slow process; for
many years I was the most obscure writer in Buenos Aires. I published a
book called *Historia de la eternidad,* (A History of Eternity) and at the end
of a year I discovered to my amazement and gratitude that I had sold forty-
seven copies. I wanted to seek out each of the purchasers and thank him
personally, and ask him to forgive me for all the mistakes in the book. On
the other hand, if one sells 470 copies, or 4,700, the number is too great for
the buyers to have faces, houses, or relations.

Nowadays, when I see that some book of mine has gone into several editions I'm not surprised; I see it all as an abstract process. Suddenly I've found
friends all over the world, and my books have been translated into many
languages. Of all the prizes I have been awarded, the one that pleased me
most was the Second Municipal Prize of Buenos Aires for a rather poor book
called *El idioma de los argentinos* (The Language of Argentines). That prize

gave me more pleasure than the Formentor, or the one awarded by the Society of Argentine Writers. Of all my publications, none pleased me more than that of a really *dreadfully* bad poem called "Himno a mar" (Hymn to the Sea), which appeared in a Sevillian magazine around 1918 or 1919.

Three Latin American writers—Borges, Asturias, and Neruda—were mentioned for the 1967 Nobel Prize. How do you feel about being nominated?

When I think of names like Bertrand Russell, Bernard Shaw, or Faulkner, to mention a few that occur to me, I think it would be absurd to give the prize to me.

How do you feel about Asturias winning the prize?

I don't know whether I would have chosen Asturias, but I would have preferred Neruda to Borges, because I consider him a better poet, although we disagree politically. I've only talked to Pablo Neruda once in my life and that was many years ago. We were both young and we came to the conclusion that nothing could be done with the Spanish language, and that we should rather attempt English. Perhaps each of us wanted to startle the other a little, and so we exaggerated our true opinions. I really know Neruda's work very little, but I think he's a worthy follower of Walt Whitman, or perhaps Carl Sandburg.

In a review of your Personal Anthology, Time *magazine for March 24, 1967, wrote that Argentina had produced a personality in Borges, but that she had no national literature. What is your view?*

I don't think people should make sweeping statements. I ought to feel flattered because it leads to the conclusion that Argentine literature started with me, but as that is obviously absurd I don't see why I should be grateful for such an inconvenient and outside present—a gigantic present.

Then can we speak of a national literature?

I believe so. We can be prouder of our literature than of some of our other activities. For instance, in the nineteenth century we produced *Facundo* and the gauchesco poets, and later on there was a great revival of literature in the Spanish language on our side of the Atlantic. Then came modernism, beginning with Darío, Lugones, and others. I think we've achieved something. But when I began to write my tales of imagination I was quite unaware of an Argentine tradition, a tradition started by Lugones.

What do you think of literary criticism in Latin America?

Well, I don't want to offend any critics, but those who write in the daily papers are very cautious. Their watchword seems to be neither to blame nor praise excessively. The newspapers do their utmost not to commit themselves. It's different here in the United States, but there are probably economic interests involved as well.

Do you think this economic factor has a great influence on critics?

Maybe. It can also influence writers. Perhaps a writer feels freer when he knows that his work won't earn him much. I remember a time, about 1920 or 1925, when books brought in very little or nothing. This gave a writer great freedom. He couldn't pander to the mob because there was nothing to pander himself for.

Would you say there's greater interest in Latin American literature today?

Yes. For instance, writers like Eduardo Mallea, Bioy Casares, Manuel Mujica Láinez, Julio Cortázar, and myself are pretty well known in Europe, and this has never happened before. When I was in Spain in 1920, talking to Spanish writers, I thought I would casually mention the name of Lugones, and I came to the conclusion that it meant very little to them, or else they thought of him merely as a follower of Herrera y Reissig. On the other hand, when I went to Spain about three years ago and again talked to Spanish writers, they often introduced quotations from Lugones into their conversation, not out of condescension or politeness but quite spontaneously. The fact that an important writer like Lugones used to be unknown in Europe, whereas nowadays between six and a dozen South American writers are well known there, is evidence of this increased interest.

For instance, five volumes of my stories and poems have been published here in the United States in paperback, and their sales seem to be going up. This never happened to Lugones. Many of my books have been translated in European countries and published in London as well as New York. Such a thing never happened to an Argentine writer thirty years ago. A book like *Don Segundo Sombra* was translated into French, and I think into English as well, but hardly any notice was taken of it at the time. Today people are not merely interested in reading books with local color or social significance; they also want to find out what Latin Americans are thinking or dreaming about.

Would you like to say something about contemporary Latin American literature?

I can't speak about contemporary Latin American literature. For instance, I don't know Cortázar's work at all well, but the little I do know, a few stories, seems to be admirable. I'm proud of the fact that I was the first to publish any work by him. When I was editing a magazine called *Los anales de Buenos Aires,* I remember a tall young man presenting himself in the office and handing me a manuscript. I said I would read it and he came back after a week. The story was called "La casa tomada" (The Occupied House). I told him it was excellent; my sister Norah illustrated it. When I was in Paris we met once or twice, but I've not read his most recent work.

I ought to speak about writers of another generation. In my opinion the best writer of Spanish prose on either side of the Atlantic is still the Mexican Alfonso Reyes. I have very pleasant memories of his friendship and his good nature, but I'm not sure if my memories are accurate. Reyes's works are important for America as well as for Mexico, and they should be for Spain as well. His prose is elegant, economical, and at the same time full of subtlety, irony, and feeling. There is a sort of understatement in Reyes's emotional response. One may read a page which seems cold, and suddenly one becomes aware that there is an underlying current of great sensitivity, that the author feels and perhaps suffers, but doesn't want to show it. It's a sort of modesty. I don't know what is thought of him. Maybe it has been held against him that he doesn't concern himself exclusively and continuously with Mexican themes, although he has written a lot on Mexico. Some people refuse to forgive him for translating the *Iliad* and the *Odyssey.* One thing is certain, and that is that ever since Reyes the Spanish language has had to be written differently. He was a very cosmopolitan writer who had explored many cultures.

Do you think that the spread of works by Latin American writers inside Latin America could have the effect of creating a more unified continental culture?

That's a hard question. We Argentines have a lot in common with Uruguayans, a little with Chileans, and not much I think with Peruvians, Venezuelans, or Mexicans. I therefore don't feel sure to what extent this Latin American awareness may not be a sham, or a generalization in the course of which much could be lost. Take Mexico, for example. There can't be a great similarity between a country of secondary importance like ours and one with a very different history, a very different past. In any case, perhaps the diffusion you mention may lead to the conclusion that we resemble each other very little, that we are different.

What is your view of Spanish literature?

I think that from the beginning of the nineteenth century the Spanish literature of South America has been more important than what Spain herself has produced. Of course, this doesn't mean that I don't admire Unamuno, whom I have read and reread. Though it is years since I opened his pages, I still retain a very vivid impression of him today. Probably his most important achievement was to leave us an impression of his personality, quite apart from his opinions, with which one may disagree—as with all opinions. I would say that when one thinks of English literature one generally thinks of individuals, just as one thinks of the characters of Shakespeare and Dickens. One tends to think of other literatures in terms of books. This is why one is very grateful that other literatures possess writers who do not make one think of a series of books, but whom we are aware of as men, and one of those men—from his conversation, he must have known it—is Miguel de Unamuno. Ortega y Gasset was a man who thought intelligently, a man who never stopped thinking, but as a writer he doesn't strike me as irreproachable. He ought to have found a man of letters to put his ideas into words. I admire him as a thinker, however. García Lorca seems to me quite a minor poet. His tragic death has favored his reputation. Of course, I like Lorca's poems, but they don't seem to me very important. His poetry is visual, decorative, not entirely serious; it's a sort of baroque entertainment.

I think Spanish literature has been in decline almost since the seventeenth century; the nineteenth century was extremely unproductive and there is nothing much better today, certainly nothing more important than what we have on this side of the Atlantic.

There are several names of Spanish poets that it would be unforgivable not to mention. Manuel and Antonio Machado, for instance. (Manuel was an Andalusian who remained one; Antonio was an Andalusian who made himself into a Castilian.) I would like to add the name of Jorge Guillén, who is here in Cambridge and has honored me with his friendship. It's a very pleasant experience, and not without some small surprises, to meet someone whom one already seems to know intimately through his writing. As a result of personal contact, one discovers that his character harmonizes with everything he has written, but not at all with the image one had formed of him.

What advice would you give a young writer?

I would give him a very simple piece of advice: not to think about publication but about his work. Not to be in a hurry to rush into print, and not to forget the reader, and also—if he attempts fiction—to try and describe nothing that he can't honestly imagine. Not to write about events merely because they seem to him surprising, but about those which give his imagination creative scope. As for style, I should advise poverty of vocabulary rather than too much richness. If there's one moral defect that's usually obvious in a work, it is vanity. One of the reasons why I don't altogether like Lugones, although of course I don't deny his talent or even genius, is that I notice a certain vanity in his manner of writing. When all the adjectives and all the metaphors on a single page are new ones, it usually indicates vanity, and a desire to astonish the reader. The reader ought never to feel that the writer is skillful. A writer ought to be skillful, but in an unobtrusive way. When things are extremely well done they seem inevitable as well as easy. If you are aware of a sense of effort, it means failure on the writer's part. Nor do I want to imply that a writer must be spontaneous, because that would mean he hit on the right word straightaway, which is very unlikely. When a piece of work is finished it ought to seem spontaneous, even though it may really be full of secret artifices and modest (not conceited) ingenuity.

You mentioned a project of yours for bilingual education, and the need for teaching English and Spanish in both Americas.

Three years ago I had occasion to travel in the Scandinavian countries—countries I am very fond of. In Sweden and Denmark, I discovered that every one spoke English. English is taught in the primary schools there, so that every Scandinavian is bilingual. It would be extraordinarily useful if English were taught in the primary schools of our republics, and Spanish in the United States and Canada. Then we should have a bilingual continent, since Portuguese is a sort of variation on Spanish or vice versa. If every American possessed two languages, a much wider world would be opened to him; he would have access to two cultures. Perhaps that would be the best means of exorcising the worst enemy in the world—nationalism. I believe it would be of the utmost importance for the history of the world if every man born in America had access to two cultures, the English and the Spanish. For me, knowledge of two languages doesn't mean the possession of a repertory of synonyms; it doesn't mean knowing that in Spanish you say "*ancho*" and in English "wide" or "broad." What is important is to learn to think in two different ways, and to have access to two literatures. If a man grows up within a single culture, if he gets used to seeing other languages as hostile or arbitrary dialects, his mental development will be constricted. If, however, he gets used to thinking in two languages and to the idea that his mind has developed from two great literatures, that must surely benefit him. To teach

English in the primary schools of Latin America, and eventually of Spain,
and to teach Spanish in the primary schools of the United States, Canada,
and eventually of Great Britain, would be a simple matter involving no difficulty. You will say that it's easier for a Dane to study English than for a
Spanish-speaking person to learn English or an Englishman Spanish; but I
don't think this is true, because English is a Latin language as well as a
Germanic one. At least half the English vocabulary is Latin. Remember that
in English there are two words for every idea: one Saxon and one Latin. You
can say "Holy Ghost" or "Holy Spirit," "sacred" or "holy." There's always
a slight difference, but one that's very important for poetry, the difference
between "dark" and "obscure" for instance, or "regal" and "kingly," or
"fraternal" and "brotherly." In the English language almost all words representing abstract ideas come from Latin, and those for concrete ideas from
Saxon, but there aren't so very many concrete ideas. This experiment ought
to be carried out at once. I suggest it to the Argentine Academy of Letters in
Buenos Aires, and now that I'm in the United States I shall not lose the
opportunity of suggesting it again. I believe it would be one means of achieving world peace.

What's your political position?
   I belong to the Conservative Party and I'll explain why. I joined the Conservative Party a few days before the presidential elections. I've always been
a radical, but by family tradition. My maternal grandfather, Acevedo, was a
great friend of Alem's, so that it was a case of loyalty rather than conviction
or judgment. Later on, I got the impression that the radicals wanted to come
to terms with the communists. Four or five days before the elections I went
to see Hardoy and told him I wanted to join the conservatives. He looked at
me in horror and said: "But we haven't a chance of winning." My answer
was: "A gentleman is only interested in lost causes." "Well, if you're out for
lost causes," he said, "don't go a step farther, you've got one right here."
We both laughed, and I joined—to the obvious advantage of the radicals. I've
had to explain to lots of people, especially here, that to be a conservative in
Argentina is not to belong to the right but the center. I detest the nationalists
and fascists just as much as I do the communists, so that I think I'm still in
the position I've always held. I more or less believe in democracy, and of
course I've always been against Peronism. Perón's government never had any
doubts about that. They attacked me by throwing me out of a small post I
held, and my mother, sister, and one of my nephews were imprisoned.

Who are the communists in Argentina?

All the communists are intellectuals, not working class. The communists of today are also nationalists, so of course they are against the United States.

What do you think is the reason for this anti-Yankee feeling?

I would say that in the Argentine Republic this feeling is artificial. Formerly it didn't exist; I think it's due to communist influence. In our country there used to be no hostility to America, but now, through Cuban influence perhaps, and of course through Russian influence, it does exist. But at the same time the very people who hate the United States want them to help us economically; they are the ones who spend their lives trying to be like Americans. It's very strange, but I think this feeling is mostly artificial. It's like anti-Semitism in our country.

Is there much anti-Semitism?

Only among small groups of nationalists. If there's one thing that interests nobody in our country, it's what race a person belongs to. During the war in the Middle East we all felt great sympathy for Israel. I remember that on the day war was declared I signed a declaration in favor of Israel; next day I was walking along Corrientes and I suddenly felt that something was about to happen. What actually happened was a sonnet about Israel. As soon as I had it worked out in my head, I went to the offices of *Davar,* asked for the director and said to him: "Have you a typewriter in the house?" "Certainly, we have seventy or eighty," he told me. "I need one." "What for?" "Because I've just produced a poem on Israel." "What's it like?" "I don't know if it's good or bad, but as it came to me spontaneously it shouldn't be too bad." I dictated it and *Davar* published it.

Do you believe in the literature of commitment?

My only commitment is to literature and my own sincerity. As for my political attitude, I've always made it perfectly clear: I've been anti-communist, anti-Hitler, anti-Peronist, and anti-nationalist, but I've done my best to prevent these opinions of mine (which are merely opinions, and may well be superficial) from intruding into what may be called my aesthetic output. A writer can satisfy his conscience and act as he believes is right, but I do not think literature should consist in fables or tracts. A writer should preserve the freedom of the imagination, the freedom of dreams. I have tried never to let my opinions on politics intrude into my work; I would almost prefer people to be unaware of what these opinions are. If a story or a poem

of mine is successful, its success springs from a deeper source than my political views, which may be erroneous and are dictated by circumstances. In my
case, my knowledge of what is called political reality is very incomplete. My
life is really spent among books, many of them from a past age, so that I may
well be mistaken.

Are you religious?
No.

*You said in the course of our conversation that you weren't sure whether you
were a Christian? Why is that?*
There are moments when I feel I am a Christian, and then when I reflect
that to admit it involves accepting a whole theological system, I see that I'm
not really one. I feel attracted to Protestantism, or to certain forms of it, and
what attracts me is its absence of hierarchy. Many people are drawn to the
Catholic Church by its pageantry, its ritual, its ecclesiastic hierarchy and
splendid architecture. These things are precisely what repel me. As I've said,
I don't know whether I am a Christian, but if I am I'm closer to Methodism
than to the Catholic Church. I say this with all respect. I'm expressing what
I feel, a spiritual tendency.
I've also done all I could to become a Jew. I've never stopped searching
for Jewish ancestors. My mother's family is called Acevedo, and they may
have been Portuguese Jews. I've given a great many lectures to the Argentine
Jewish Society; I'm deeply interested in the Cabala and in Spinoza's philosophy, and I have sometimes thought of writing a book about him. I have written a poem about Spinoza.
Apart from the accidents of blood, we are all both Greeks and Hebrews.
We are Greeks because Rome was merely an extension of Greece. One can't
conceive of the *Aeneid* without the *Iliad,* the poetry of Lucretius without
Epicurean philosophy, or Seneca without the Stoics. All Latin literature and
philosophy is based on Greek literature and philosophy. On the other hand,
whether we believe in Christianity or not, we cannot deny that it was derived
from Judaism.

*Do you believe that the current liberal movement in the Catholic Church is
important?*
I think it's a sign of weakness. When the Church was strong it was intoler-
ant; it went in for burning and persecution. It seems to me that the Church's
present tolerance largely derives from weakness; it's not that it has become

more broad-minded, because that's impossible. No church—whether Catholic or Protestant—has ever been tolerant, nor is there any reason for them to be tolerant. If I believe I am in possession of the truth there is no reason for me to be tolerant of those who are risking their own salvation by holding erroneous beliefs. On the contrary, it's my duty to persecute them. I can't say: "It doesn't matter that you are a Protestant because we're all brothers of Christ in the end." No, that would be a proof of skepticism.

I believe you travel a lot. Do you enjoy it?

I don't enjoy traveling one bit, but I very much like having traveled. One travels for the sake of one's memories, but of course for something to exist in the past it must once have been the present.

Which of the countries that you don't know would you like to visit?

I would like to imitate William Morris, who made a pilgrimage to Iceland in the last century. The word "pilgrimage" is not an overstatement here, or a pointless exaggeration. I've begun studying Icelandic, and I believe that the literature produced during the Middle Ages in that remote island close to the Arctic Circle is one of the most important in the world. I would like to get to know Norway and Israel too, and to return to the countries I love most, Scotland and England. These are my geographical ambitions.

Have you been to Russia?

No. I've been invited by some of the countries on the other side of the Iron Curtain, but I thought that as I should go with a bias against them my visit might not be pleasant either for my hosts or for me. I preferred to abstain, because I think one should travel in a cordial frame of mind, and in the case of Russia I don't know to what extent I should be capable of it. If I make an experiment, I'd rather make one that is likely to succeed.

Your life must be full of interesting anecdotes. Can you remember any?

I can't remember anecdotes. One thing that has always amazed me has been the extraordinary patience and kindness people have shown and still show me. I try to think about my enemies and I can hardly think of any—in fact, I can't think of one. Some of the articles written about me have been considered too savage, but I've thought to myself: "Good Lord, if I'd written that article I would have made it a lot more savage!" When I think about my contemporaries, it's with a feeling of gratitude, a somewhat amazed gratitude. People have, on the whole, treated me better than I deserve.

I remember the case of Ricardo Güiraldes. He and I edited the magazine

Proa together for a year. I was writing some undoubtedly mediocre poems at the time, which were afterwards published in a book called *Luna de enfrente* (Moon Across the Way). I showed Güiraldes these poems; he read them and divined what I had wanted to say, not what my clumsiness had prevented me from saying. Afterwards, Güiraldes discussed my poems with other people, but instead of talking about the poem I had written, he talked about the one I had wanted to write and which he had perceived in the very awkward draft I had shown him. The people he talked to became enthusiastic about my poem, looked for it in the book I had published, and of course failed to find it. It was as if Güiraldes had given me a gift, and I think that was what he was unconsciously doing. I may say that I have the warmest recollections of Güiraldes, of his generous friendship and his strange destiny; though all destinies are strange.

Have you a message for the younger generation?

No, I don't think I can give advice to other people. I've hardly been able to manage my own life. I've drifted somewhat.

Jorge Luis Borges: An Interview

Patricia Marx and John Simon / 1968

From *Commonweal,* Vol. 89, No. 4, 25 October 1968, pp. 107–10. Reprinted by permission.

Often considered the greatest living writer of Spanish prose, Jorge Luis Borges was born in 1899 in Buenos Aires. In reviewing a volume of Borges' "fictions within fictions" in the September 29, 1967 *Commonweal,* Ronald Christ called the term *"Borgesian,"* like *Kafkaesque,* "indispensable for the specification and clarification of our awareness." In 1961, Borges shared the International Publishers Prize with Samuel Beckett. Several collections of his stories and poems have been translated into English: *Labyrinths, Ficciones, Other Inquisitions, Dream Tigers, A Personal Anthology.* Mr. Borges was interviewed by Patricia Marx, weekly interviewer for WNYC, and John Simon, drama critic for *New York Magazine.*

Mr. Borges, you recently spent quite some time visiting Harvard University as the Charles Eliot Norton Professor of Poetry. I wonder what your impressions were of students there.

Borges: I found the students very keen. One of them wrote a parody of my stuff, and I was introduced as one of the characters. He also gave me some fine lines of verse. For example this one—I wish I had written it, and anybody would say the same—it's a pity it wasn't written in the 17th or maybe in the 18th century: "So chaste was she that lilies were her roses."

You began writing as a poet and essayist, and it was not until after a serious illness that you started writing stories. Do you value one form of writing more than another?

Borges: Well, I suppose that they're all essentially the same. In fact, I hardly know what I'm going to write—an article, a story, a poem in free verse—or in some regular form. I only know that when I have the first sentence. And when the first sentence makes a kind of pattern. Then I find out the kind of rhythm I'm looking for. And then I go on. But I don't think there's any essential difference, at least for me, between writing poetry or writing prose.

76

So you evolve the form and the content as you go along?

Borges: Yes. When I feel I'm going to write something, then I just am quiet and I try to listen. Then something comes through. And I do what I can in order not to tamper with it. And then, when I begin to hear what's coming through, I write it down. I try to avoid purple patches, fine writing, all that kind of thing, because I think they're a mistake. And then sometimes it comes through and sometimes it doesn't, but that's not up to me. It's up to chance.

Does this kind of inspiration . . .

Borges: Well inspiration I think is too—too ambitious a word.

This process—is this something that is regular in your life?

Borges: No, it comes and goes. Sometimes there are periods of aridity, periods where nothing happens. But then I know those periods are real. I know that when I think of myself as being utterly worn out, when I think that somehow I have nothing more to write, then something is happening within me. And, in due course, it bubbles up; it comes to the surface, and then I do my best to listen. But there's nothing mystical about all this. I suppose all writers do the same.

In his review of your Personal Anthology *John Simon made the point that in contrast to so many other writers who make distinctions between reality and illusion, in your writing, reality is illusion, and illusion is reality, being one and the same.*

Borges: Well I wonder whether we can make a distinction. Because in order to make that distinction we would have to know whether we are real or unreal. And, I suppose, as philosophers have been bickering and quarreling over that for the last 2,000 or 3,000 years, it's not up to me to decide.

Let's say that the words "an unreal thing" or "an unreal happening"—are a contradiction in terms. Because if you can speak about something, or even dream something, then that something is real. Unless of course you have a different meaning for the word "real." But I don't see how things can be unreal. I don't see any valid reason why Hamlet, for example, should be less real than Lloyd George.

You've been attracted to fantastic writings. Does this same concept apply to the fantastic?

Borges: I am attracted to fantastic writing, and fantastic reading, of course. But I think things that we call fantastic may be real, in the sense of being real symbols. If I write a fantastic story, I'm not writing something willful. On the contrary, I am writing something that stands for my feelings, or for my thoughts. So that, in a sense, a fantastic story is as real and perhaps more real than a mere circumstantial story. Because after all, circumstances come and go, and symbols remain. Symbols are there all the time. If I write about a certain street corner in Buenos Aires, that street corner may pass away for all I know. But if I write about mazes, or about mirrors, or about the night, or about evil, and fear, those things are everlasting—I mean they will be always with us. So, in a sense, I suppose a writer of the fantastic is writing of things far more real than, well, what newspapermen write about. Because they're always writing about mere accidents, circumstances. But, of course, we all live in time. I think that when we write about the fantastic, we're trying to get away from time and to write about everlasting things. I mean we do our best to be in eternity, though we may not quite succeed in our attempt.

Do you feel any kinship with Pirandello, by any chance?

Borges: I have greatly enjoyed Pirandello. I mean that game, for example, between the actors and the spectators. But I do not think he invented that game. Because in a sense you're getting that game all the time in Cervantes. I wonder if you remember that the characters in Cervantes have read *Don Quixote*. And that some characters speak about Cervantes, and even poke fun at him. That is the same kind of game.

What about people like E.T.A. Hoffmann and the German romantics? Have you felt any sympathy with them?

Borges: Well I have done my best to admire Hoffmann, but he's always defeated me. Because I think of him as being quite irresponsible. At the same time I don't think of him as being particularly amusing. Of course you might say that Lewis Carroll is irresponsible, but I feel attracted to him, and I don't feel attracted to Hoffmann. But that, of course, is my personal mistake, or my personal heresy, I should say.

What do you mean by Hoffmann's irresponsibility, Mr. Borges?

Borges: Well, if I may use old-fashioned and rather phony American slang, I shall accuse him of piling on the agonies. I remember that Poe was asked about his horror, and they thought that his horror came out of German romantics. He said, "Horror belongs not to Germany but to the soul." I suppose personally his life was awful enough, he had no need of looking for that horror in books.

You have said that the purpose of your writing is "to explore the literary possibilities of certain philosophical systems."

Borges: Many people have thought of me—of course, I can only be grateful to them—as a thinker, as a philosopher, or even as a mystic. Well the truth is that though I have found reality perplexing enough—in fact, I find it gets more perplexing all the time—I never think of myself as a thinker. But people think that I've committed myself to idealism, to solipsism, or to doctrines of the cabala, because I've used them in my tales. But really I was only trying to see what could be done with them. On the other hand, it might be argued that if I use them it's because I was feeling an affinity to them. Of course, that's true. But in fact I'm in too much of a mental muddle to know where I am—an idealist or not. I'm a mere man of letters, and I do what I can with those subjects.

Do you have a personal religion?

Borges: No, I don't have, but I hope to have one. Of course, I can believe in God, in the sense that Matthew Arnold gave to that word, something not ourselves that makes for righteousness. But I suppose that that's rather shadowy. I suppose you want more on that. Now as to a personal god, I don't like to think of God as a person—though I'm quite fond of people, and I suppose I'm a person myself, after all. But I don't think I have any use for a god who is very much interested, let us say, in ethics, in what I am doing. I would rather like to think of God as being a kind of adventurer—even as Wells thought about him—or perhaps as something within us making for some unknown purpose. I don't think I can really believe in doomsday; I could hardly believe in rewards and punishments, in heaven or hell. As I wrote down in one of my sonnets—I seem to be always plagiarizing, imitating myself or somebody else for that matter—I think I am quite unworthy of heaven or of hell, and even of immortality. I mean I might accept immortality, if I had to do it. But I would prefer—if there is any after-life—to know nothing whatever about Borges, about his experiences in this world. But I suppose identity depends on memory. And if my memory is blotted out, then I wonder if I exist—I mean, if I am the same person. Of course, I don't have to solve that problem. It's up to God, if any. So that I ask of any God, of any gods, that if they give immortality, I hope to be granted oblivion also.

Perhaps in a reincarnation you wouldn't mind reading Borges.

Borges: Well no, I look forward to a better literary future than that.

Let me ask about one more German that I'm curious how you feel about, I mean Rainer Maria Rilke.

Borges: I don't know. I have a feeling that he's been greatly over-rated. I think of him as a very pleasant poet. I know some of his pieces by heart, or

at least I did. But I never could be very interested in him. But if I have to
speak of German writers, there is one German writer that I would like to
speak about. And I think I spent most of my life reading and rereading
him—at first in English and now in German. And that writer is, as you may
have guessed, Arthur Schopenhauer. I think that if I had to choose one philosopher, one metaphysician, I would choose Schopenhauer. Or if not, I suppose
I would fall back—and be very happy about it—on Berkeley or on Hume. So
you see that I'm quite old-fashioned. But I think of Schopenhauer as belonging to the 18th century. I think his irony and his pleasant style—and the word
"pleasant" means much to me—belong rather to the 18th than to the 19th
century. And certainly they don't belong to the cumbrous dialect of his German contemporaries. I think that, in a sense, he was more of a contemporary
of Gibbon or of Voltaire than of Hegel or Fichte, whom he hated, as you all
know.

*Mr. Borges, do you feel in any way indebted to surrealism? Either through
Ultraism or some other form.*

Borges: Well, as a matter of fact, I know very little about surrealism. But
I hope it's better than Ultraism, because I think of Ultraism as being sheer
stuff and nonsense. And that's the feeling most of us old Ultraists have. It
was merely a boyish joke, and I hope we've grown out of it. And yet now
and then when I write, I evolve very silly metaphors, and then I know that's
my old self—that's the man I was let's say around 1920—who's still lurking
somewhere and who's trying to spoil everything I write.

*Well, what do you do with those metaphors—do you keep them or do you
throw them out?*

Borges: Yes, I keep them, and I attribute them to imaginary writers, so that
I use them for the sake of parody. Because after all I've got to put them to
some use. And maybe in a sneaking way I'm fond of them.

*Are there any contemporary writers that you are attracted to and feel an
affinity for?*

Borges: Well, if I have to speak of contemporary writers, I should be thinking about Plato, about Sir Thomas Browne, about Spinoza, about Thomas De
Quincy, about Emerson, about Schopenhauer, of course. Maybe, why not?
about Angelus Silesius, about Flaubert. That's as far as I care to go. But here
I'm merely repeating what Ezra Pound said. He said, "All art is contemporary"—and I think he was right. I don't see why a man, by the mere fact of

sharing my experiences of living in the same century, should be more important to me than somebody who died many years ago. [After all, if I am
reading somebody, that writer is a contemporary—I mean he belongs to the
present.] So that I think the word "modern" means nothing whatever; and
the word "contemporary," of course, is a mere synonym of "modern." I
think they're both meaningless.

You're renowned for your knowledge of literature and philosophy. Are there
other arts that are as meaningful to you—painting or music?
   Borges: Well, I'm very ignorant of music. I can only plead the doctrine of
invincible ignorance. But when we were writing, Bioy Casares and I, we were
hearing records. And then we found out there were some records that stimu-
lated us, that gave us a sense of power, of passion, of might. So we wrote
better when we were hearing them. Then we found out where those records
came from. And they were records by Brahms. And that's all I know of
music. There my knowledge stops. But in a sense I should be grateful to
Brahms. Because I feel a stronger and happier man and a more passionate
man when I am hearing his music. So I suppose I should thank him for that
gift. But, of course, I cannot understand that gift or explain it.

Mr. Borges, one subject very rarely, if at all, shows up in your work, and that
is sex. What would you say was the reason for that?
   Borges: I suppose the reason is that I think too much about it. When I
write, I try to get away from personal feelings. I suppose that's the reason.
But there has to be another reason. The other reason may be that it's been
worked to death, and I know that I can't say anything new or very interesting
about it. Of course, you may say that the other subjects I treat have also been
worked to death. For example, loneliness, identity. And yet, somehow I feel
that I can do more with the problems of time and identity than with what was
treated by Blake when he spoke of "weaving through dreams a sexual strife,
and weeping o'er the web of life." Well, I wonder if I have woven through
dreams the sexual strife. I don't think so. But after all, my business is to
weave dreams. I suppose I may be allowed to choose the material.

In an interview for the Paris Review *you were mocking the concern about*
the audience you reach. And you were saying that, only 37 copies of your
first book had been sold, and that . . . you liked that because you could
identify yourself with 37 people.
   Borges: Because after all, if you sell a thousand copies you might as well

sell no copy at all, no? Infinity and zero come together. But 37 people—with faces, with circumstances, with likes, with dislikes, with relatives and so on. So I was very grateful when I had sold 37 copies. But I think I was exaggerating, it may have been 21 only, or 17 for that matter.

But is it really of little concern to you to reach a large audience?

Borges: I think that what I'm really concerned about is reaching one person. And that person may be myself, for all I know. In my country writers hardly worry about audiences. Perhaps because they know they'll never get any. Not out of modesty, but self-knowledge. But I think it's all to the good that a writer shouldn't be too famous. Because, in a country where a writer may be famous, he may be pandering to the mob, celebrity and so on. But in my country, I write for myself, and perhaps for half a dozen friends. And that should be enough. And that might improve the quality of my writing. But if I were writing for thousands of people, then I would write what might please them. And as I know nothing about them, and maybe I'd have a rather low opinion of them, I don't think that would do any good to my work.

There are many of us who are afraid about the directions that art—or the arts in general—have been taken most recently, and there's the feeling that there may be a dehumanization in the arts, to use Ortega's term. Do you feel that danger?

Borges: Well I see no reason whatever why that danger should be specially active today. After all, there are thousands of people writing away, and if we evolve one or two writers, that should be enough. I mean, we're always thinking highly of the past, because we say Shakespeare, Marlowe and so on. But after all, we are thinking of the ones who have come down to us. I suppose that in any special time art must have been really quite rubbishy. But if we manage to evolve one or two writers, and those writers should be thought worthy of being read in time to come, I don't think we need worry about there being many quite bad writers.

I was thinking not so much of the quantity of bad writers but the direction in which perhaps even good art or so-called good art is going, which seems to become progressively beset by scientific or anti-intellectual or self-destructive values, which might in time lead to a preponderance of anti-art.

Borges: Well I wonder if you're thinking, let's say, of art being written in a very special way. For example, of literature being merely verbal. Or painting merely concerned with shapes, with lines, with certain patterns.

But I think that something should come through in spite of the artist's theories. Suppose a writer may think that he's writing meaningless verse, or that he's only out, let's say, for verbal patterns, and at the same time he may be saying something, or rather suggesting something, very meaningful. Because art is very mysterious. I wonder if you can really do any damage to art. I think that to have that opinion is to think too highly of reason. I think that when we're writing, something comes through or should come through, in spite of our theories. So theories are not really important. I don't think esthetic schools are important. What is important is the use that is made of them, or whatever the individual writer does. I'm not interested in the fact that a writer may label himself as being intellectual or anti-intellectual. I'm really interested in the stuff he's turning out.

At this point, what are you attracted to—where is your sense of adventure leading you now?

Borges: Well, I have several plans. One of them is to write a volume of straightforward stories. I think I'm rather tired of mazes and mirrors and people who are somebody else. And I was rereading some months ago the *Plain Tales From the Hills,* these very straightforward stories that Kipling wrote when he was a young man—afterward, of course, he went on to very intricate schemes—and I thought I would try my hand at writing a straightforward story, and I wrote one. And I'm thinking of writing more stories in that style. I mean stories with simple characters—if there be such a thing as a simple character. That's one of my plans. And the other plan would be to write a book on Old English and Old Norse literature. Not a book of information, but rather a book with my personal opinions, a book wherein I try to say what I thought that poetry might have meant to the Saxons and to the Norsemen. So that I have those two books in mind.

And also, perhaps, I'll fall back on my old schemes, because one never knows. I might write one or two fantastic stories. But I'll do my best to avoid them. I'll only write them down if they insist on my writing them.

Jorge Luis Borges

L. S. Dembo / 1969

From *The Contemporary Writer: Interviews with Sixteen Novelists and Poets,* by L. S. Dembo and Cyrena N. Pondrom, The University of Wisconsin Press, pp. 113–21. Copyright 1972. Reprinted by permission of The University of Wisconsin Press.

Interview conducted by L. S. Dembo on 21 November 1969, in Madison, Wisconsin. The interview was held in English.

Q. In your essay, "Valéry as Symbol," you wrote that Valéry was "the symbol of a man infinitely sensitive to every phenomenon and for whom every phenomenon is a stimulus capable of provoking an infinite series of thoughts. Of a man who transcends the differential traits of self and of whom we can say . . . he is nothing in himself." What would you say of Borges as symbol?

A. Well, I don't think I can say very much, because that symbol has been invented for me by other people; I mean, I don't think about myself, but many people seem to be thinking about me. So I am, in a sense, their handiwork, not my own. When I write a story or a poem I am simply concerned about that story or that poem, but I have no general philosophy; I have no message to convey. I am not really a thinker. I am a man who is very puzzled—and generally speaking, very pleasantly puzzled—by life and by things, especially by books. My father had a fine English library, and I've always been reading and rereading those books. I was introduced to America by one of the first novels I ever read in that library: *Huckleberry Finn.* And afterwards I read *Roughing It* and other books by Twain. And then, of course, I came to Edgar Allen Poe, and also—I wonder how you'll take this—to Longfellow. Since then, of course, I discovered other writers: Emerson, Melville, Hawthorne, Thoreau, and Henry James. The very first lectures I gave when I was obliged to do so, because, well, I had to earn a living somehow, and I was hounded out of a small job I held by the dictator—the first lectures I gave were on *literatura norteamericana clásica,* and then I spoke on those authors. I had not spoken in public before and of course I was full of fear and trembling, even as I am full of fear and trembling now when I speak here. I'm always afraid the words will stick in my throat.

Q. They somehow don't.

A. No, but in a sense, I am quite a veteran in everything concerned with stage fright. I get more and more afraid as the years go on.

Q. It certainly isn't obvious.

A. Well, it's obvious to me.

Q. Anyway, let me continue with this question: One of your chief themes seems to be the ability of the mind to influence or recreate reality. I am thinking of the consummate recreation of the world in "Tlön, Uqbar, and Orbis Tertius." The philosophy of idealism prevalent on the imaginary planet Tlön seems to be vindicated when the actual world begins to transform itself in Tlön's image. Are you in fact a philosophic idealist or do you simply delight in paradoxes made possible by idealistic reasoning, or both?

A. Well, my father—I seem to be referring to him all the time; I greatly loved him, and I think of him as living—my father was a professor of psychology, and I remember—I was quite a small boy—when he began trying to teach me something of the puzzles that constitute the idealisitc philosophy. And I remember once he explained to me, or he tried to explain to me, with the chessboard, the paradoxes of Xeno, Achilles and the Tortoise, and so on. I also remember that he held an orange in his hand and asked me, "Would you think of the taste of the orange as belonging to it?" And I said, "Well, I hardly know that. I suppose I'd have to taste the orange. I don't think the orange is tasting itself all the time." He replied, "That's quite a good answer," and then he went on to the color of the orange and asked, "Well, if you close your eyes, and if I put out the light, what color is the orange?" He didn't say a word about Berkeley or Hume, but he was really teaching me the philosophy of idealism, although, of course, he never used those words, because he thought they might scare me away. But he was teaching me a good many things, and he taught them as if they were of no importance at all. He was teaching me philosophy and psychology—that was his province—and he used William James as his textbook. He was teaching me all those things, and yet not allowing me to suspect that he was teaching me something.

Q. But you would say that you more or less were brought up on idealism?

A. Yes, and now when people tell me that they're down-to-earth and they tell me that I should be down-to-earth and think of reality, I wonder why a dream or an idea should be less real than this table for example, or why Macbeth should be less real than today's newspaper. I cannot quite understand this. I suppose if I had to define myself, I would define myself as an idealist, philosophically speaking. But I'm not sure I have to define myself. I'd rather go on wondering and puzzling about things, for I find that very enjoyable.

Q. That reminds me of the image of the labyrinth that recurs throughout your work.

A. Yes, it keeps cropping up all the time. It's the most obvious symbol of feeling puzzled and baffled, isn't it? It came to me through an engraving when I was a boy, an engraving of the seven wonders of the world, and there was one of the labyrinth. It was a circular building, and there were some palm trees near. Anyway, I thought that if I looked into it, if I peered into it very closely, perhaps I might make out the minotaur at the center. Somehow I was rather frightened of that engraving, and so when my mother said, "Since you like the book, you can keep it in your room," I answered, "No, no, it better stay in the library," because I was afraid of the minotaur coming out. Of course, I never told her the reason. Children are very shy. You don't say those things when you are really afraid of something happening. It really was an uncanny picture.

There was also an English dictionary, with a picture of the sphinx. Then I would play with my terrors; I would say to myself, now I will look up the word "six" and see that very tiny little illustration, and then I opened the book and closed it at once.

Q. Has the minotaur ever come out of the labyrinth?

A. Well, I have written two sonnets; in the first, a man is supposed to be making his way through the dusty and stony corridors, and he hears a distant bellowing in the night. And then he makes out footprints in the sand and he knows that they belong to the minotaur, that the minotaur is after him, and, in a sense, he, too, is after the minotaur. The minotaur, of course, wants to devour him, and since his only aim in life is to go on wandering and wandering, he also longs for the moment. In the second sonnet, I had a still more gruesome idea—the idea that there was no minotaur—that the man would go on endlessly wandering. That may have been suggested by a phrase in one of Chesterton's Father Brown books. Chesterton said, "What a man is really afraid of is a maze without a center." I suppose he was thinking of a godless universe, but I was thinking of the labyrinth without a minotaur. I mean, if anything is terrible, it is terrible because it is meaningless.

Q. Yes, that's what I was driving at. . . .

A. . . . Because the minotaur justifies the labyrinth; at least one thinks of it as being the right kind of inhabitant for that weird kind of building.

Q. If the minotaur is in the labyrinth, the labyrinth makes sense.

A. Yes, if there's no minotaur, then the whole thing's incredible. You have a monstrous building built round a monster, and that in a sense is logical. But if there is no monster, then the whole thing is senseless, and that would be the case for the universe, for all we know.

Q. Doesn't Thomas Hardy express a similar idea in one of his poems—I think it's called "Hap"—in which he says that if he knew that the universe were malevolent, he could resign himself, but he knows that it's haphazard, and that is the real cause of his despair?

A. I admire Hardy's poems but I haven't come across that one. You see, I lost my sight in 1955 and, of course, I had to fall back on other readers and young minds—young eyes and young memories—and so I depend on things already read. But my consolation lies in the fact that my memory's rather poor, so when I think I'm remembering something, I'm surely distorting it and perhaps inventing something new.

Q. Perhaps that's what it means to be an artist.

A. Yes, well, if I could verify every one of my memories, I should be less fanciful than I am or less inventive.

Q. Well, you're apt to turn into Funes, the Immemorious.

A. No, in the case of Funes I think of a man being killed by his memory and of a man being unable to think, since he can possess no general ideas; that is, in order to think, you must forget the small individual differences between things. Of course, Funes couldn't do that. But that story came to me as a kind of metaphor for sleeplessness, because I suffered greatly from insomnia.

Q. Yes, you speak about the "terrible lucidity of insomnia."

A. The terrible lucidity of insomnia. And there is a common word in Argentine Spanish for "awaken": *recordarse,* to remember oneself. When you're sleeping, you can't remember yourself—in fact, you're nobody, although you may be anybody in a dream. Then suddenly you wake up and "remember yourself"; you say, "I am so-and-so; I'm staying in such-and-such a place; I'm living in such-and-such a year." But *recordarse* is used as a common word and I don't think anybody has worked out all its implications.

Q. Getting back to the labyrinth, it seems to me that this image was not only generally appropriate to your work but represented the central paradox in it; that "the rich symmetries" of the mind, and of history, and of the world, end only in confusion or mystery.

A. But I really enjoy that mystery. I not only feel the terror of it; I not only feel now and then the anguish, but also, well, the kind of pleasure you get, let's say, from a chess puzzle or from a good detective novel.

Q. In other words, you don't feel "angst"?

A. No, I don't. Or if I feel it, I feel it now and then, but I don't try to cherish it nor do I feel especially proud of it. It comes on me, let's say, as a headache or toothache might come, and I do my best to discourage it.

Q. I notice that from time to time the narrator of a story will identify himself as Borges, but, as the parable "Borges and I" seems to illustrate, Borges is more than one man. Are the characters of the *ficciones* sometimes Borges' nightmares or dreams or are they in fact the works of a detached creator intellectually interested in their dilemmas?

A. Sometimes I have been influenced by dreams. But only twice have I written down actual dreams. One was in the sketch called "Episode of the Enemy"; and the other dream I had I gave the Norse name of *Ragnarök*, "The Twilight of the Gods." And those two dreams were written much as they occurred. I worked in a few details to make them more credible. In other cases I may have been influenced by dreams without being quite aware of it.

Q. I meant dreams in the broader sense of the word.

A. Well, I don't think of literature and dreams as being very different. Of course, life has been compared to a dream many times over. But I think that in the case where you're imagining a story, you are actually dreaming it; at the same time you're dreaming it in a rather self-conscious way. I mean, you're dreaming and you're trying to direct the dream, to give it an end. Now, it is quite a common experience of mine—I suppose it has happened to you also—to dream and to know that I am dreaming. And also this has happened only during the last few years of my life: to begin dreaming before I begin to go to sleep. I know, for example, that I am in bed; I know where I am, and that somebody has come into the room, that somebody belongs to a dream; and then I know that very soon I will fall fast asleep. That's a sign that sleep's coming on. I asked one of my nephews and he told me that he had the same feeling. Sometimes he had dreams not only the moment before waking but before going to sleep.

When one dreams before going to sleep, one knows that one shouldn't worry about insomnia because in two or three minutes one will be fast asleep, and then one will be dreaming in a more intricate way, with different characters, different people speaking, and so on.

Q. Would you say that your characters represent a part of you?

A. Yes, they do—all of them. But I have a trick of my characters poking fun at me. I am also contemptible in my stories. Many of the characters are fools and they are always playing tricks on me and treating me badly. Actually, I often play a very poor part in my stories.

Q. Well, as intellectually impressive as they are, all the characters seem to have some sort of weakness: Averroes, for instance. He can never determine what Aristotle meant by "tragedy" and "comedy" because he has never seen the theater, and he's limited by the concepts of Islam.

A. Yes, in that story I write of a very intelligent man, as I imagine Averroes to have been, and yet a man who cannot possibly know what tragedy and comedy stood for, since he had never seen a tragedy or a comedy being acted. He couldn't possibly guess at the whole thing. If the story is pathetic, it is pathetic because a very intelligent man commits a very elementary blunder. That's the whole point to the story.

Q. Would you call it a blunder or is it a necessary fallacy in his thinking? No matter what he could do, he was still limited by his environment and his experience.

A. I also think of him as being a symbol of everybody, because after all, what any single individual must know is very little as compared to the sum of all things. But in that story you are made to feel, at least if the story's successful, that the hero is very intelligent, and yet that he could by no means understand what tragedy meant, because, as I read in Renard's book on Averroes, when he speaks of comedy, he speaks of fate as panegyric, and when he speaks of tragedy, he speaks of it as satire, because he knew about those things but not about the stage.

Q. Well, maybe the point is that he does represent everybody. Does he represent the author, too, in the same way?

A. Yes, of course he does.

Q. The author himself is in a labyrinth, following casuistic reasoning, but bound by the limitations of the tunnels in that labyrinth. He can never really get out and find reality.

A. But of course. When I say everybody, I include myself. I should say so. Let me tell you an anecdote now, if you don't mind anecdotes. This happened in the province of Buenos Aires. There was an actor who went all over the country, playing the story of a brave gaucho hunted down by the people. When he came to a certain town he was told to change the name of the hero to that of the local, well, the local "Billy the Kid," in order that the people might better enjoy it. Then two or three days before the play was about to be shown, an old man came to see the actor. He was a very timid man; I've seen pictures of him. He had killed many men in his day; he had a grey mustache; he was a smallish man. He didn't know quite how to speak—he had spent all his life killing or being hunted by the police. Then he said, "I heard that somebody will appear on the stage and will say that he's me. But I want to warn you beforehand that you will deceive nobody, because I have lived in this town and everybody knows who I am." The actor tried to explain to him the whole art of stagecraft, but how could this poor old gaucho understand that? Finally, he said, "Well, maybe you're right. You're a learned man, and I'm very ignorant. I spent all my life being hunted by the police and fighting them; but I want to warn you that even though I am an old man, I can still take care of myself, and if anybody appears on the stage and says he's me, then I will come on the stage and fight him." And so the play couldn't be acted.

Q. So for all his intellect, Averroes suffered from the same problem an illiterate gaucho did. But let me ask you something on a different subject. In an essay on Coleridge you examined the idea that all literary works are one work and that all writers are one impersonal writer.

A. Yes, I got that idea from Emerson, who said they were the work of one single all-knowing or all-thinking "gentleman." The word "gentleman" is beautiful there. Because if he had written "man" it would have meant very little, but the idea of a gentleman writing, well, let's say, all Shakespeare's tragedies for him. . . .

Q. Well, the word probably speaks for Emerson's own gentility.

A. Yes, but I don't want to blame gentility. I think it should be encouraged. At least I try to be a gentleman, though I never quite succeed in that ambition.

Q. In any case, what would you say is the contribution of *Ficciones* to this universal work? Is it part of traditional literature?

A. Oh, I think it's made of half-forgotten memories. I wonder if there is a single original line in the book. I suppose a source can be found for every line I've written, or perhaps that's what we call inventing—mixing up memories. I don't think we're capable of creation in the way that God created the world.

Jorge Luis Borges
Selden Rodman / 1969

From *Tongues of Fallen Angels,* pp. 5–37. Copyright © 1974 by Selden Rodman. Reprinted by permission of New Directions Publishing Corporation.

"I was quite old when it occurred to me that poetry could be written in a language other than English."

I

The first time I saw Borges he was seated at a large conference table in Buenos Aires's National Library staring into space. He looks at first more like a harassed, tired executive than Argentina's great poet who, in middle age, had received world-wide renown for his "metaphysical" fables of circular time, and now almost blind in his seventies was beginning to write poems again. It was only when he got up to lean on his cane, grasped me just above the elbow, and started to pour over me (at very close range) his passion for literature and his distaste for most things contemporary, that I caught a gleam in those piercing blue eyes under their drooping lids, and a sense of the dedicated, almost Gothic bony structure of that long, slightly pouchy aristocratic face under sparse gray hairs and unruly eyebrows. He talks fluently in English but with an accent, almost a Scottish burr. And it's not easy to stop him once he starts, because he has a disconcerting way of looking you straight in the eye, holding you close to him, and occasionally laughing at his own sallies with a flash of white teeth; you can never rid yourself of the notion that he really sees you.

When he heard that I'd been with Pablo Neruda recently, he started to say something about his great Chilean antagonist, but then broke off to approach the subject more indirectly.

"You've come from Chile by way of Brazil," he said. "What difference strikes you most entering Argentina?"

"Not seeing a single black on the streets of Buenos Aires," I said. "I can't get used to it. Weren't there any slaves here? Didn't they have children?"

"I can't explain it either," he said. "In my childhood one saw them every-

where. All our servants and laborers were Negroes. Maybe this was one reason we began to think of ourselves as close to you. This was white man's
country, not a country of Indians and half-breeds like Peru or Bolivia—or
Brazil, which is just an extension of Africa, no?"

"Hardly," I said, "though the blacks provide the most vital element in that
unique culture. You know their literature, I suppose."

"They have a literature?"

"A rich one, classics included. You must have read Machado de Assis."

"No."

"Euclides da Cunha?"

"Yes. His book is a kind of sociological curiosity, isn't it? I was impressed
until I read Cunningham-Graham's version of the same episode and saw how
a real writer could handle it."

He hadn't heard of the distinguished modern poets like Cabral de Melo or
Vinícius either but had been "once familiar" with some poems of Carlos
Drummond de Andrade. I mentioned that Drummond, at least during the
Thirties when he was a member of the Communist party, had been quite
close to Neruda. "But Neruda," I added, "when I expressed admiration for
your writing, made a remark that I know won't surprise you. 'Literature,' he
said, 'is like a good beefsteak and can't be put together out of other literatures.' "

He smiled. "There are several answers to that remark." He paused.

"While you're selecting the best one," I said, "tell me what that ancient
tome lying in front of you is."

"It's Dr. Johnson's *Dictionary,*" he said. "The preface—made up of many
literatures—is a great piece of prose. This copy was sent to me by a man
from Sing Sing."

"The prison?"

"No. The town."

"But there is no town by that name any more. They renamed it Ossining.
It must have been a prisoner who sent it to you, Borges!"

He liked the idea. "Yes. A prisoner of the eighteenth century. What a good
place to be imprisoned. With all those Latinisms!"

"Can I ask you a Johnsonian question?"

"Like: What would I do if locked up in a tower with a baby?"

"Exactly. I'm writing a travel book, you know. What does Argentina need
most?"

He pondered. "More curious minds, perhaps—like yours. You saw that girl

at the desk when you came in? Can you believe it? Her mother burned her
books one day. She said to her: 'We're simple folk. We don't need books.'
That's what we're up against."

"You were saying about Neruda—?"

"He's a fine poet, of course. Some of his early poems are very good. But
then he wrote a book denouncing the South American dictators—and left out
Juan Perón."

"Why?"

"Perón was then in power. It seems that Neruda had a lawsuit pending with
his publisher in Buenos Aires. That publisher, as you probably know, has
always been his principal source of income."

I questioned the accuracy of this observation, its implications at any rate;
perhaps only outsiders can have ambivalent feelings about the aging dictator
who had so radically undercut the old landed oligarchy at the behest of his
militant mistress, the late Evita Duarte. And I thought, too, of Borges's little
essay about the mourning general who set up a tiny shrine in the Chaco one
day in 1952 and accepted contributions, candles, and flowers from the poor
who came to worship the blond doll inside:

> What kind of man, I ask myself, conceived and executed that funeral farce? a
> fanatic, a pitiful wretch, or an imposter and cynic? Did he believe he was Perón
> as he played his suffering role as the macabre widower? The story is incredible
> but it happened, and perhaps not once but many times, with different actors in
> different locales. It contains the perfect cipher of an unreal epoch, it is like the
> reflection of a dream or like that drama-within-drama we see in *Hamlet*. The
> mourner was not Perón and the blond doll was not the woman Eva Duarte, but
> nèither was Perón, Perón, nor was Eva, Eva. They were, rather, unknown indi-
> viduals—or anonymous ones whose secret names and true faces we do not
> know—who acted out, for the credulous love of the lower middle classes, a
> crass mythology.
>
> "The Sham," *Dreamtigers*

I asked Borges if the tale was true. He said it was; he had had it from two
men in the Chaco who didn't know each other. He gave me a long account
he had had from a friend of torture by electric wires in one of Perón's prisons.
He described the various parts of the body shocked, almost clinically. He told
with relish several stories making fun of Evita Perón as an ex-prostitute who
had put on airs. He spoke lightly of the constitutional presidents who had
bumbled in the wake of Perón, but with respect of the current military strong

man, General Onganía. "He is a gentleman. He does not raise his voice or
strike poses . . ."

Borges's conservatism is moral. He is offended by Perón's morality—his
lack of morals. There are overtones of snobbism in the description of the
religious Peronista—the use of the words "the woman" and "credulous." He
is not interested in the social welfare, labor benefits, and public works of the
first Perón period. He is concerned only about the means—which is a tenable
philosophical position, of course.

We went to pay a call on Borges's mother who lives nearby and who is
astonishingly alert at ninety-three. She moves, in fact, more nimbly than her
son. Borges's sister Norah, who paints, was leaving as we entered the eighth-
floor apartment. Señora Borges told us that she was reading English again—
"lest I forget." ("Mother often calls me a quadroon," Borges confided behind
his hand, "for being a fourth part English.") He had always lived with his
mother, until two years ago his marriage to a widowed boyhood sweetheart
in her fifties surprised his friends.

I asked Borges on the way down in the crowded elevator if my favorite
among his stories, "El Sur" ("The South"), was autobiographical. Did it
reflect a physical accident that had turned him from poetry to prose? "Yes,
yes! of course, and it is one of my favorites too, because it is on so many
levels—the autobiographical, the man who kills the thing he loves, the—"

The elevator came to a jerking stop, and we were spilled out into the lobby
without my finding out what the other levels were.

2

Fame came to Borges as a young poet in Argentina. Years later it was his
"metaphysical" tales that aroused awe and admiration throughout the world.
Today the *avant-garde,* paradoxically, is making a culture hero of the arch-
conservative. But there is another Borges who deserves to be at least as well
known: Borges, the wit; Borges, the nonconformist who delights in poking
fun at Latin America's fetishes; Borges, conversationalist extraordinary.

My talks with Borges were spread out over three week-long visits to Buenos Aires in 1969, 1970, and 1972. No doubt they would read well enough
as unadorned dialogue. But to present them that way, divorced from the Victorian *décor* and courtly ballet that make Borges, Borges, and without intro-
ducing Norman Thomas di Giovanni who made the encounters possible and

at whose home Borges sometimes held forth while I was guest, would be awkward and ungracious.

Though my first visit to Buenos Aires was to "research" a travel book, on which I was then working with Bill Negron as illustrator, my goal from the start had been to meet the poet-fabulist and try to convey Argentina's essence through his eyes. I had loved the stories for years. But behind the intricacy of their plots, behind their philosophical implications—that time is circular, that everything that happens has happened before and will happen again—I sensed a human warmth transcending Borges's passion for literature, an affection for Argentina transcending (if indeed it wasn't dictated by) the writer's despair over his country's tawdry politics and its capital's decay.

Though we bore no introductions, Negron and I had taken a taxi directly to the National Library. There we were informed that Borges was "being taped" by some French T.V. crew but that his aide would speak to us. A stocky young man with thick black hair and eyebrows and burning eyes came out, and when I had introduced myself he said: "You wouldn't remember it, but I visited your house in New Jersey ten years ago with Mark Strand and Rico Lebrun. But long before that your *100 Modern Poems* changed my life. I doubt whether I'd be here in Argentina were it not for that anthology. Borges will be happy to see you, I know; but while he's tied up in there let's go out and have a drink."

Over *chopps* the story of Norman Thomas di Giovanni began to unfold. It threw a good deal of light on Borges's personality and on Argentina. In New Hampshire where he had been working on a novel, Norman had heard that Borges was lecturing at Harvard and had gone to see him. Soon after Borges left he decided to chuck everything and fly to Buenos Aires. He had majored in Spanish at school, he loved Borges's work, and he saw no reason why the poems, on which Borges's early fame in Argentina rested, shouldn't receive as much recognition in the English-speaking world as the stories. He would try to convince Borges of this, and then he would organize poet-translators from all over the world to prepare a book, under his and Borges's supervision.

He succeeded beyond his wildest expectations. Borges was delighted with the idea. So delighted, in fact, that he soon began concentrating on writing poems again. The result was Borges's first new book in nine years, *In Praise of Darkness*. Translators began sending in their versions which Borges and Norman would scrutinize, mailing them back for improvement whenever necessary. Happily for both men, the younger quickly became indispensable to the older, as go-between with the increasingly unwieldy flow of visitors, promoters, lecture-agents, and publishers; and as friend, for the Argentine writer has always felt closer in spirit to the Anglo-American literary world than to the French-oriented one traditional in Argentina.

But Norman's sudden eminence baffled the intellectual community of Buenos Aires. Who was this upstart—from North America of all places— attached to their great man? It made them feel better about it to invent all kinds of academic credentials for Norman. He began to be referred to in the press as "Dr. di Giovanni" or as "the well-known scholar from Harvard." And Norman, with a typically American contempt for titles, would have none of it, though Borges said, "Can't you see it makes them happy to call you Doctor, Norman? Go along with them. Play their little game." One day when they were sitting next to each other at a T.V. panel interview, Norman had lunged forward to protest his Harvard indentification; Borges seized him by the elbow and whispered in his ear: "Norman! . . . Avoid veracity!"

A friend in Chile, Nena Ossa, had already told me something about Borges's humility. She had met him in Santiago and taken him to a television studio where he was to be interviewed. "I was trying to guide him across the streets, but he insisted on guiding me. I was with him when the girl was putting pancake make-up on his face. "I'll never forget the way he apologized to her for 'this indignity—having to touch this old and ugly visage.' The girl, thrilled by the privilege of so intimate a contact with such a great man, was speechless."

Norman confirmed the genuineness of Borges's reaction by telling us of the time he had accompanied Borges and his wife on a speaking engagement to a town in the south of Argentina that involved an exhausting six-hour journey by rail. They arrived only to discover that a mistake had been made in the invitation: the lecture was to have taken place the day before. The college officials were furious. "We'll get to the bottom of this unforgivable insult, Dr. Borges. The secretary responsible for the error will be fired!" Borges turned to them open-mouthed. "But why?" he said. "Can't you understand that I'm delighted? I won't have to lecture now!" But their outrage—and Señora Borges's—persisted. "At least the offender must be exposed—" "Please, no, no," Borges insisted. "Can't you see that I'm grateful to her? She's my benefactor. If you punish her, I'll never come back."

3

Walking to the Library, we re-entered the gloomy structure that was once the National Lottery, its brass balustrades on the grand staircase having as their motif the spherical baskets in which the tickets are shuffled. The Director's office, with twenty-foot ceilings and ornately carved wainscoting, has a curved desk designed for Paul Groussac, Borges's predecessor, who was also blind. (Was there something symbolic, I wondered, about these blind librarians in a Latin American institution devoted more to reverence than to use?)

The restaurant to which Borges invited us to dine with him is a homely establishment called the Caserio. On the way to it, he never stopped talking. Bill and Norman would get a block ahead of us and then stop to let us catch up. Borges tugged at my elbow so hard it was difficult to avoid lampposts and keep out of the gutter. (Norman told me that he had a sore arm for a week after arriving in Buenos Aires and that he still walks like a crab.) Once we were agreeing that Goethe was overrated as a poet, and I delighted him by quoting the passage from *Faust,* Part II, beginning *Wenn im unendlichen dasselbe* to prove that Goethe was best in philosophical nuggets like that, he pulled me off the curb and with taxis barreling by intoned a dozen lines from *Beowulf* to indicate the bridge between the Teuton and English tongues. At an intersection he stopped me in the middle of the street to quote José Hernández—the idea being that *Martin Fierro* was somewhat cheapened by its propaganda content—"The poem was written, you know, to stop the killing of the Indians by the Gauchos. Hernández's Gaucho complains too much. Real Gauchos are not so self-pitying."

"Is the Gaucho in *The Purple Land* more real?" I asked.

"No. Less so. Hudson was a first-rate naturalist but not a first-rate novelist. His memory of the Banda Oriental played him tricks. I could give you a dozen instances of inaccuracy. He romanticized the Uruguayan back country hopelessly, all those silly loves, and so on."

By the time we were seated for dinner we were quoting and counterquoting. He'd quote Tennyson; I'd quote "a better poet of the same time, Hopkins." He'd quote a war poem by Browning; I'd quote "a better poet, Owen." He'd cite Kipling or Chesterton or Stevenson; I'd cite Stephen Crane. I asked him whether he admired César Vallejo's poetry. "Vallejo? Never heard of him." I couldn't believe my ears. "García Márquez's fiction?" I ventured. "Never heard of him either." I retreated to safer ground. "Leopoldo Lugones?"

"Of course. Lugones was our greatest poet. But very limited, very Paris-oriented, by way of Rubén Darío who worked for years in Buenos Aires as a journalist. Lugones showed his basic insecurity by frequently prefacing a sententious remark with 'As Rubén Darío, my master and friend, and I agree. . . .' Ah, he was a very distasteful person, Lugones, very negative. His mouth seemed shaped by nature to pronounce the word 'No.' Later on he would invent reasons to justify this word that his soul and facial muscles so automatically shaped."

Borges had to admit that he had read some Cortazar but he didn't like the expatriate Argentine novelist. "He is trying so hard on every page to be original that it becomes a tiresome battle of wits, no?"

When discussing English or American literature, Borges's whole personality changes. He beams, he expands, he glows. "You know I was brought up on English in my father's library. I was quite old when it occurred to me that poetry could be written in a language other than English."

He ordered a plate of rice, butter, and cheese, while our mouths watered at the thought of the Argentine steaks we'd soon be served. "I hate steaks," Borges said. "They are so common in this country. I can't eat more than one or two a year."

Norman said: "Borges, I heard you mention Eliot a while back—"

"Eliot is a little dry, don't you think?" Borges said. "I prefer Frost. You like Frost, Rodman?" He was glad that I preferred Frost to Eliot. He asked me how Frost looked and talked. Did I think that Frost's reserved Americanism had any kinship with Whitman's boisterous brand?

"I think Frost was a direct descendant of Emerson," I said.

"And Whitman was influenced by Emerson more than by anyone! That essay about the ideal American democrat, pioneer, truthteller, yea-sayer— with a bit of Asiatic-Indian philosophy thrown in—"

" 'I greet you at the beginning of a great career,' " I quoted.

"—And how distressed Emerson was that Whitman made bit publicity out of that letter!" Borges said. "Yet why not? If Emerson didn't expect it, why did he write it? Whitman was right . . . but don't you think Whitman *tries* too hard, that he's really a quite unspontaneous writer?"

"Not in 'Song of Myself,' " I said. "That's the most spontaneous poem in the language. Even some of the lines in the later poems are pure magic, impossible to will."

"For instance?"

" 'I repose by the sills of the exquisite flexible doors.' "

Borges said it over several times. "I don't get it. What's so wonderful about it?"

"You've revealed to me at last that English is only your adopted language," I said.

He laughed. "They didn't find me out at Harvard, or at Texas either." The lectures he had delivered at Austin had been a great experience, he added. "Every South American should visit the United States to see how perverted by lying Communist propaganda the local image of America is. The students, compared with ours, are so alert. I'll not forget the one who pointed out in class that my story 'The Golem' was a reworking of 'The Circular Ruins.' I was amazed! 'My God,' I said, 'you're right! I've never thought of it, but it's true. Well, I only wrote it—once. You've probably read both stories many times.' "

He leaned toward Bill to answer a question, and Norman said to me: "He says things like that all the time. He really means them. He thinks his present fame is a matter of luck, not necessarily deserved, and that any day the bubble may pop and he'll be forgotten, or relegated to a very minor role. Of course he's enjoying it while it lasts, rather astonished by the adulation, the translators all over the world haggling over the meaning of this or that arcane phrase—but not at all taken in by it, or spoiled, as you can see."

"Here," said Borges turning back to me, "examinations are like lottery tickets. In Texas a student wanted me to give a course all over again, unsure that he'd profited by it thoroughly, unconcerned about quick credits . . . That could never happen here."

4

We had been to Borges's apartment on Belgrano several times, but one day the maid, who always rushed to the door and then looked as though she'd been interrupted at an embalming, said that only Señora Borges was in. Never having met her, we said we'd be pleased to have that privilege. She could not be disturbed but we could wait in the parlor. Bill escaped and I settled down, making a *catalogue raisonné* of the premises to pass the time: two potted rubber palms, two green-cushioned Morris chairs, a spindly dining room set, two glass-enclosed bookcases, two etchings in the style of Whistler, two eighteenth-century engravings (Arch of Titus, Pyramid of Caius Cestius), a Dürer etching, a painting of angels by Borges's sister, a student exercise by Silvana Ocampo of a woman's back from the waist up, a cabinet containing Borges's medals and other literary awards, a wall rack with brandy decanters and glasses of red glass in brass holders, a Harvard shield, a glass coffee table containing an ash tray, Joyce's *Ulysses* (Borges thinks Joyce should have filled it with character studies rather than catalogues), Apollinaire in Spanish *(El Heresiarca y Cia)*, and the complete works of Dürer in folio.

Presently Borges came in and I made a date to meet him here at four in the afternoon and then go to the Library for drawings and photos. I told him I'd like to meet his wife. He went through one of the closed doors and came back, closing it after him.

"She excuses herself. She just had a bath."

"I'm beginning to think you don't have a wife, Borges."

He smiled wryly. "Maybe it's better if we keep up the mystery."

He took me to the elevator and I had trouble closing the accordion gate which has to be shut before any Argentine elevator will start. "Is this some diabolical Argentine invention?" I said.

"Heavens no," he said, as my head began to disappear below floor level, "the Argentines could never invent something as complicated as an elevator—or for that matter anything at all."

At four o'clock I picked up Bill and drove back to Belgrano. This time La Señora emerged and greeted us. She is a buxom, rather handsome woman in her fifties. She surrendered her husband to his guests unceremoniously. To get Borges across the street to a taxi was, as always, a tug of war. This time he was talking about his story "Funes the Memorious" and about what a terrible thing it was to have insomnia.

At the Library, we rang the bell but no one answered. Borges had no key. Finally a man came up to us from across the street, concerned to see the old man with a cane standing hatless under the fierce sun, and asked us if we'd like to have a whisky or a Coke. Borges said we'd like to have a Coke but that was the last we saw of our presumptive benefactor. Borges, by now engaged in quoting Longfellow's translation of an Old English poem, "The Grave," showed very little interest when the watchman, who should have been on duty, finally arrived with the key. To get the natural light for photography and drawing, we took three chairs out on to the narrow balcony that runs around the top of the huge, glass-domed main reading room.

I asked Borges how important in shaping Argentina's history was the fact that the Argentine was a dependency of Peru from 1563 to 1776.

"Not at all," he said. "Communications were much too difficult in those days to give Argentina much sense of inferiority. We were pretty much on our own, with Spain giving us most of the trouble. In the War of the Pacific in 1879, everybody here sided with Peru against Chile. But the city of Buenos Aires has always been democratic compared with aristocratic Lima . . . Argentina has always been far too large, I've always thought. Our northwestern provinces, with their surviving Indians, would be better off as parts of Indian Paraguay or Bolivia."

I asked him whether he thought the nineteenth-century domination of Argentina, by the British economically and the French culturally, had had a schizophrenic effect on his country.

"I don't think so," he said. "Both influences were accepted quite naturally, in my family at least. But we were not devoted to Spain. We thought of Spaniards as servants. I recall someone coming back from meeting the Infanta and reporting scornfully 'She talks like a *gallego*'—the equivalent of saying that a British princess talks like a limey."

He went on to say that Paris had had a bad influence on intellectuals and poets—"Like your Ezra Pound, for instance, who adopted his ridiculous pose there. Or was it in London that he first affected cowboy dress and talk? . . . Even Victor Hugo felt he had to strike an attitude, though he was a serious poet and a great one."

I reminded him of André Gide's famous remark—"Victor Hugo, alas"— when asked who he thought was France's greatest poet. "Do you think Baudelaire and Rimbaud were better poets?" I asked.

"Of course not," he said. "Baudelaire is overrated, and Rimbaud was a mere freak . . . Do you know Hugo's splendid poem 'Boaz Endormi'?" I didn't and he quoted it all, with its ending: "L'herbe était noire; C'était l'heure tranquille quand les lions vont boire."

I told Borges that I was haunted by his story "El Aleph," especially by the passage describing the magical appearance on the cellar step of the small iridescent sphere "whose center is everywhere and its circumference nowhere." I asked him about the connection between the first part of the story and the last. "It's not clear to me." And I explained why.

"Now that you mention it, it's not clear to me either," he said. "I think I'll change it and put in a much clearer relation between the buyer of the house and the seller, a hint at the very beginning that someone is going to buy the house. And I will put your name in it too, if you have no objection, as a tribute to you for improving it."

I laughed. Was he pulling my leg, mildly making fun of me—which he had every right to do? He told me about a reporter in Madrid who had come to him and asked him seriously whether the Aleph existed in fact. "Later on I wished I had encouraged him in this tomfoolery, but at the time I said, 'Of course not,' and he left quite crestfallen, and even disgusted with me for

making such a deception! Tomfoolery should always be encouraged, don't
you agree? But I let the poor man down and he felt disconsolate." He added
that the poet satirized at the beginning of the story was drawn from life and
that his mother had begged him not to make it so obvious. "But I said to her:
'He'll never recognize himself'—and he didn't!" I asked him where he found
the title. "I took it from Bertrand Russell's Introduction to his *Philosophy of
Mathematics,* where it is used as the symbol for transfinite numbers."

"Why is the house in which the Aleph appears destroyed in the end?" I
asked.

"It had to be destroyed," he said, "because you can't leave things like an
Aleph lying around in this day and age, the way Aladdin left his lamp lying
around. Not any more. The premises have to be tidied up, the supernatural
suitably disposed of, the reader's mind set at rest."

Which, of course, is exactly what Borges doesn't do. For part of his genius
is to leave the mysteries suspended, very disquietingly suspended, in these
"real" settings which make the metaphysical content so alarmingly believ-
able. Untypical in this respect is "La Intrusa," which I'd just read after being
told that Borges regarded it as his best story. I told him that I liked it less
than the earlier stories, and he asked me why.

"The woman's reactions to what the two brothers are doing to her are
never hinted at," I said, "with the result that I can't feel any involvement in
her fate. I'm stunned by the conclusion, but emotionally indifferent to what
happens to the woman. Why would it detract from the story if you presented
her as a human being rather than as the animal they feel she is?"

"The more we are made to think of the woman as a kind of thing," Borges
replied, "the easier it is for the reader to feel about her as the brothers did—
and to understand that the essential subject of this story is friendship, not
brutality. I wonder if you noticed, by the way, that the older brother is the
only one whose words we are allowed to hear? It is he who dominates the
story, finds the woman, invents the scheme of sharing her with his brother,
sells her to the brothel, buys her back, and in the end knifes or strangles her."

While he was saying this, I had a close look at Borges's eyes. No wonder
he looks just a little mad! The pupil of the right eye is so enlarged it almost
fills the iris. The pupil of the left eye is very small and a little off center.

5

Borges asked me where I'd been the past week when I came to his apartment
to say good-bye. I'd been to Bariloche in the Andes and to Montevideo.

"What has Bariloche to do with Argentina?" he said. "In my childhood it didn't even exist. It is an invention of the Swiss and is populated with tourists and those who live off them. Of course it has mountains. But I spent the most impressionable years of my boyhood in Geneva where there are mountains just as good and a civilized society as well.

"Uruguay is something else again," he continued. "It is a very small and poor country, so things like poetry and football are taken overseriously. They say—as they never would here, or with you—'I want you to meet my friend the poet so-and-so.' You can't joke about the Gauchos or their national heroes, either. But it's like that all over South America, isn't it? In Peru they asked me seriously: 'Are you on the side of Pizarro or Atahualpa?' We don't think of such ethnic absurdities here. My best friend, the poet Carlos Mastronardi, comes of Italian stock on both sides. I'm all mixed up racially myself. It doesn't matter. We're all Argentinians. So we never think of it. In Berlin Miguel Angel Asturias made a speech beginning, 'I want to tell you I'm an Indian.' He'd be laughed off the stage if he said that here. I'd say to him: 'Then why do you publish books and not *quipos?*' In Colombia, though there's an enormous gap between the rich and the poor—and that terrible *violéncia*—they're more sensible. They say: 'The only hope for us is the American Marines.' " He smiled mischievously. "—And the only hope for South America as a whole is that you can conquer it. Nowadays you fight only small wars which you're not very good at, and which you wage half-heartedly, with a sense of guilt—like the British in South Africa when they almost lost to the Boers. You both win the big wars, of course; and if you were to conquer South America in the same spirit, without any misgivings, you'd be universally admired for it, you can be sure!"

"You've got to be kidding, Borges," I said.

"Not so much as you might think," he said with a smile.

I showed him a copy of a book by Fernando Guiberts called *Compadrito,* which I'd picked up in San Carlos de Bariloche, asking him whether the following description of the hoodlum of the Buenos Aires outskirts was accurate: his betrayal and oblivion of the pampas, where this without-a-horse man was born . . . this dismounted peasant no longer riding his destiny . . . his mother out for hire by day, dragging her tasks along; the father only a forsaken portrait in the bureau drawer . . . his passion servile and sticky, a craving to be the man he will never become . . . attending to the drama of his own vital impotence . . ."

I had seen enough of the deracinated slum-dweller in Lima, Mexico City, and Santiago to be sure that there was some truth in this deception, but I knew Borges well enough by this time to know that he wouldn't recognize it as his truth. He said he had lived in those neighborhoods "in the time the writer pretends to describe," and that it was not like that. He had me read another bit, about knife fights. He went out and came back with two wicked-looking silver-handled poniards. He demonstrated that instead of holding the point down as Guiberts indicates, it should be held up—"to get up under the shield of the poncho wrapped around the left forearm. Of course there are instances of all these attitudes he describes, but to harp on them only produces caricature."

The knives reminded me of the fatal encounter at the end of his story "El Sur."

"What were the other levels," I asked Borges, "on which that story was written—the levels you were starting to tell me about the other day?"

"Well," he said, "one is that it was all perhaps a dream. You remember there's a circumstance hinted at in the beginning—that the protagonist may have died under the surgeon's knife. Then, at the inn, the protagonist has the *Arabian Nights* with him again, and the storekeeper is like the intern at the hospital, and the store reminds him of an engraving. So couldn't it all be a dream at the moment of dying? . . . The autobiographical level is in the thinking of the violent death of his grandfather—as I did so often of mine. A student once asked me in Texas: 'When did the protagonist die?' I answered: 'You pays your money and you takes your choice! . . .' Still another level is the protagonist's love for the South—and its symbolic knife. He loves it, and it kills him."

I thought of the exaltation of courage in Borges's poems, not the physical courage he may have lacked, or thought he lacked as a young man—as some have conjectured—but courage as a spiritual legacy, as in the poem about his great-grandfather, who turned the tide during the Battle of Junín:

> . . . His great-grandson is writing these lines,
> and a silent voice comes to him out of the past,
> out of the blood:

> "What does my battle at Junín matter if it is only
> a glorious memory, or a date learned by rote
> for an examination, or a place in the atlas?
> The battle is everlasting and can do without

the pomp of actual armies and of trumpets.
Junín is two civilians cursing a tyrant
on a street corner,
or an unknown man somewhere dying in prison."

"A Page to Commemorate Colonel Suárez,
Victor at Junín," Selected Poems 1923–1967

Or the poem about the dying thoughts of Doctor Francisco Laprida, set upon and killed September 22, 1829, by a band of Gaucho militia, which Norman had translated from the same book:

> . . . I who longed to be someone else, to weigh
> judgments, to read books, to hand down the law,
> will lie in the open out in these swamps;
> I see at last that I am face to face
> with my South American destiny.
> I was carried to this ruinous hour
> by the intricate labyrinth of steps
> woven by my days from a day that goes
> back to my birth . . .

We told him we must leave, but he wanted us to stay and have tea. We declined, thinking we'd stayed too long already and were tiring him. As we edged our way toward the elevator, I asked him whether he'd like to have a copy of the biography of Byron's sister which I had ordered for Neruda.

"Some poets, like Byron," he said, "are so much more interesting than their poetry, aren't they?"

"Hemingway, for instance," I said.

"Yes," he said. "A very uninteresting writer, really."

"It was a great pleasure meeting you, Borges," I said lamely as we stepped into the cage and pulled the accordion doors shut.

"It was a pleasure and great honor meeting you," he replied graciously.

"We'll always remember it," said Bill in a louder voice as we started down.

"If you do forget," we heard his laughing voice say as we plunged out of sight, "write it down and remember the spelling—B-O-R-G-E-S—Borges!"

On the plane to Lima, quite possibly directly over Junín, I translated the last four lines from one of his poems:

> I seem to hear a stirring in the dawn
> of multitudes departing; I perceive
> the loves and memories that now are gone;
> space, time, and Borges take their leave.

6

When I returned to Buenos Aires two years later, Borges hadn't changed but the circumstances of his life had. He was back with his mother, and he was not contesting his wife's demands for exorbitant alimony. I asked di Giovanni why.

"He's been living in constant fear that he *won't* have to pay alimony! He feels guilty as hell. He thinks he alone is responsible for the failure of the marriage and should pay for it. Also, don't forget that while Borges is kind, generous, humble, imaginative, and noble, courage isn't part of his character. When his wife cursed him loudly at the airport once, with people all about listening in, he just stood there next to me with head bowed taking it without a word of rejoinder. He'll do anything to avoid facing up to a situation and asserting himself."

"Does his religion have anything to do with this self-abnegation?" I asked.

"Not really," Norman replied. "But his religion is one of the things that makes Borges so different from other Latin American intellectuals. Though his mother is a devout Catholic and his father was an atheist, Borges is a Portestant at heart. 'What Protestant church do you think I should join?' he once asked me only half jokingly. Ethics and belief in the value of *work* are central with Borges. When we were working on the autobiography last year, I wrote the phrase 'Amateur Protestant that I am . . . ,' and he exclaimed with delight: 'That's it! That's exactly it!' "

The moment Borges arrived for dinner, we started arguing. I'd just come back from Mar del Plata with Norman and his wife, Heather, and remarked about Buenos Aires's clammy heat.

"In my childhood we were not aware of such changes in the weather," Borges said. "At least it was not the custom to mention them. My father wore a thick coat with a high collar and a neckerchief at all times. Maybe it was cooler that way."

"Take your coat off and relax, Borges," I said, mopping my forehead.

"I'll take my coat off, but not my tie," he said. "Don't move me ahead too fast! Where have you been besides Mar del Plata? And what's new in poetry?"

I read him a poem by Stanley Kunitz, "After Pastor Bonhoeffer," and I told him I'd had a talk with García Márquez. "I know you won't read *Cien Años de Soledad*," I said, "in view of what Bioy Cáseres has told you about it—a bad novel, incompetently written—but he's wrong. It's a great novel, comparable to *Don Quixote*. García Márquez, by the way, is a great admirer of yours."

He looked pleased. "How can we judge the work of others when we can't even judge our own? Cervantes thought that his only good book was a dull, obscure work entitled *Trabajos de Persiles y Sigismunda: un novela septentrional*. I've been rereading Sinclair Lewis recently. Did you ever know him?"

I told him about the time I was an undergraduate at Yale and accompanied Lewis to the library to present (unsuccessfully) his Nobel medal.

"He's not a great writer," Borges said, "but he's a good one. The best thing about him is that he makes you sympathize with even the characters he ridicules, like Babbitt. He must have been a kind man."

"When he wasn't drunk," Norman said.

"Do you know why I don't drink?" Borges said. "Because when I was a young man I used to drink a lot of whisky Saturday nights, and one day I heard myself referred to as 'that drunkard, Borges.' Naturally I didn't want to go through life being considered a drunkard, so I stopped drinking."

"Lewis wasn't a drunkard but he certainly was drunk that day at Yale. But now let me ask you one. Did you ever meet Stevenson? And how can you consider him a major writer? For me he's minor—compared to you, for instance!"

"Thank you very much," he said, with a courtly smile in my direction. "I'm grateful, and sorry for you at the same time!—As I was when you referred to Neruda as a major poet. I think Neruda was a poet of some talent, derivative of Whitman, who gave up writing poems for political tracts. To me a 'major' poem is any very good poem, so a man who writes even one good poem, like George Meredith, for example, may be classified major. No?"

"Emphatically no," I said. "The distinction has to do with the whole body of a poet's work. If it changes poetry, the times, the race, it's major. Whitman and Neruda are major, no matter how many bad poems they wrote—and they wrote a lot, though Neruda has written some of his best in this decade, unlike Whitman who wrote very few after 'Song of Myself.' Poe, on the other hand, is minor—except perhaps to the French."

"Yes, I agree with that. Only his stories survive," Borges said.

"And a very few poems, like 'Sonnet to Science,' with magical lines—"

"Like that one of Whitman I didn't get? How did it go?"

" 'I repose by the sills of the exquisite flexible doors,' " Norman said. "Not bad as an epitaph for an elevator operator!"

"The line the French consider their greatest—'*La fille de Minos et de Pasiphaë*'—doesn't even sound like a good epitaph for Racine's heroine," I said. "But would any French poet be stunned by Milton's 'Smoothing the raven down of darkness till it smiled'?"

"I am," Borges said, "that's major!"

"Thanks for putting that word back in circulation, Borges," I said. "You consider *Don Segundo Sombra* a major novel?"

"Certainly not," Borges said, "though a quite interesting one. But it came out of *Kim,* a better book, just as *Kim* came out of *Huckleberry Finn,* a still better one. It was based on an actual character, you know. Don Segundo Ramírez Sombra actually existed. Maybe that is why the character is not larger than life. The book is an elegy for a vanished time. Daydreaming, wishful thinking by a conservative about the *criollo* past. Güiraldes died in 1927 of cancer, the year after this best of his books came out here."

"You know him?"

"He came to our house in Montevideo once on his way to Europe. He was very sad to be leaving and asked if he could leave his guitar on our sofa as a kind of symbolic pledge that he would return. He was a gentleman, never saying an unkind word about anyone."

"Speaking of gentlemen," I said, "I remember that that was the word you used to describe Juan Onganía two years ago. You regard the present strong man as highly?"

"I had an audience with President Levingston some weeks ago," Borges replied, "hoping to get him to raise the salaries of the Library employees who get an average $65 a month. You know what came of it? He raised *my* salary of $200 a month, which was perfectly adequate, and none of the others . . . No, it's a big step backward. They don't have any ideas for spending that make any sense. Like this repaving of Calle Florida, which only causes confusion. My chain of command used to go from me to the Minister of Education and then to the President. Now it's an organigram. There are seven links—seven dead bodies I must step over, and all receiving big salaries for doing nothing."

"Well," I said, "Chile has finally gotten Allende. Argentina's turn may be next."

"They've gotten what they wanted by way of free elections," Borges said, "—the fetish that brought us Perón, twice! We'll go to the dogs, if we go, via free elections. . . . But my philosophy is that some day we will deserve *not* to have governments."

7

"You really turn him on," Norman said, after we'd taken Borges back to his mother's apartment. "I haven't seen him so animated in months. Here they fawn on him and bore the hell out of him. He loves being told he's all wet once in a while, being introduced to new things. I wish I could accompany you to the Library to say good-by to him."

Borges was standing up, talking to Bioy Cáseres on the phone, when I entered his office. When he'd finished he apologized and sat down with me at the long table. "How did you come up?" he asked.

"On foot," I said, "the elevator wasn't working."

He chuckled. "Why don't you say 'lift'? It's so much shorter. But Americans, though always in a hurry, use the four-syllable 'elevator.' You use 'garbage can' too, though there's a shorter word for that. But maybe you don't use it at all, it's such a disagreeable word!"

I assured him we had plenty of short words—"like 'can' for *escusado,* 'balls' for *cojones,* 'lab' for 'labóratory,' and so on. But we have lots of words that are much too long, I agree; like 'explicate' for what a professor does to a poem he can't get through his senses—"

" 'Explicate'?" he said, "not just 'explain'? That's fantastic!"

"What are you working on now, Borges?"

"An article on Keats."

"Saying—?"

"I don't know. I'll find out when I start writing it."

"I'm relieved to hear you say what I've said so often. To publishers especially."

"They think a book starts with an outline."

"Instead of a feeling."

"You like Keats?" Borges asked.

"Tremendously. The letters, which reveal the man, are the best in the language. The longer poems, well—"

"They're not very good, are they? Not many long poems are—"

"But the shorter ones, beginning with 'Chapman's Homer'—"

"Even that one is a little dated, isn't it? 'Much have I travelled in the realms of gold' has an artificial ring, hasn't it?"

"Perhaps deliberately," I said, "but the sestet is superb, with one unforget-table line—"

" 'Looked at each other with a wild surmise'?"

"Yes. The syllables trip over each other to convey the excitement. Just as the line from Blake I quoted to you last week—'The lost traveller's dream under the hill'—has the opposite effect, interminably stretched out to suggest death. I'm more moved by Blake at this point in my life."

"He got all that from Swedenborg, didn't he?" Borges said.

"Only what he found usable, what echoed his own philosophy. Sweden-borg didn't see those 'dark Satanic mills' as the obverse side of the 'garden of love' . . . By the way, I've never heard you mention Emily Dickinson."

"I like her, of course," Borges said, "but not as much as Emerson, a happier spirit."

"Were you pulling my leg two years ago when you said you'd never heard of Vallejo?"

"No!" he looked deliberately startled. "Not at all. Who is he?"

"Come on, Borges, you must have at least *heard* of the most famous South American poet after Neruda."

He laughed. "What the hell do I have to do with South America?"

"But he is a great poet, Borges, and not at all a public, declamatory one like Neruda. You might even like him!"

"Great poets are overrated. Whom would you consider the great Spanish poets?"

"Quevedo? Góngora?—"

"Very overrated, both. Góngora is famous for his influence on the Elizabe-than poets of England. Quevedo is not interesting. I much prefer Fray Luis de León—"

"*Who?*"

"You see! Never heard of him?"

"Never. What is his poetry like?"

"Full of serenity. Unobtrusive rhymes . . . Beauty is very common actually. In the future maybe everyone will be a poet . . . But to come back to Keats, do you know Kipling's story 'Wireless'? It's about Keats and Fanny Brawne. You must read it. Come. I'll show you."

We went into a dark corridor and I guided him through two closed doors to a book-lined chamber. He went to a shelf containing a thirty-volume set of Kipling in red. "Which volume, Borges?"

"No idea. Let's start with the first."

"I'll miss my plane to Rio!" I read him the table of contents of the first three volumes while he stopped to give me the plot of several favorites. Fortunately 'Wireless' was in the fourth volume. I skimmed through it. We walked down into the lobby and he accompanied me to the revolving door.

"I hate to put you in this," I said.

"It's like a whirlpool. I may be scrambled."

"You may come out changed."

"I hope so."

8

The talks I had with Borges during my third and last visit to Buenos Aires, in 1972, revolved about the book of new stories he'd just published [*Doctor Brodie's Report*], and an anthology of English poets I was then working on and which he asked me to read him.

When I arrived at the Library about nine in the evening he'd just finished a session with María Kodama with whom he was studying Norse and Old English. We took a taxi to a restaurant. The street was torn up, and as we stumbled over potholes to the entrance he said: "This country is going to the dogs, isn't it? First we gave up being Spanish. Then we became amateur Frenchmen. Then came the English stage, followed by the Hollywood one. Now—mere ignorance! . . . Of course," he added, as we selected a table, "no one admires commercial empires, and that's the only side of the United States most Argentines ever see. Besides, you're a Protestant country. Catholics don't think in terms of right and wrong."

As he settled down to his frugal repast of honeydew melon draped with thin slices of ham, I asked him for his version of Neruda's Paris-bound transit of Buenos Aires some months ago. "Ask him," Norman had said, after telling me with considerable outrage of Borges's failure to respond to the generous telegram the Nobel laureate had dispatched from Santiago requesting an audience with "Argentina's greatest poet."

"Of course I couldn't see the ambassador of a Communist government," Borges said; and then, perhaps recalling my friendship with Neruda, he added: "To be sure, he's a fine writer. We did meet forty years ago. At that time we were both influenced by Whitman and I said, jokingly in part, 'I don't think anything can be done in Spanish, do you?' Neruda agreed, but we decided it was too late for us to write our verse in English. We'd have to make the best of a second-rate literature."

"It's that poor, Spanish?" I said.

"Of course. For one thing, the words are too long. English has the short Saxon words. Then a Milton comes along and mixes them with the long Latin ones. Or take Shakespeare's 'seas incarnadine.' Speaking of which," he added, "Pound inverts words so badly in his version of that great poem, 'The Seafarer': 'May I for myself songs truth reckon . . .' "

I thought of Borges's *mot,* "writers invent their own forerunners," when he next proceeded to tell me that a Southern soldier in our Civil War, Henry Timrod, "is one of the fine American poets."

"I finished *Doctor Brodie's Report* on the plane from Rio, Borges," I said. "I couldn't help wondering how you reconcile such overwhelming pessimism with such a hopeful statement as 'Some day we will deserve not to have governments.' "

"It's inconsistent, I admit," he said. "My father was an anarchist. I prefer to think that about future governments rather than abandon myself to the more probable fate of the Yahoos."

"You said in one of the stories, 'lost, as some day all things will be lost.' You believe that?"

"I *hope* all things will be lost?"

"Then why do you write?"

"What else have I got to do? Wasn't it Carlyle who said: 'Any human achievement is worthless, but the achieving is worthwhile'?"

"Shakespeare seemed convinced he would survive through his poems."

"*Aere monumenta?* That was a hoary literary convention. He stopped writing when he'd made enough money to retire, and he surely didn't expect that the 1623 Folio would ever be published. Writing was not taken too seriously then, and I don't take it too seriously."

"I was thinking as I drove over this afternoon—did you ever consider writing a story about one of these underground Nazis in B.A.? One who had finally become a decent human being, for instance, only to discover that society wouldn't let him?"

"No, I don't like the Germans," he said. "I went there six or seven years ago and found them so cringing, so wallowing in self-pity. I never heard one say a bad word about the German character—or even about Hitler."

"Your new stories are full of knife fights. Did you ever see one?"

"No. But I did see a man shot in a senseless vendetta once, in Uruguay."

My next question was triggered by a talk I had had the day before with Alastair Reid, about the lack of "motivation" in the characters of these new stories. "North Americans," Reid said, "have been brought up in a psychoanalytic world where everything must have an explanation—a rational one. Life, however, is what happens, not what can be explained. These are Borges's greatest stories because they are purified of motivational or metaphysical props. Borges likes to call Kipling's *Plain Tales from the Hills* the ultimate stories because they are the simplest. Latin American literature— whether Borges, García Márquez, Neruda—is written from the posture of humanity, and against theories of any kind which are death."

"Why does the protagonist of 'An Unworthy Friend' turn on his friend?" I asked Borges. "It seems an inexplicable act."

"The story is confessional," Borges replied. "When I was a student in Switzerland during the First War, a boy wanted to be my friend and I rebuffed him—feeling that I was unworthy. So in the story I made myself a Jew boy, to dramatize it, and went further than rebuffing, to actual betrayal. But it's still a confession!"

"In 'The Gospel According to St. Mark'—"

"I think I should rewrite that one," Borges said. "The climax [when the boy who's been reading the account of the Crucifixion to the credulous peasant family is led to the cross on which they will re-enact the drama] is too abrupt and tricky. There are hints, but I think I should make it clear that he suspects what will happen, and then bamboozles himself into believing that he's safe."

"It's a great story as it is," I said. "Why cushion the reader's shock?"

"You think so? Then I won't tamper with it."

"It may be your best."

"I think 'The Intruder' is better. It's my most economical story. We aren't told about the way the woman is killed. That's better than melodrama, don't you think? You've noticed the older brother is the only one who speaks? It's always 'they talked' but 'he says.' So the reader is made aware that the decisions are his; the others have no authority. But people read into it such absurdities! Someone actually said to me 'Those two brothers were in love with each other.' Some people have to find homosexuality or incest or hidden meanings in everything. They can't accept a good story as a good story."

"What touched off 'La Intrusa'?"

"I'd just read Kipling's 'Beyond the Pale,' impressed by its terseness. I said to Vlady who happened to be with me, 'Now I'll write something . . .' "

"And 'Guayaquil'?"

"The point of that story is that the two of them *become* Bolívar and San Martín, and as it happened historically, the better man won. I was also taking a dig at the Argentine nationalists for their hero-worship of General San Martín. Why did his alter ego yield? He was a pompous fool from the start. The story would have broken down if their conversation had been longer."

I took him home in a taxi about eleven. The driver dropped us quite a way from his door. He said he'd walk by himself, but I wouldn't let him. "How do you know we're even on the right street, Borges?"

"I know."

"You could see me, at the restaurant—in outline?"

"Only your hands."

"If I lie down on this doorstep you may see my face."

"Don't do it," he said, as his key slipped into the lock, "what *you'd* see would be even more ugly than what you see now!"

9

At the Library the next afternoon I read Borges the contents of my new British anthology and then those poems which he remembered or asked to hear. It was hard to wrench him beyond *Beowulf.* He liked my version of *Piers Ploughman,* and he said that Dunbar was an old favorite of his. He wanted to hear the one Shakespearean song he didn't know ("The master, the swabber, the boatswain and I . . ."). He approved my choice among the several versions of "Tom O'Bedlam." He quoted almost flawlessly Milton's "Sonnet on His Blindness." He speculated about the inferiority of *Paradise Regained,* quoting from memory,

. . . He, unobserved,
Home to his mother's house private returned.

"How could he? How could he! After the splendid conclusion to *Paradise Lost!* Surely it wasn't his blindness, for he was blind writing both poems."

Of Grey's "Elegy" he remarked: "Valéry's 'Cimitière Marin,' an inferior poem, is based on it, don't you think? There really are no first-rate French poets—Hugo included."

"You almost convinced me of the contrary three years ago," I said. "Do you approve my large selection of Burns?"

"Burns was only a great song writer, and popular songs can't be judged any longer as poetry. For instance 'Drink to me only with thine eyes,' which may once have been thrilling."

I read him the bawdy 'Is there for honest poverty . . .' to see whether he'd be as shocked by the four-letter words as Norman said he would be, but he made no comment. When I came to Blake, he urged me to include the passage from 'Uthune' ('Uriel'?), intoning

> . . . But nets of steel and traps of adamant
> . . . Girls of mild silver or of furious gold
> . . . I'll lie beside thee on a bank
> in lovely copulation, bliss on bliss . . .

—repeating the last line over and over, with evident relish.

(I recalled that when a daring student in Oklahoma had once asked Borges, "Why is there so little sex in your stories?" Borges had replied, "Perhaps because I am thinking about it too much." And I remembered Norman telling me that Borges called this ditty which he'd found in a Buenos Aires men's room—

> La mierda no la pintura,
> El dedo no lo pincel;
> No sea hijo de puta,
> Limpiesa con papel—

"excellent didactic verse" and that he'd suggested to Norman that he write it on the wall of an American college lavatory "as a gesture of cultural exchange," which Norman gladly did.)

Among the poets of this century Borges, not surprisingly, showed little interest in Owen, Hardy, or Lawrence, but berated me for not having included Kipling's "best poem" ("Harp Song of the Dane Women") or anything of G. K. Chesterton at all.

As I was getting up to go I remembered what we'd been talking about yesterday. "I think you're of two minds about immortality, Borges," I said.

"Can you prove it?"

"In 'Delia Elena San Marco,' which I read last night for the first time, you say, 'Man invents farewells because he knows he's immortal," and in another of your poems, 'The Saxon Poet,' aren't you positing a kind of immortality when you say, 'Today you are *my* voice,' and then ask that 'some verse of mine survive on a night favorable to memory'?"

"Well," he said, after some thought, "I suppose *that* kind of immortality I do believe in. It's not personal. I won't be aware of it. And I certainly won't get a kick out of it!

"I wrote a poem yesterday," he confided, as we walked toward the door, "with a deliberately flat beginning. My idea is to work up to ecstasy at the end. The first part was very easy!"

10

"I spent a good part of last night in bed thinking about your anthology," Borges said when Norman and I met him in the park the following morning for some pictures. "Instead of poems that seem 'modern' I would have adopted the reverse principle. I mean I would have selected poems that seem completey *un*-modern: about old virtues like loyalty, and so on. We shouldn't be reminded of what we are—I mean like that stanza from Byron's *Don Juan* about the blacks, or Shelley's description of the London slums—but of what we were."

"But were we ever?" I said. "I'm more interested in the similarities. The constant is our common perversity and humanity. And the discovery of those ties will draw the reader from the new to the old, through what never changes."

"Well, maybe," he said dubiously, "but it wouldn't be my touchstone."

"It surely wouldn't," said Norman as we crossed the square, with Borges tapping his way ahead of us with his cane. "When Borges makes an anthology his criticism is narrower: he selects only what reminds him of himself."

"That Burns poem you read me," Borges said as we caught up with him, "is really nonsensical, isn't it?"

"Didn't I tell you," Norman whispered, "that he'd never accept those dirty words! It took him a whole day to come out and tell you!"

"Those figures you were giving me on the phone, Norman," Borges said. "It can't be possible—46,000 copies of our new book before publication?"

"Before any are even *bought,* Borges."

"Before anybody even *reads* them," I added.

"When they do, they'll throw the book away," said Borges, smiling.

"But it will be too late!" I said.

"Yes," he chuckled, "they won't be able to get their money back, will they?"

Borges at N.Y.U.

Ronald Christ, Alexander Coleman, and Norman Thomas di Giovanni / 1971

From *TriQuarterly*, Number 25, Fall 1972, pp. 444–59. This interview was edited for publication by Ronald Christ. Reprinted by permission of Ronald Christ.

On April 8, 1971, at the invitation of Professor Alexander Coleman, Borges came to the Washington Square campus of New York University, accompanied by Norman Thomas di Giovanni, to appear briefly before a group of students and answer their questions about his work. The questions had been submitted beforehand, and near the beginning of the program di Giovanni called me to the platform to help him sort and perhaps invent a few questions, so I was in a good position to tape Borges' replies. What follows is a transcript of that tape.

But a few words of clarification might be useful, and some explanations are necessary. The occasion, like many another academic affair, was not especially brilliant—either because the students avoided Borges (who he is and what he has written) or because they asked after matters already well known. (In preparing their questions the students had more often than not questioned their own responses to Borges' work or reviewed what they knew about him, rather than inquiring into Borges' intentions, methods, or pleasures,) Those questions implied a monologue, really, on the part of the students; but Borges is an old hand at monologues and so he was, perhaps, more than usually willing to enter playfully into the pseudo-dialogue.

At any rate, what the occasion lacked in profundity it made up for in range of expression. More than most other question-and-answer sessions (including interviews), this one presents Borges in a lively and characterizing performance. On the one hand he answers a question about the figures in his work with a straightforward seriousness and accuracy that are rare in his oral comments on his own writing; on the other he coyly dodges an inquiry into the escapist nature of his fiction. Then, too, he acts out his timidity and ironic remove from what he has done, only minutes before he tearfully stutters a response to an *engagé* questioner from the floor. In short, what you may get from a reading of these remarks is a sense of person rather than a set of facts useful for critical evaluation. Some of those facts are here, all right, but the real attraction is the style of their exhibition.

But if you are going to realize that attraction, you will have to treat the following pages not as transcript but as script. You will have to play the strenuous formality in Borges' put-ons and take-offs, the measured authority of his slight misquotation of Rossetti; the genial mockery in his use of Johnson's "Sir"; you will have to supply the glimmers of irritation in his voice, his constant search for the iamb of any thought, the tenacity of his diversionary humor—all of which I have foregone emphasizing with complicated punctuation or awkward stage directions. Most of all, however, you will have to imagine the laughter echoing from platform to auditorium and back, because, from the very first moments, Borges won his audience with fooling and held them, sometimes against their own interests, with his humor.

In addition to all that laughter, some unimportant things are missing. I have edited the other speakers' remarks, condensed the questions, and in some few instances deleted the unintelligible or inconsequential while, as a general rule, I have omitted the merely repetitious. What follows, though, is essentially what was said, and the participants required no small bravery or humility to lend themselves to this *phono-verité*. Borges himself summarized their attitude when he replied to my request for permission to record what he had said. "Publish away!" he laughed.

Since Borges needs no introduction, as Alexander Coleman indicated in his, we start with the end of Coleman's opening remarks:

Coleman: . . . and therefore ditnyrambs and poems of praise in wild meters simply cannot be used in praise of Borges. Borges hardly needs any praise. But I would like to introduce to you Norman Thomas di Giovanni, to Borges' right—

Borges: Fancy *needing* praise! You gush all over!

Coleman: —who, with Borges, is in charge of the complete re-edition of Borges' work in English. Now, Borges, I think the only thing I can do is just tell you what sort of inquisitorial army you're facing.

Borges: Yes.

Coleman: It looks like around two hundred people.

Borges: Oh, *really!* Well, I have to face them, eh? In fact, I'm doing it.

Coleman: Let me tell you who they are. Fifty or sixty of them are students who just began Spanish last September, and they will be finishing their year by reading five of your pieces, beginning with "Borges y yo"—

Borges: Oh, *really!*

Coleman: —and then ending with "La intrusa." Okay?

Borges: Yes. Good. I'm very fond of "La intrusa."

Coleman: But I don't think there are any enemies here.

Borges: No.

Coleman: There may be a Maoist lurking under a seat, but I don't think he's appeared yet.
Borges: What! Only one?

Coleman: Now, the only other classification—
Borges: I thought China had a larger population.

Coleman: It's true China has a large population, but somehow the distances reduce the possibilities of immigration.
Borges: Yes.

Coleman: The only other possibilities I can describe to you are the twenty maniacs—
Borges: Only twenty?

Coleman: Yes, only twenty, who are at least theoretically under my charge. They have been doing nothing for the last semester but reading the works of Jorge Luis Borges.
Borges: Well, I'm awfully sorry. But I'm not to blame, eh?

Coleman: No, no, hardly. But that's all I can say about this *aglomeración*.
Borges: That sounds pretty impressive, eh?

Coleman: I think Norman is sifting out the questions.

di Giovanni: I can't find any literary questions. They're all about imperialism, about Latin America—
Borges: I'm not an authority on Latin America.

di Giovanni: "Borges, what is your role in the Vietnam war?"
Borges: Well, I think I got killed off last year, no? . . . Are they all like that?

Coleman: Well, Norman, you have "real" questions to ask of Borges?
Borges: Do you?

di Giovanni: I can't find one interesting one.
Borges: Well, you shouldn't say that, eh?

di Giovanni: Why not?

Coleman: Can I start? You can use me as a straight man if you wish. It's okay.
Borges: Yes. Well, go ahead.

Coleman: I was wondering if behind any of your stories, after you had written them, you felt you had emitted a moral judgment. Do you feel that one might argue the impossible by arguing for a moral purpose in literature?

Borges: I can only speak about myself. I don't think I have any moral purpose when I write. When I write, I'm trying to set down some kind of tale, not some kind of fable, but if the reader wants to read something moral into the text, that's all to the good. When I'm writing a story, I'm not thinking in terms, let's say, of political or ethical opinions: I'm merely trying to be true, let's say, to the plot, to the dream, perhaps. Of course, if my writing is any good, then I suppose many purposes should be creeping in; but that's up to them, not to me. I'm merely trying to be sincere to the plot, to the dream. And as to my political opinions, I have them, but I don't let them interfere, I don't let them tamper with my literature.

Coleman: But you're asking the reader to take part in the reading of the story almost as much as you have in the writing of it.

Borges: The reader, of course, is allowed his freedom, as I'm allowed mine. If people find more in a story than what I intended to put in there, well, that's all to the good, because I think any story or any poem should have more in it than what was intended by the writer; because, if not, it would be a very poor one. I think that's all I have to say. —But when I'm writing a story or a poem, I'm concerned about that story and about that poem, and I try to forget my convictions, my opinions, even my personal feelings. To be honest only. It's a kind of willful . . . well, willful dreaming, I should say, in writing a story; but I let myself go. At least I do my best.

di Giovanni: May I read a question?
Borges: And I'll try to find an answer.

di Giovanni: I don't think you need answer this.
Borges: Well, why not?

di Giovanni: Because this is the most incredible question. "Last year you refused to come to the United States of America because of the war in Vietnam—"
Borges: *Did* I?

di Giovanni: "—and other govenment policies. What changes in America allowed you to reconsider and come now to speak?"
Borges: I don't know. What changes made me reconsider a decision I never took? —All this is fancy work.

Coleman: I tell you what's happened. Borges, you've been confused with Carlos Fuentes.

Borges: Or with Charlie Chaplin, if you want. Or with King Charles I. Or any other Charles.

Coleman: May I ask you a question about Valéry? In looking at "Pierre Menard" and even at "Funes," I was wondering if not only *Monsieur Teste* but also the first pages of the *Introduction to the Method of Leonardo da Vinci* might have somehow goaded you to the elaboration of a monstrous mind, such as Monsieur Teste—a man who's not very human, you have to admit.

Borges: He's not very human and he's not very intelligent, either. No, I'm sorry to say that I haven't been goaded on in my writing by Valéry. Valéry is hardly to blame for my writing. I'm to blame. And as to Funes, I don't think of him as being intelligent. On the contrary, he was simply a gigantic memory, and as such incapable of intelligence, because in order to think you have to, well, let's say, make certain mistakes, you have to forget, you have to connect, and he couldn't do that. He said his memory was full of mere facts and naturally those hindered him from thinking.

di Giovanni: I've got a few questions. "What is the relevance of character in your work?"

Borges: This is a hard nut to crack, because I'm afraid there are no characters in my work. I'm afraid *I'm* the only character; or rather, I should say, a kind of wishful thinking. For example, my forefathers were military men— I'm not much of a military man myself, as such—I'm merely a librarian—so I suppose there's some wishful thinking in what I write. But as to characters, I don't think I have evolved a single character. I think I'm always thinking in terms of myself, of my limitations, and of the possible lives I should have lived and haven't.

di Giovanni: How about your new stories? Those aren't about yourself, are they?

Borges: . . . No. The problem is that I've quite forgotten all about them. I never think about my own work; I prefer remembering other writers. And I'm a very poor hand when it comes to being asked questions about my own work since I do my best, my successful best, to forget it once it's written.

Coleman: But you know, the most wonderful thing is that you really *do* forget your stories.

Borges: Yes.

Coleman: You can find thousands of students who can remind you of details and you've honestly forgotten them—for good reasons in some cases and in others not.

Borges: Well, I suppose the real reason is that I want to write new ones. If I'm to be recalling my old ones, how can I go on? I'd be hampered by that.

di Giovanni: That comes up so many times when we're translating. Sometimes he'll come upon a sentence and say, "Hey, that's pretty good, isn't it?" as though it were somebody else's, and sometimes he says, "We've got to make that better."

Coleman: Ronald Christ has written about the remarkable translation you gave *"unánime noche,"* which has puzzled many a commentator, and now in English—

Borges: Well, to tell you the truth, it has puzzled *me!* I wrote it down because I thought it had a fine sound, hadn't been used before. But I wonder what it really means, if it means anything.

Coleman: —in English it comes out "encompassing night"—
Borges: That's far better.

Coleman: —which is lovely.
Borges: Of course. I'm very sorry I wrote *"unánime."* But there is no word for "encompassing" in Spanish.

di Giovanni: A mere rough draft.
Borges: A mere rough draft, yes. I was doing my best in a Romance language, say.

di Giovanni: Here's a question: "What do you think of space?" Not NASA, I suppose.
Borges: I tend to be always thinking of time, not of space. When I hear the words "time" and "space" used together, I feel as Nietzsche felt when he heard people talking about Goethe and Schiller—a kind of blasphemy. I think that the central riddle, the central problem of metaphysics—let us call it thinking—is time, not space. Space is one of the many things to be found inside of time—as you find, for example, color or shapes or sizes or feelings. But I think the real problem, the problem we have to grapple with, and of course the problem whose solution we'll never find, is the problem of time,

of successive time, and, therein, the problem of personal identity, which is but a part of the problem of time.

Coleman: Do you like the South? It is very much the preferred geographic space in your writing.

Borges: Yes, it is; but this has a quite simple explanation. I think of myself as being a man of Buenos Aires. When I think of Buenos Aires, I'm not thinking of that awful, large, shabby, sprawling city. I'm thinking also of the Province of Buenos Aires. The North is full of agriculture and so on, while to the west and to the south—of course, the word *"oeste"* is rather an uncouth word, while the word *"sur"* is a fine word—there you come across the large, open spaces; there, if we're very lucky, we may get a gaucho or so. And so I think of the South in terms of the past of my country. That is to say, when the country was a country of horsemen and large, empty *estancias*.

Coleman: Just think what the South means to us.

Borges: Oh, it means something very important. It means the Deep South. I know. Yes, I can feel that kind of south also.

di Giovanni: "Do you ever feel that you can travel through time or that events recurring exactly create an impression of time travel?"

Borges: Of course, the most obvious answer would be that we're traveling in time all the time, just as we're doing now. But as to the idea of things coming back, I wonder if that isn't a mere laziness of the imagination. I think that we should expect at least some novelty or novelties, perhaps, in the same cyclic pattern.

Coleman: But you have felt the sense of *déjà vu;* it's not absent from your own work.

Borges: Well, it's not absent from my own life, but I'm not looking for it. It has been given me, several times.

Coleman: Is there the possibility, twenty years hence, of occupying the same space and conditions you did twenty years ago at the exact same moment?

Borges: Yes. But if things were exactly the same I wouldn't be aware of it. Let's suppose that it has happened. We're now living in nineteen hundred and . . . and ninety-two. Now, of course, I can't remember it because if I could remember it, if I could recall it, there would be a difference. But if the moment is exactly the same, I can't be expected to remember it. Of course, we all know about that feeling. I'm very fond of a quite forgotten poet, Rossetti, who expressed all that when he said—

> I have been here before,
> But when or how I cannot tell,
> I know the grass beyond the door,
> The sweet, keen smell,
> The sighing wind, the lights around the shore

—in a poem called "Sudden Light" about the *déjà vu.* I think there's also a passage in Dickens' *David Copperfield* about it, so he must have got the same feeling. But I think that the theory was really worked out logically by David Hume in a book called, I think, *Treatise Concerning Natural Religion,* or some such title. Then it was rediscovered by Nietzsche; and, well, many people have gone over that. Sir Thomas Browne also.

Coleman: I remember "Feeling in Death" from your "New Refutation of Time."

Borges: Exactly. That was back when I got that feeling. That was years and years ago, on the Northside of Buenos Aires.

Coleman: It's just magnificent.

Borges: Yes, I know. One of my best pieces of writing, yes?

Coleman: I think so.

Borges: Well, it was when I wrote it, but still that was ever so long ago.

Coleman: There seems to be a topic that connects with this one.

di Giovanni: "Could you please tell us of your own feelings about death? Do they agree with the statement in one of your stories that refers to death as 'the oblivion that awaits us all'?"

Borges: I think of death as oblivion. I am hungering and thirsting after oblivion. I do not want to be remembered; and—this is most important—I am tired of being myself. In fact, I am tired of being an ego, an "I"; and I suppose that when I'm dust and ashes, then I'll be nothing. I'm looking forward to that prospect. But of course I won't be able to enjoy it because I won't be there.

Coleman: You don't want any repeats in the future life?

Borges: No. I don't want to be threatened by personal immortality of any kind. I only think of an afterlife as a kind of awful possibility, but I think we should rather speak of it as a kind of awful *im*possibility.

di Giovanni: "Does God play an important part in your mystic themes?"

Borges: Well, if you, Sir, are thinking of a personal God, the answer is decidedly no. If you think of God as an ethical purpose, as an intellectual purpose, as what Matthew Arnold called "the something not ourselves that makes for righteousness," in that case I believe in God. Perhaps there is a moral purpose or intellectual purpose to the universe; however, I know nothing about that. I know that I am attempting in my own tiny way to further that purpose by writing quite unimportant short stories.

di Giovanni: "If you were to write in English, would your work have a different impact?"

Borges: Yes, it would, because it would have the full strength of the English language behind it. But I respect English too much to attempt the writing of English. Although I have done most of my reading in English.

di Giovanni: "You've often talked about the 'verbal music of English' and its effect on you. What exactly is that 'verbal music'?"

Borges: When I wrote that down, I wasn't thinking of myself as a writer, but as a reader. I think that English *has* a word music of its own; and it springs, of course, from the fact that it is not merely a Germanic tongue but also a Romance language. To quote the most obvious of all examples, it might make all the difference in the world were I to use, in a poem written in English—but I don't write poems in English—the word "Holy Ghost" or "Holy Spirit," because those words have the same logical meaning and quite a different, let's say, spiritual or literary connotation. You see, the word "ghost" is a fine and a dark word, while the word "spirit" has something light and shining about it. Yet those words are supposed to be synonyms. Of course, far more is the case with such words as "royal" and "kingly" or "brotherly" and "fraternal" or "folk" and "people," and so on. If you read your Bible, you are finding that continual shifting, that rich music, of the Saxon and of the Latin element.

Coleman: I remember an etymology you gave of the Spengler title.

Borges: *Der Untergang des Abendlandes.* That would be "The Down Going of the Evening Lands," which is far better than *The Decline of the West.* In the German you are made to feel *Untergang* = "under" and "going down." By the way, the word "gangster" comes from the same root, because people thought of those men as walking together. Then there's the same thing in the Scots: *gang* is "to go." *Abendland* is a beautiful word, but it's only used, I think, for literary purposes. I don't think any German would speak of *Abendland* or *Morgenland.* But in Old English I found quite a fine word for the morning—the *morgentid,* "morningtime," or "morningtide." Tennyson translated it as "But when first the great sunstar of morningtide," where he is hinting at a metaphor, where the idea is not only of "tide" in the sense of time, but also the idea of the day as breaking forth in a kind of tide. And then "sunstar"—that's a fine word. In the Saxon we have something perhaps stronger, but different. In the Saxon text of the "Battle of Brunanburh" we read something like "The sun, that famous star"—which is quite fine in its own way.

di Giovanni: "Do you think that the presence of Ortega y Gasset had an intellectual influence in Argentina?"
Borges: Well, I suppose he did, but not for me. I merely had some five minutes' talk with him, and, I think, well—period, full stop.

di Giovanni: "How do you feel about your name's having become an adjective—Borgesian—like other adjectives: Kafkaesque, Dickensian?"
Borges: I think that all those words are impartially ugly, I should say, and I should avoid them. Still, I'm not to blame for that kind of thing.

di Giovanni: "What is mythology to the writer?"
Borges: I am trying to think, and I'm hardly accustomed to that operation. But I think—you see, here I am trying to think *again*—whether he knows it or not, every writer is attempting a mythology. I mean, if we are to live at all, then our work is to become a kind of myth, as even, for example, in the case of Dr. Watson and Sherlock Holmes, Boswell and Johnson. I suppose that every writer creates, even if he doesn't intend to, a small but worldwide mythology of his own. Every writer lives in some kind of inside world; that should be his mythology. But I don't think a writer should take any pains about that, or worry about it. If he's a good writer, that kind of thing is bound to happen.

Coleman: Do you think the worst writers are the ones who end their life in *costumbrismo* or local color or anecdote?
Borges: I dare say you're right, Sir. And you're very brave, because I've always thought the same thing but I've never dared to say so. Here you're saying it before a number of people.

Coleman: But I'm supposed to be the straight man in all this.

Borges: . . . I quite agree with you.

Coleman: I always thought so, reading you, because you escape the vices that have plagued so many different kinds of literature.

Borges: I *think* I escaped them because I began by committing them. According to the Gnostics, you can't get rid of a sin until you've committed it. You're a possible murderer until you have murdered somebody. After the murder, then you're purified and—

Coleman: —you're a saint.

Borges: Yes, yes, maybe you're a saint. So we should try, as Luther had it, *pecca fortiter,* no? Sin strongly. And then in the end you'll be a saint.

di Giovanni: "Could you explain your idea of literary inspiration and shed light on the existing unity between author and work?"

Borges: I can only say that when I am writing, I feel I am being led somewhere by something. I can't go beyond that. I don't think I should talk in terms of the Muse or the Holy Ghost or the subconscious. I know that when I am writing, I am merely a tool, but as to the real name of the tool, I know nothing whatever. So that would be inspiration. But I think that there's another part of the question that I have utterly forgotten. How does it run?

di Giovanni: ". . . and shed light on the existing unity between author and work."

Borges: Well, I fail to see the link between the two parts of the question. I'm being very, very dull, no? After a heavy lunch and so on.

di Giovanni: Well, try this one: "What is the cause-effect relationship in your world of labyrinths?"

Borges: That should be an easy one. I am continually feeling perplexity. I feel, of course, all the common emotions of mankind, but perplexity would be the chief—or, as Chesterton had it, *wonder.* And of course the most obvious symbol of perplexity, the obvious token of amazement, is a maze. So you find only too many mazes in my work, but I'll do my best to get rid of them if I can—to find other symbols—because I'm already a bit tired of my pet symbols.

di Giovanni: "Mallarmé said a poet sculpts his tomb. Would you agree?"

Borges: I wonder what Mallarmé meant by that? And then I might agree or disagree.

di Giovanni: Maybe that means the same thing you wrote in the last paragraph of *El hacedor*.

Borges: But what on earth *did* I say in my last paragraph? That's another big mystery!

di Giovanni: About all the elements you write about in your lifetime, and then in the end you find that they trace your own face.

Borges: That's possibly the quotation, but I wonder whether my own face is a tomb? At least I hope it isn't.

di Giovanni: So much for Mallarmé. "Your stories are filled with murders, defenestrations"—what's that?

Borges: That means being thrown out of the window. There are no windows here, so there is no danger.

di Giovanni: Your stories are?

Borges: I don't know. I have never—

Coleman: You have never defenestrated anyone.

Borges: No, not to my knowledge. In any case, I have forgotten it. Well, my stories are full of defenestrations—why not? It's a fine word.

di Giovanni: ". . . and very little sex. How do you feel about humanity?"

Borges: The answer is obvious. I have been worried all my life by falling in love, sex, and that kind of thing.

di Giovanni: Falling out of windows?

Borges: Not yet, but it may happen at any moment. And as to murder, I wonder. I don't think there are many murders. I rather think in terms of men getting themselves killed, but not of men killing other men. I rather think in, let's say, ethical terms. And even in such stories as "La intrusa"—which you will read in due time, as I am told—there is a murder, but I have purposely left out the way it was committed, because I don't go in for being blood-and-thundery. In fact, I rather dislike that kind of thing. We know that "A" killed "B," but we are not told how he did it, and in fact I don't know because I am not too curious about my own creatures. As to love, I think I have written any amount of poems on the subject—not of stories. Perhaps I have written too much. I accuse myself of thinking all the time of some woman or other.

di Giovanni: "Do you see mysticism as a way out of the maze?"

Borges: For all I know, mysticism is the only way; but my gods, whoever they may be, have not allowed me that particular way. So that, as mysticism is denied me, I have to go in for being an amateur student of metaphysics, being a reader of Schopenhauer, of Hume, of Bradley; but except for that one strange experience I had that my friend has remembered ["Feeling in Death"], really I can say very little about mysticism personally, though of course I have studied, I have read my *Varieties of Religious Experience,* and I have done much reading in the mystics, especially Swedenborg, also Blake.

di Giovanni: "Some Argentine writers accuse you of being too abstract and too little of an Argentine. Do you feel at one with your country?"

Borges: Only too much so. At this moment I am not crying for the Carolines, as the song has it, but I'm thinking back on Buenos Aires. I know that Buenos Aires is perhaps the ugliest city on earth; I know it's far too straggling, too uneven, too shabby-genteel also, and yet I love it. Perhaps I am too much of an Argentine. But I should be excused for this since I also think of myself as a citizen of Austin, a citizen of Cambridge, Massachusetts, a citizen of Geneva, a citizen of Montevideo, a citizen of Edinburgh, and at this moment, of course, as a citizen of the capital city of the world—New York.

di Giovanni: Do you think that behind the question there's this—that it's impossible to be abstract *and* an Argentine? Is it written somewhere that you can't be both things?

Borges: Well, perhaps it is written somewhere; it's laid up in heaven! But why not be an Argentine and also go in for abstractions? For example, I was a good student of algebra and that doesn't make me less of an Argentine. Also, what does it mean to be an Argentine? It means to be the inheritor of what might be called "Western culture." (And of course if we can get anything from the East, we should grab as much of it as we can.) So that I don't think being Argentine is necessarily a limitation, except in the sense that belonging to some country, some land, is a limitation. Those things can't be helped. I was born in Buenos Aires, so were my people before me, and I may be allowed to be an Argentine, I suppose. In fact, I am—what can I do about it?

di Giovanni: "If you could spend an afternoon in your garden with the beings and beasts from your *Book of Imaginary Beings*—"
Borges: I'd be frightened to death!

di Giovanni: "—or with the beasts from T. H. White's *Bestiary* or with real animals, which would you choose?"

Borges: The answer is easy: I would choose something else.

di Giovanni: "What ever happened to the translation of Whitman's 'Song of Myself' that you undertook many years ago?"

Borges: I'm sorry to say I undertook it, being quite unworthy of the task, and I'm sorry to say it found its way into print. I translated the "Song of Myself" and the "Children of Adam" and then some pieces chosen at random, and they were published in Buenos Aires in a far too expensive edition.

Coleman: Did you take up the translation of Faulkner because you felt it had to be done, or someone asked you, or—

di Giovanni: Or you needed the money?

Borges: At first it was merely hack work. I was asked to do it, and I needed the money. As I went on, I felt I was doing right, and I did my best to do full justice to Faulkner. Of course, once the translation came out in Buenos Aires, people said that I had been betraying Faulkner because they said the sentences were far too long and too involved. Then I had to remind them that perhaps long and involved sentences might be found in the text. Translators are always blamed, no? Texts are always perfect.

di Giovanni: How many translations of Faulkner, Virginia Woolf, and other American writers—

Borges: Virginia Woolf is hardly an American writer.

di Giovanni: —and other writers *in English* were done by Leonor Acevedo de Borges?

Borges: Yes, she did the translations, but I *signed* them!

di Giovanni: Did you really do them, or did your mother help you with them? Or did she do them and you polish them?

Borges: No, I think the truth—and I owe you the truth—is that I did some of them and that she polished them.

Coleman: Borges, can I ask you—

Borges: Of course you can!

Coleman: I was just going to ask about your seemingly real attraction to Melville and Hawthorne. I think the nineteenth century in North America attracts you more than the twentieth?

Borges: Oh, far more. No question about it.

Coleman: Could you speak of your interest in Hawthorne as is shown in your lecture in, I guess it's *Other Inquisitions?*

Borges: I guess it is. As a matter of fact, I was quite a small boy when I read Edgar Allan Poe, and it was many years after that I came to Hawthorne, and I saw that in spite—at least I divined it or I had it—that despite the fact that Hawthorne was thinking along moral lines all the time (most of his stories were intended to be fables or allegories) and Poe wasn't, I think there is a kinship between them—a kinship in the style—but here I'm speaking as a mere foreigner and I may be making any amount of mistakes. Besides, I discovered a story—"discovered" is too ambitious a word—a story by Hawthorne called "Wakefield," and that story is one of the most remarkable stories I've ever read. There I found one of the many forerunners of Kafka, and, strange to say, he wrote that one quite different story when he was a young man. Then he went on to write such books as *The Scarlet Letter, Twice-told Tales,* and so on.

But in the case of nineteenth- and twentieth-century American literature, I don't think we should set one against the other. What I know is this fact: that at least two or perhaps three of America's nineteenth-century writers have had an influence all over the world. I'm speaking, of course, of Poe. Poe was the begetter of Baudelaire, was the begetter of the Symbolists, of Valéry, and so on. Then, of couse, I'm thinking in terms of Walt Whitman, and I'm not sure that there are any contemporary American writers who have that kind of interest.

Coleman: You seem to read Henry James in a very dark manner.

Borges: In a very dark manner? Well, he *wrote* in a very dark manner.

Coleman: Most people here in the United States don't look on him as a dark writer.

Borges: Well, I suppose I'm very dull, but I find him dark. I don't only find him dark but also very mazy and very intricate. I find him as intricate, for example, as Frost. When you read Frost and take him at his face value, he seems a quite simple kind of poet. But he's deceptively simple. When I think of Henry James, I'm not thinking of his novels—I think they are rather boring—but of his short stories, and in those stories I think you get labyrinths and mazes, endlessly. But I haven't invented a fancy Henry James for myself.

Coleman: The tales are given short shrift here.

Borges: Well, they shouldn't be, if I may be allowed to make that remark.

di Giovanni: "Would you object if your work in its totality were to be classified as escapist, anti-realist, and neocolonial?"

Borges: No, I shouldn't object. I don't object to *anything* people say about my work, even if they find it good; but if they point out something derogatory to me, I fully agree with them, of course—being a modest man.

di Giovanni: Part two: "If so, is there any aspect of Argentine reality that you have not treated as a mere vehicle for metaphysical 'tripping'?" (I don't think he knows what "tripping" means.)

Borges: "Tripping"? Yes, I know what that means.

Coleman: *Viaje en el espacio.*

di Giovanni: No, not in this sense you don't.

Borges: Thinking of the light fantastic, too?

Coleman: It's an imaginary voyage induced by drugs.

Borges: In that case I know nothing whatever about it—drugs. Here is my glass of *water* before me. But I may be allowed to say something that may smack of vanity—I *am* a part of Argentine reality.

di Giovanni: "Many of your earlier works reflect the books you read, but your recent works don't—at least not to the same extent. What are the books or authors that interest you now?"

Borges: I lost my sight, for reading and writing purposes, way back in 1955—the year of the revolution. Since then I've had little time for my contemporaries, so I may have done some rereading or very little reading. And my time is busy. In the morning I work at my own stuff in the National Library; every afternoon I work with my friend Norman Thomas di Giovanni on translating and, I hope, bettering my stuff in English; and at night I may meet a few friends—I'm meeting one at a time because I don't think I know more than six or seven people in Buenos Aires. So all this kind of experience—having to answer questions—is quite new to me. Those things don't happen to me in Buenos Aires, for nobody would stay for an answer, and that's all I can say.

Coleman: When you dictate a story, is it different from when you actually wrote it down?

Borges: The answer to this particular question was revealed to me—was given unto me, may I say biblically—by Norman Thomas di Giovanni last night. He told me—and I think he was telling me the truth—that the simplification that came to me through the fact of living in a colorless world (the only color I can make out is yellow; all the others are much the same) also stands for a simplification in my vision of the world in a metaphysical sense, and in my style also. Even as when nighttime comes and things are simplified, so when night fell on my eyes, things were also simplified for me. As I want to know what I'm writing, as I want to be gazing at what I'm writing, I couldn't very well go in for elaborate, baroque writing; I couldn't go on aping Sir Thomas Browne, for example, or even De Quincey's amazing sentences; and so I fell back on simplicity, and, naturally, not only in style, but I fell back on quite simple, straightforward plots such as in "La intrusa."

di Giovanni: Of course, I was also thinking of the most physical sense of all, having seen Borges' early manuscripts, which were written in the most minuscule possible hand and were keyed in with various kinds of symbols, interpolations, additions, contradictions, and which it would now be physically impossible for him to dictate or to do himself. In other words, he was forced—

Borges: No, no secretary would stand that kind of thing.

di Giovanni: The kind of secretary he has now is very amusing.

Borges: Yes, she is. I feel I have found the right person, because I feel I am quite alone when I am with her. For example, if I dictate a sentence to her and then say "semicolon" or "period," she writes those words down. I tried dictating to my mother, but she was always saying, "No, that's the wrong rhythm," or "That's the wrong word," or "You shouldn't write that." While with my secretary, who shall be nameless here, and to whom I am duly grateful, I feel quite at home. I feel quite at ease, quite alone with myself.

Coleman: You've spoken about how you were stuck at one point in "La intrusa."

Borges: Yes, and my mother gave me the words. "La intrusa" is a rather nasty story about hoodlums, and my mother hated it thoroughly. I was dictating it to her, and she said: "God, what an awful story! Promise me this is the last time you'll try your hand at this kind of stuff." I said yes, dutifully, knowing I was lying all the time. But there was a moment when something quite important had to be said by one of the characters, and then I stopped. My mother said, "Well, what has happened to you?" And I said, "I don't know what the man said." She said: "I know quite well what he said," and then she gave me the key word I was looking for. Now, of course, she denies the anecdote, saying it was made up by myself because she is thoroughly ashamed of the story.

Coleman: How does the line go? *"A trabajar, hermano"?*

Borges: That's it. A man has to tell his brother that he has killed the woman they are both in love with. He has done that out of friendship, because he thinks that the friendship is far more important than the woman or than any woman. Now the man had to blurt that out to his brother, and I would have committed the capital sin of saying, "I killed her," and that would have spoiled the whole story; but my mother found—being a *criolla,* coming from old Argentine and Uruguayan stock—she found the right word. She made him say: "Now, to work, brother. I killed her this morning." And then they go on to bury her. I have to thank her for that gift—well, for many gifts.

Coleman: We're coming to the end—

di Giovanni: I think we have more time—

Coleman: No, we're being thrown out at four-thirty.

di Giovanni: Out the window.

Borges: We're being defenestrated. . . . I'm quite enjoying all this. . . . I wonder where the Chinaman is, eh? He hasn't shown up yet.

Coleman: Oh, the Maoist. I can see him. In fact, I'm looking at him right now.

Man from audience: A Maoist is convenient; a Castroite is convenient.

Coleman: I'm sure we have other adversaries of your literary principles, but they're being very courteous.

Borges: Well, I suppose they're as timid as I am, and I can beat anyone at timidity. That, of course, is a form of boasting also.

Coleman: Norman, do you have one more question?

di Giovanni: "Could you write a story about revolution and still view it in metaphysical terms?"

Borges: As a matter of fact, I am going to write a story about a revolution, about our revolution in 1955, and it won't be metaphysical. I have a plot. That plot has been haunting me since—since 1955. When I get back to Buenos Aires, I'll set it down and it will be, I think, my finest story, because it is a story of friendship, and friendship is perhaps the best thing to be had in my country. The story will be called, as a matter of fact, "Los amigos"— "The Friends." That's all I'm allowed to reveal now.

Man from audience: May a Maoist ask a question? How do you define revolution? I've heard of the revolution of 1955, but as far as I am concerned it would not be a revolution at all—

Borges: Wasn't it? They threw Perón out!

Man: However you might want to characterize—

Borges: It *was* a revolution. I have known people—

Man: A social revolution? What changes were there, really?

Borges: Well, there was a big change. Now we have gentlemen governing us, and then we had hoodlums. I think, ethically, that should be enough.

Man: They are the same *military* gentlemen.

Borges: No. They are not.

Man: You've had a series—nine, I think, in the last three years.

Borges: No. But if you think of military men, you should think of the military men we have in the Argentine. They are quite mild and quite harmless and well meaning. But Perón was a hoodlum, a rascal. Well, I . . . I . . . I . . . I . . . I . . . I . . . I can hardly mention his name because I think . . . I think his . . . his name is obscene, somehow. Perhaps because my sister was in prison, my mother was in prison, my nephew was in prison, I was . . . I was being followed by a detective; and still more because I have known people who were tortured to death. And even during Perón's regime no man dared to say that he was a *peronista* because people would have laughed at him. They made it very clear that if they were *peronistas,* it was because it suited their convenience, because he was filling their pockets. And I had to live all through that time, and in fact I should know something about it.

di Giovanni: Borges, would you like to say something about your newest story?

Borges: "El Congreso" is a story that has been haunting me for the last thirty or forty years. I thought I should be worthy of that plot, but as time went on I felt that I had no such hope. I was always telling it to my friends, and then one of my friends said: "Well, the story is already there. Why don't you write it down?" And so I did. It is a story about a mystical experience.

(The Congress is not the Argentine Congress, of course.) The story is about a mystical experience I never had, but maybe before I die I'll be allowed to have it. I can say no more—the story hasn't been published as yet. It may be, for all I know, my best story or my justification as a storyteller.

With Borges in Buenos Aires

Willis Barnstone / 1975

From *Denver Quarterly,* The University of Denver, Vol. 15, No. 1,
Spring 1980, pp. 48–57. Reprinted by permission.

Borges waited behind the door, by the large portrait of his late mother.
Dressed in his usual black suit, neat but one shoelace untied, he tottered a bit
without his cane. The darkness of his clothes contrasted with the pallor of his
face. His head tilted sideways and upward, he smiled like a child, yet se-
verely, and his blind eyes glowed. He took me by the arm and said come, sit
down on the couch, and I found myself guided by and guiding him to the
couch under the window.

"Don't you think English has developed toward a monosyllabic language?" he said. "Take the word *laugh.* In Old English it had two phonemes
hlehhan or *hlyhhan,* and also two in Old High German, *lachen.* Yet just one
syllable in modern English. Remarkable, no?"

"Like Chinese," I said, "but going the other way in time. Classical *wen-
yen,* the old literary language, was virtually monosyllabic. But with the need
to make up new words and because of the limited number of sounds—about
sixteen hundred I believe—they had to combine sounds, putting two or more
characters together, and so modern Chinese has moved toward the use of
more polysyllables."

I had not seen Jorge Luis Borges in six years, yet he was chatting about
language as if not a second had elapsed since our last words. I thought of the
Spanish mystical poet Fray Luis de León, who on returning to his classroom
at the University of Salamanca, after five years in an Inquisitional prison, is
said to have begun his first lecture with: "As I was saying yesterday."

"But English is really monosyllabic, even when it is not," Borges coun-
tered eagerly. "Take the adverb *quickly.* You hear only *quick.* The *ly* is very
weak and unimportant. But in Spanish we must say *rápidamente.* The *mente*
is as loud as the *rápida.* English is a remarkable language. Back in 1927
when I first talked to Pablo Neruda we said how much we admired English
and what a pity we were writing in Spanish, an impossible language. But
since we were stuck with it, we did what we could. I myself first read *Don
Quijote* in English. It was one of those books in my father's library, a room

138

from which I may never have come out. Later when I read Cervantes in Spanish I felt I was reading an uncertain translation from English."

"Do you like Neruda?"

"He wrote all those silly sentimental love poems at the beginning, you know, *Veinte poemas de amor y una canción desesperada (Twenty Love Poems and a Desperate Song),* but when he became a Communist his poems became very strong. I like Neruda the Communist poet."

"Both you and Neruda wrote about animals as in the old bestiaries. Do you remember the two and a half bestiary poems in Anglo-Saxon?"

"O yes," Borges replied. " 'The Phoenix.' A long poem. And then 'The Whale.' He's the devil. And the panther is Christ. Why did Eliot use the leopard and not the panther when he wrote 'three white leopards sat under a juniper-tree'? Maybe the panther was too obvious," he said, answering himself.

We talked about Old English. Borges delighted in every word, and each etymology he treated as a friend. "What do you think the word *bonfire* comes from?"

"From the French *bon* plus *feu*," I guessed, falling into his trap.

"No, it's from Anglo-Saxon *Bān fȳr.* A *bonefire.* I suppose they got some big horse bones and burned them outdoors to keep warm."

"When did you learn Anglo-Saxon?"

"In 1955 when I was fifty-six. I couldn't read by then. My eyes had gone. But a priest here in Buenos Aires helped me. I don't have much to do with priests, but this one was very patient with me."

"Do you know it well?"

"The grammar's hard, you know. This Jesuit had a very deep knowledge of it. Then I went on to Old Norse and Icelandic, but I have to struggle with them. I put things in order when I wrote a small volume on Old Germanic literatures."

Every Sunday afternoon from six to nine, Borges still gives classes in Old English in his house. He knows the texts by heart. I attended these classes for five months. The student of course paid nothing. They were his friends. When an argument arose, he would ask someone to go to one of his ponderous old reference books to settle an outcome of a battle or the rivalry of kings and lords. The acts of plunder, cowardice, the enumeration of flights across the sea, the stabbings, the counting of jewels, gold, and black horses, somehow gave rise to constant laughter and Borges laughed the loudest. Brugos, a clerk in one of the ministeries, would shove a text in front of Borges and say, "Just look at this." And Borges turned his blind eyes to the text, and remembered.

Today, a Monday, Borges's tongue was filled with verses from Icelandic and Old English as during those unusual classes at the bottom of the New World celebrating the old barbaric north. He spoke the lines with ceremony and humor, like a priest.

"Come have some tea," he said.

Borges rose fragilely. He took an arm and we walked to the table which Fanny, his Guaraní-speaking housekeeper, had set with many silver pieces for the biscuits and tea. Borges is a partisan of cold cereals and his breakfast each morning includes Corn Flakes or another cereal which he eats dry, without milk or sugar. When we were seated he asked me to read two sonnets I had translated into English, one from his recent *La rosa profunda,* the other from *La Nación,* the national Argentine newspaper in which he publishes new poems. I read aloud:

Remorse

I have committed the worst sin of all
That a man can commit. I have not been
Happy. Let the glaciers of oblivion
Drag me and mercilessly let me fall.
My parents bred and bore me for a higher
Faith in the human game of nights and days;
For earth, for air, for water, and for fire.
I let them down. I wasn't happy. My ways
Have not fulfilled their youthful hope. I gave
My mind to the symmetric stubbornness
Of art, and all its webs of pettiness.
They willed me bravery. I wasn't brave.
It never leaves my side, since I began:
This shadow of having been a brooding man.

and

A Blind Man

I do not know what face looks back at me
When I look at the mirrored face, nor know
What aged man conspires in the glow
Of the glass, with tired silent fury.

Slow in shadows, with my hand I explore
My invisible features. A sparkling ray
Reaches me. A glimmer of your hair is gray.
And some is even gold. I've lost no more
Than just the useless surfaces of things.
This consolation is of great import:
It is the comfort Milton had. I resort
To letters and to roses—my wonderings.
I think . . . if I could see my face I soon
Would know who I am on this rare afternoon.

"You see, these poems," he began with characteristic humor, "which were not worth much, now are good in English." His dead eyes (to use his term) glowed, and his face was animated. Then I read the poems to him in Spanish, which he said he hardly remembered. Borges normally keeps no copies of his works, and as soon as a publisher sends him something he gives it away to the first guest who enters his house. But after each line or two, he repeated the lines resonantly and with admiration, as if hearing them for the first time, and said, "¡Ay, qué lindo!" ("Oh, how beautiful!"). As he listened to the poems and repeated them, again he tilted his head sideways and upward, smiling wide as Fernandel, yet excess was curiously mingled with understatement and austere dignity so characteristic of Borges's changing face.

"You new sonnets in *La rosa profunda* are perfectly traditional," I said, "black as Quevedo and more personal than earlier poems. They have a narrative pathos disguised in a sonnet form which is almost invisible because of run-on lines and their spoken quality. Invisible sonnets."

"Well, I use only simple rhymes in Spanish, the obvious ones everybody knows, which call no attention to themselves. If I used the complicated rhymes of Lugones, rhyming *reloj* (watch) with I don't know what, the rhymes would stand out. Anyway, here in Argentina no one reads poetry so I can do what I want. I'm safe. No one will criticize the poems because they will go unknown."

"Borges, in *Elogio de la sombra (In Praise of Darkness)* you write that you don't distinguish between poetry and prose . . ."

"No," he interrupted. "I don't distinguish between *my* poetry and fiction, but others may do so."

"I think you also do. Because when you write poems you are not all those people, all those Borges's you can't keep track of that run through your fiction. In the poems there is a character who is Borges, though he may be a Saxon in battle, a Spanish Jew from Salonika. And the *you, he,* or *other* is talking about history, time, or himself with a pathos and personal identity not usually found in the more elusive stories."

"Then you like the poems?"

"Yes."

"My friends say that they are not much good. They are being sincere. They say I should write more stories and not waste my time on those verses. I think of myself first as a poet."

"You and Cervantes," I said. "Except that poor Cervantes really *was* wrong, because he did not write good poems."

"Yes, Cervantes was a terrible poet," Borges said. "He wrote only one good line—but that was pretty good. Now the English poets were much better. When Marlowe speaks of topless towers, he means that the tower was infinitely high, like Babel, but he didn't have to say *infinite.* Or when Chapman translated the *Iliad,* and talked about *gelding* that fellow, he said 'they lopped off the man.' "

Borges felt his way to his library and pulled out a heavy volume of the first half of Samuel Johnson's dictionary.

"A friend gave this to me. Not the first edition, but from that time. They haven't reprinted it, they should, you know." Borges took my arm and we went out for the elevator, about ten steps from his door.

It took us a very long time to reach the elevator because he was speaking avidly about Samuel Johnson. Finally, we were in the street, on the way to the newspaper offices of *La Nación,* where he had to deliver a poem to the literary editor.

Guiding Jorge Luis Borges through the streets of Buenos Aires was dangerous, at least for me, and perhaps I was delinquent, for although I paid attention to where we were going, it was not easy. Borges didn't stop dialoguing for a second, even when we might be caught in the middle of a major street, with fat buses plunging toward us. Another friend walked ahead, attempting to hold up traffic, for we could never cross any street in time before the light gave out. Words were always more important than the machines rushing near us.

Yet Borges knows the streets very well, knows when to step up or down. Much of the pavement however is broken, and there are pits every ten or fifteen feet. I was reminded of a powerful dark poem in *La rosa profunda:*

The Blind Man

The varied world was plundered. Gone the sweep
Of faces (that are what they were before),
The nearby streets, today remote. And more,
The hollow blue that yesterday was deep.
Yet in the books is only what remains
In memory—that form of forgetfulness
Which keeps the format but undoes the sense,
Reflecting mere titles. The street contains
Ambushing breaks and holes. And each step won
May be a fall. I am the very slow
Prisoner of a dreamlike time, who has no
Way to mark his dawn or his declining sun.
It is night. No one is here. With my verse
I must work out my insipid universe.

"The sidewalks are broken like my country," Borges said.

"What is its future?"

"We had a past."

"Yes, everyone here now talks about the national depression. Nothing's going well—except the kiosks that sell everything from light bulbs to Kafka."

"That's the only good thing we have had for ten years," he said, "the kiosks. But in the nineteenth century we fought everywhere for Argentina's independence. My grandfather died with bullets in his chest, in battle. No we have had that *cornudo* (cuckold) Perón. The only battle he ever fought was to try to rename the city of La Plata for his wife Evita, and he even failed at that. He wanted to call it *La Puta* (The Whore) in her honor but wouldn't accept the compromise of *La Pluta*. After all, in Argentina (silver country) La Pluta—a silver prostitute—is quite fine."

As we walked the crowded sidewalk, people generally moved aside. A few policemen, planted with their backs to us, stood in the middle of Florida, the main shopping street. People were walking around them. We walked directly into their midst and they hopped aside as they heard and, at the last instant, saw the old gentlemen coming upon them. People came up to Borges frequently and shook his hand. Borges said he hired all these pedestrians to do this. They were the same ones coming round and round the block. "I do what Perón did. He hired people to come to rallies and shout." A man came up to us and rhetorically addressed Borges, seizing his hand and shaking it furiously. "Borges, you are immortal."

"Don't be a pessimist, sir," Borges gently replied.

When Perón first came to power, Borges was fired from his position in a small library in Buenos Aires. He was assigned the position of inspector of chickens and rabbits at outdoor street markets. Hardly the position for a librarian with poor eyes. He declined. When Perón fell in 1959, Borges was appointed director of the National Library, but by this time he could perceive only a bit of light in his left eye. They returned him, he told me several times, to the library with a hundred thousand books to look at in the darkness. This obsession is recorded in his well-known "Poem of the Gifts" which begins:

> Let no one with tears or disapproval slight
> This declaration of the majesty
> Of God, who with magnificent irony
> Granted me books and, at the same time, night.
> He made this set of lightless eyes the lord
> In this city of books, and they can only read
> In the library of dreams where the dawns cede
> These senseless paragraphs to unexplored . . .

"When I was in Paris as a young man, I knew a very correct poet. Poor man, he had nothing left but perfection." We talked about Yeats who got better as he got older and e. e. cummings who did not, and Eliot who stopped altogether.

"Cummings and Pound put their masks on when they write poems and you take yours off," I said.

"Eliot is a good poet, no? but a stuffy critic. But Frost is a *fine* poet. I would like to have known him personally."

"Frost wrote in a simple language," I said, "which at the time was thought old-fashioned and which now again is modern. It has aged well."

"Frost is a very good poet," Borges added, "but you know he was an awful farmer."

Another old man took Borges's hand and congratulated him for taking a political stand against Perón. Borges asked him his name, as he did most people who spoke to him in the street. He always smiled fully and held the passerby's hand firmly. Borges told the gentleman that he (Borges) was a bit beyond *la primavera* (the spring) for politics. When one lady hysterically called him Argentina's greatest writer, he answered softly: "What you say is clear proof that our country is going through a difficult period."

When we reached the building of *La Nación,* the elevator was not working so we walked the three flights. He did not want to rest, he said, because it might make him tired. "We better keep moving before the stairs break down too. Buenos Aires is the only city in the world where they discovered stairs after they invented the elevator. But elevators work only when they are out of order." As we went up the long flight in the dark—for the lights were also out—Borges was serene and sure. It was the same to him, with or without light.

"Why aren't you out of breath?" I asked at the top of the stairs, which he said were also tired with all of us.

In a deep, mock-reverent voice, he answered, "I'm afraid I've gone beyond the age of panting."

Once in the office of the literary editor, Borges pulled his poem from a pocket. The editor read it out loud.

"Do you like it?" Borges asked. "Do you think you might possibly use it?"

"Yes, very possibly," he answered ceremonially. Borges's constant spoofing almost always provoked a similar tone. "Well, Borges, if we can sneak it in, would you like it Monday or Sunday?"

"Are you taking it as an act of literary clarity," I asked, "or as an example of literary justice?"

"My editor is a very charitable chap," Borges answered.

When we went down the stairs, Borges had no handrail to hold on to, and the steep steps were harder to descend.

"We are walking down into Hell," I commented.

"Buenos Aires is Hell. But Dante was joking when he asked people to give up hope when they entered down there. Actually he was trying to comfort them."

I mentioned García Lorca's lines about a staircase, *barandas, barandales de la luna / por donde retumba el agua* (stairway, balustrades of the moon where water resounds).

"Not a very intelligent man, that Lorca," Borges said. "He was hopeless. A year in New York and didn't learn a word of English."

As we walked back along Florida, the street where no cars run, we bantered about Spanish poetry. Borges said Scottish ballads were better than those old Spanish *romances.* "The *romances* are not very good, you know."

"How terrible of you."

"Well, we know those Spanish poems so well because they are in our blood, so we don't even have to read them. And so we really don't know them." Then with heavy Gaelic slurs, he recited, " 'To Norway, to Norway, to Norway o'er the foam.' Emily Dickinson comes right out of Emerson, no?"

Borges shifted poets as quickly as he talked, and he rarely mentioned a poet's name without citing four or five lines. He quoted Hölderlin, Rilke, Frost, Lugones, *Beowulf,* Baudelaire—"a clumsy poet, don't you agree?"— reciting in German, English, Spanish, Anglo-Saxon, Latin, and French. After melodiously citing a poem by Hölderlin, he said, "The poor Germans have managed pretty well writing in their dialect of Yiddish. Do you like Cicero? After all, he did more for prose than the Greeks. I mean, Cicero made Latin prose sing. There is a Uruguayan poetess, Delmira Agostini, she wrote only one good line—but that was fifty years ago, in Montevideo. *En la noche tu llave de oro cantó en mi cerradura* (In the night your gold key sang in my lock). Now that took courage fifty years ago."

"Yes, because she did not write it 2,500 years ago in Mytilene. By the way, Borges, in *La rosa profunda* there is a brief, terrifying poem, the epigram 'To the Minor Poet': *La meta es el olvido / Yo he llegado antes.* (The goal is oblivion. I got there beforehand.)"

"The theme is from the Greek Anthology. Of course I don't know Greek, , but there is the Loeb and the German translations. I don't have Hebrew either, although I am interested in the Kabbalah. I do what I can without Hebrew. Since I became blind," he said suddenly, sadly, "I can no longer read or write."

"You think and feel."

"Yes, only think and feel."

As we neared his house, I asked if the peoms came to him like birds, perhaps like the vultures attacking the Parsi towers of silence, about which we had just talked.

"I walk around with them until they overpower me. Then I dictate them, because I can't keep them in the dark anymore."

"Why not?" I asked.

"Because since I am blind I have lost the darkness, I don't know what night is, for everything is a greenish blue, a mist, and never black."

"When you dream?"

"I dream in all colors. Very intense colors."

"Do you also dream in Anglo-Saxon?"

"I don't know Anglo-Saxon quite that well." He recited the first lines of the *Battle of Malden:*

> brocen wurde
> Hēt pā hyssa hwǣne hors forlǣtan,
> feor āfȳsan, ond foro gangan,
> hiegan to handum ond tō hige gōdum

Several hours had passed. Borges was leaving that evening for America where he would stay five days. When the car came to take us to the airport, the driver said his paper called for him to pick up a Mr. Bones. Borges thought this misspelling amusing, but, as we sat in the front seat for the forty-minute ride, his mood was grave. He spoke about his mother.

"She was ninety-nine when she died a few months ago. She suffered so much during the last six months that each night she used to pray for that night to be her last night. And when she woke in the morning and found herself alive she said that God must be punishing her for some sin which she could not remember. I told her she was foolish, that there was no God anyway, and she had not sinned."

"It is your story in which one-hundred- and two-hundred-year-olds are condemned to the fate of living, unable to die."

"That's true. But when I wrote that story I was quite happy. I was spoofing. I never dreamed it would really happen to us."

"Your new book is obsessed with blindness," I said.

"Yes, it is an obsessed book. But I don't speak about blindness in order to complain. I am simply telling people something I know about, what it is like to be blind."

"Has your blindness affected your other senses?"

"Perhaps my memory is a little better. It has to be, since I have to remember things. You know I have to keep all those things in my mind. I can concentrate better, perhaps."

The subject of suicide came up. I mentioned a suicide in my family. He told me that his grandfather had killed himself after the battle was over.

"What do you mean?"

"Well, my grandfather Colonel Francisco Borges Lafinur was only 24 when his side lost the battle of La Verde in 1874. Wearing a white poncho he mounted a gray dapple and charged the enemy trenches, with his arms crossed. Of course they filled his chest with bullets. He committed suicide but didn't jump or use a revolver. He used a whole army. As a young man I used to think of suicide too. Everyone does, doesn't he? But as you grow older you learn that what is terrible now may not be later on, and so you learn to control your moods."

We were speaking now about his own person. Neither modest nor arrogant—the terms are irrelevant, for Borges is himself, whatever that may be—he remarked that people write many books about him and his work, but he had read only one, the first, and wouldn't read any more.

"They see a lot of things in me. And they see many things in my work. That's fine, because I only start the process. But really, why must they say *problematics* or *novelistic?* Sometimes they write very nasty things in a review and I feel bad that they didn't call me first, because I usually agree, and I could tell them even more. Really, we could collaborate. I could help them a lot and they would not have to guess."

"How has it come about that you are going to a conference and that they are going to talk about you?"

"Things like this always happen because I think no and always say yes. I don't know why I am here, getting on this plane."

We were climbing up the metal steps to the plane. There was a particularly difficult part on the ramp, just before we went inside.

"Where am I?" Borges looked around at the night, his head tilting upward. It was November and the air was very warm.

"About one foot ahead you must step up and you will be inside."

Borges gauged the distance with his dutiful mahogany cane and stepped carefully into the cabin.

A Colloquy with Jorge Luis Borges

Donald Yates / 1976

From *The Gypsy Scholar,* Vol. 3, 1976, pp. 65–76. Reprinted by permission.

On February 6, 1976, Jorge Luis Borges accepted an invitation to participate in an informal discussion with the University of Michigan English Department faculty members, graduate students, and the editors of the *Gypsy Scholar.* He was accompanied by Professor Donald Yates of the Department of Romance Languages who is currently preparing a critical biography on Borges. The following colloquium represents the essence of that talk with the Argentine poet and writer.

Question: We are interested in your comments on how you view yourself as a writer in the 20th century.

Borges: Firstly I think of myself as a 19th century writer; I don't think of myself as being modern. I am 76. I was born way back in 1899 so I have a right to be thought of as an old fogey. Now I'll answer your questions.

Question: Well, the first thing that occurs to me as I read over your essays in *Other Inquisitions,* for instance, is the people you refer to in the 19th century; De Quincey, very often, Robert L. Stevenson, but not so much other people you might expect, like Jane Austen or George Eliot. Of course, I'm talking about that one collection primarily.

Borges: Well they came before my time, no?

Yates: You might tell the story about Jane Austen's library of books . . .

Borges: Yes, I remember now Mark Twain's joke. He said, and I think he was demonstrably wrong, that a very fine library might be made by leaving out the works of Jane Austen. And if that library contained no other books, it would still be the finest library in the world. I don't agree with him; I don't suppose anyone does.

Question: Well, I guess what I was thinking was that if we were going to make an undergraduate course in 19th century British literature, these would be the main figures. You refer to De Quincey, Robert Louis Stevenson, and others, and I wondered if you had any comment on that or if there is anything you particularly enjoyed about these authors?

Borges: In the case of, say, Thomas De Quincey, I think he is essential for me. I think I have read and reread *The Confessions of an English Opium Eater,*—one of the saddest books in the world, or saddest papers rather, or a small book in a sense. In "The Last Days of Immanuel Kant" we see a man of great intelligence, a man of genius, very slowly falling to pieces before the eyes of the reader, and then, at last becoming something like a mere mechanism. I think that's one of the finest pieces in De Quincey. There is a very fine translation, a very curious one, of Jean Paul Richter's *Laocöon,* but much later they compared the De Quincey translation to the German text. And I see that De Quincey was enriching the subject all the time because he said what he found least satisfying about the Germans was that they rarely used examples. I mean, they just gave you a bare statement and then you had to find an example yourself. But he was working in examples and, of course, the rather dry prose of Lessing is changed into De Quincey's wonderful prose, I should say. I think that the chief thing to be noted in De Quincey is his style; the style, especially when he spoke of nightmares, mazes, and that kind of thing; the sentences are also mazes. I have some passages I might quote to you by heart—I read and reread them—I have thought of him as if I knew him. I mean I loved him whether as a contemporary or a person one has known. I should say that his influence may have been greater than Chesterton's, greater even than the influence of Robert Louis Stevenson was. Now, De Quincey was a very strange man. For example, he tells us that the one thing admirable in *The Arabian Nights* is the fact that the magician, in order to find out the one man who would be able to unearth the lamp, put his ear to the ground and heard millions and millions of footsteps. Then he detected the footsteps of Aladdin in China and he knew that he was the man, the only boy on earth who could find the lamp. Then he (De Quincey) talked it over with his sister and they thought it was really the most imaginative passage in *The Arabian Nights.* Then I looked for that passage. I looked for it in Galland's translation, in Edward William Lane's translation, in Captain Burton's translation (a literal translation) and it is nowhere to be found. So this means that De Quincey has an inventive memory. And then he said "I was led to think that the smallest things may be secret mirrors of the past and that perhaps everything is a lock that might open a door somewhere or somehow." Then he writes really something very memorable. He said "I have arrived at the idea of the whole world being a kind of secret alphabet, through that passage in *The Arabian Nights*"—which is not to be found in *The Arabian Nights!*

Yates: In your own writing, in your own constellation, Stevenson is in, Chesterton is in, Kipling is in, Wells is in, but George Eliot and Jane Austen are out. Is it because they weren't part of your father's library of books that you began to read as a boy, as a very young boy?

Borges: I think Jane Austen was, but I don't think George Eliot was, but that may account for it. But really I did all my reading as a boy, when I was young. What I read afterwards has made less impression on me.

Yates: Would you say your own reading and your own reading tastes and the authors who may have influenced you most when you wrote were more your father's favorites or your grandmother's favorites?

Borges: Well, of course, for example, my grandmother was very fond of Dickens and so am I. My father never liked Dickens.

Yates: Your grandmother liked Bennett and I don't think there's any place you have ever mentioned Bennett . . .

Borges: I thought of Bennett as being, let's say, a fine novelist. Think of the stories of *The Five Towns* and *The Old Wives Tale.* They're fine books, but to me, they are not essential books. They're books that when you are young, might have been valuable for a little time, no? How about *Elmer Gantry?* Still, I could more than manage to go on living without those books. Reading Arnold Bennett, I feel he was a competent novelist, but not a very interesting person in the sense that somebody like De Quincey is interesting or Stevenson is interesting or Shaw was interesting.

Yates: Are you talking about their lives outside the books they wrote; the men behind the books?

Borges: Yes, I might be talking of that and also of the impression of the writer that the books convey.

Question: I'd like to hear something about Stevenson, something you think is particularly inspiring.

Borges: I should say that every page in Stevenson is particularly inspiring, but, of course, I wonder if literature can be argued about. I mean, if you don't like a writer I can't argue you into liking him. If you dislike Stevenson, then what can I do, it is useless. At the same time, even take such a hackneyed poem as:

> Under the wide and starry sky,
> Dig the grave and let me lie.

> Gladly I live, and gladly die,
> And I lay me down with a will.
> This be the verse you grave for me:
> Here he lies where he longed to be;
> Home is the sailor, home from the sea,
> And the hunter home from the hill.

Well, if those words will not ring out for you, I can say nothing whatever. If Stevenson fails, what can I do? But I think something else might be said about Stevenson. I think that one of the charms of Chesterton (if Chesterton is allowed, I don't know) is the fact that when you read *The Father Brown* Saga or *The Man Who Was Thursday* or *The Man Who Knew Too Much,* you feel that all of those things that are happening in London are not in real London—if there be such a thing as real London—but in fairy London. And I think that the man who invented or who discovered, let us say, that fairy London, was Stevenson, because you get that same sense of London as being a fairy city in the *New Arabian Nights* of Stevenson. I suppose an explanation might be sought in the fact that when Stevenson came to London, London was perhaps a fairy city for him, since he came from a very lovely but quite different city; he came from Edinburgh. And when he wrote stories they told stories in their very names, no—"The Adventure of the Hansom Cabs," "The Adventure of Prince Florizel," "The Suicide Club," for example.

I think in the case of Stevenson, there is one thing I greatly prize, and that's bravery. You feel all the time that Stevenson was a brave man. He speaks of a friend of his, who was perhaps as sick a man as he was; you get to the last, the will to smile, and I think he kept that will when he was dying on that island in the Pacific and wrote the story of his life, his marriage to an American Lady, and his relation with his stepson. By the way, there's a book no one seems to have read. He wrote that in collaboration with Lloyd Osbourne, a detective novel or, as he called it, a police novel—*The Wrecker.* I would like you to read that book; I think it's a very, very fine book. I have read and reread Stevenson, and I think that his touch is lighter than the touch of Chesterton. Sometimes Chesterton is rather heavy-handed. He has a joke and drives it in, but in the case of Stevenson, he has a very light touch. I remember a very fine sentence by André Gide. André Gide, who translated Stevenson, says: "Si la vie grisé . . ." I wonder how "grisé" should be translated. It's not "drunk." It's like "exhilarated," no? How would you translate that, Yates? "Si la vie grisé"—it's like champagne. Stevenson was very fond of champagne. He was always working champagne into his books. It seems the right thing for him.

Yates: I don't know. I think it must lie between what you've suggested and "drunkenness."

Borges: No, "drunk" stands for something uncomfortable, rowdiness. "Grisé" would be the beginning of drunkenness, a light drunkenness.

Yates: "Grisé de parfum" for example. Dizzied by a woman's perfume.

Borges: I think that Stevenson would have enjoyed it—that judgment of André Gide.

Question: When I listened to you this fall, I was struck by your statement that when anyone reads a poem of yours or any work you feel that the work is created anew. I was struck by the respect that you have for your reader.

Borges: Well, I should say that poems only exist when they're read, because if not, a book is a thing among things, a physical object. When somebody reads it, it comes alive. Then it comes alive in your consciousness and then you say you're reading it or collaborating with your writer, and I think that's a fact that has no need of being discussed, it's quite obvious. But Stevenson said something which has always struck me as being rather awful. He said, "What is a character in a book?" And then he answered it in this rather grave way—"A character after all is only a stream of words." Of course, a character is *created* by a stream of words, but you do not think of the character as *being* a stream of words. You do not think of Huck Finn as being a stream of words or Hamlet as being a stream of words or the Master of Ballantrae as being a stream of words. You think of them as living, let's say, not only when the writer is speaking about them, but "in between," no? For example, if in a book you read that the character goes to sleep then you're told nothing about him, but the next morning, if the character is a living character, you feel that he has been sleeping and dreaming, whether or not you're told about the dreams. So that idea, I think, Stevenson must have written when feeling desperate or disheartened—the idea that the character is only a stream of words. For no one thinks of characters as being a stream of words. Do you think Mr. Pickwick is a stream of words?

Question: With that conception of your reader, what is your view of what the profession of literary criticism is or should be, or even if it should exist?

Borges: Yes, of course it should. A literary critic is a man who invites other people to have his dreams, or maybe one who has done the creative

reading, so he gives us something different from what is to be found in the
book. For example, I remember I was disappointed in some of the dramas of
Ibsen when I had read Bernard Shaw's *Quintessence of Ibsenism.* Really, I
found that some of the plays discussed by Shaw were more interesting than
the original plays. So I think there Shaw was being a writer and a critic. Had
he stuck with telling us the plots of Ibsen's plays, that would be more or less
hack work: a very simple thing to do. You see, he was *revealing* them. There
is a famous book in Spanish called *Vida de Don Quixote y Sancho,* by Miguel
de Unamuno. I think he went to certain romantic excesses, but his idea was
a very interesting one: the idea of retelling the whole novel of *Don Quixote,*
from beginning to end, and recreating or rethinking it. Of course, perhaps he
went too far, maybe he took a wrong turn, but the book is an interesting book.
And as you're reading that book, you may or may not agree with him, but
your perception of the original work is changed.

Question: Many of your stories are allegories. Where did you learn allegory, if that question applies to you?

Borges: Well, I don't think of them as being allegories—of course they
are—but were I to say that they cannot be read as stories I don't think I would
be telling the truth. In a sense, I wonder if a writer thinks of what he writes
as being allegorical, or as being symbolical. I think that, of course, we believe
in the symbol, in the allegory, but not immediately. In the case of poets who
are not really great writers, you think of so-and-so as being merely a fable,
for virtue or for courage, or whatever you want, or some social type. But
when you read a great writer, you think of those characters, or those stories,
or those parables, as being true, beyond the other meaning, no? After all, the
outside meanings have been added by somebody. Of course, I know that the
many things I have written are parables—I have called them parables—but I
wish I could write living books; and perhaps I have succeeded now and then.
Who knows?

Question: Well, with that in mind, what do you think of, for instance, the
epic poems of Blake?

Borges: Well, I could never find my way into the mythology of Blake. But
I think of Blake as being a fine thinker, and perhaps, one of the best disciples
of Swedenborg; but as for the poems, I don't like them. There is something
very heavy-handed about them, something very cumbrous. True, you get now
and then beautiful lines: who can fail to remember the moment when the
goddess is in love with a man—her name is, I am sorry to say, Oothoon; it's

rather an uncouth name—and he says "her nets of steel, her traps of adamant will Oothoon make" and ". . . girls of mild silver or of furious gold." Isn't that wonderful—"girls of mild silver or of furious gold . . ."? But for the poems to require a dictionary for the mythology of Blake, is an argument against them. I should say if you need a dictionary for the different gods, and then if you are told that Los, for example, stands for time, or that Enitharmon stands alone before space, I think there is something wanting in the mythology. He made the mistake, I suppose, of *creating* mythology, but had he used, let's say, Greek mythology, or Roman mythology, or Christian mythology—and that's a mythology also—it might be easier to follow him.

Question: I have noticed tonight, and in some of the talks I've heard you give earlier, that your method, the means by which you praise writers you like most often, is to praise the writer rather than the work. In your own composition, do you make any attempt to convey personality or is that something that you trust will come through, or something you try to achieve?

Borges: I think what you say is very acute, even to say right. When I am writing a story, a poem, I do not think of it as a symbol of myself. I think of the story as being interesting to me and as being likely to be interesting to other readers. For example, I don't think I've ever written a fable in the sense that I have begun with something abstract and then gone on to find a symbol. I begin by a symbol. I am interested in a symbol. And then I find out the moral of the symbol that's beyond it, and it is not my task to work that out. Maybe my method is wrong, but at my age I can't find any other . . . it's rather late in the day.

Question: I was curious about this matter of personality; do you desire the reader to sense your personality behind your work?

Borges: Perhaps in the case of my poems I do. But nobody seems to care much for my poems and they're probably right. But in the case of my stories, they are interested, even as a child might be, in the plot, in the characters, Of course, I think that the mention of the very names of Stevenson or Chesterton or Kipling or Blake is to be talking of living people who stand out in your imagination. I don't think that I have to define Stevenson or to define Chesterton or to define anybody since you know them if you know their *sense.*

Question: I find it curious that all the writers you seem to admire the most, Borges, are writers who have what I would call very strong narrative gifts, the gift of telling a story—and I rather suspect from listening to you talk about your own stories, that this is what you are primarily interested in—and yet I think that your reputation and your appeal is more intellectual than it is narrative, more symbolic than narrative.

Borges: I wish I had the gift of storytelling. I wish I was Scheherazade. But I'm not. But still I must do the best I can. There's nothing wrong about storytelling. The literature we have of storytelling—the epic, a good story— why should we be ashamed of that? Especially in my country, where people seem especially fond of words, of coining words, of weaving and interweaving them. I am interested in the story, in the fact of wanting to know what will happen next. I think plots are important; besides plots are also symbols; the plot is a way of conveying something. But perhaps I am more interested in the plot than in what is conveyed by it. I think I'm keenly aware of, let us say, the beauty of words; I'm quite sensitive to word-music. You, Yates, re-marked today that my mind, my memory is full of words and quotations, and that those I can remember because I like those poems.

Yates: Why do you feel that it took you eight books and thirty-three years before you even dared try a narrative yourself?

Borges: That came out of circumstances. People thought of me as a poet, they thought of me even as a critic, but they never thought of me as a story-teller. So I felt that really I was an outsider and an intruder when I was telling a story. I'd spent all my life reading stories and I thought I was unworthy of writing them. So I found that kind of halfway house, a kind of cross between the essay and the story. You see, that was not my literary fortune, no? That came out of my shyness.

Yates: If you knew better, why would you care whether the public thought you were a poet or thought that you were a critic?

Borges: Well, my friends thought of me as a poet; they never thought of me as a storyteller. Of course, I didn't want to shock them by writing a story, because I thought I was unworthy of writing stories.

Yates: Why? Because the stories you had been reading were so good? Chesterton seemed so good he was beyond you? Stevenson was beyond you? Wells was beyond you?

Borges: Yes, and Kipling was beyond me; *The Arabian Nights* was beyond me; in fact, almost everyone was beyond me. That's the way I felt. And I felt that I could attempt poetry and criticism, of course, not much is thought of a critic. If you write in, let's say, a clear style, and you state certain opinions, that may be allowed to pass. But in the case of a story that's not enough. As for poetry, I thought I knew the tricks of poetry—of course, I didn't—I thought that I knew how to work with that kind of thing. I thought I knew rules, but the story, that was beyond my possibilities.

Yates: Two questions then immediately arise, related to this very problem: why, by the end of the 1920's, in 1930, had you stopped writing poetry? That's the first question, because you gave up writing that; and why did you reject all of the books of essays that you had published up until then—it was a sort of wiping out the traces and burning up bridges, before you got into the 1930's. I think you wrote six poems in the decade of the 1930's, after having published two books in the 1920's. Why did you negate all the essays you published in the 1920's?

Borges: Because the essays that I wrote were not very good, because they offended me, and I can't read them without blushing. You see, what I had set out to do was ridiculous—the idea of writing, let's say, of re-writing the works of Tomás Herrera de Riviera; that can't be done nowadays. I think that those books mean nothing to me. I don't share the opinions of those books. Those books are full of heresies. For example, I thought of metaphor as being essential to poetry, but having given that matter a moment's thought, it would seem that in folk poetry you get no metaphors, or only stock metaphors, so the whole theory is wrong. Now, you don't need metaphors because the real metaphors, the essential affinity, is between things that have already been discovered.

Question: In what does the writer's originality consist, then? If it's all been discovered, if it's all just a re-ordering of an ideal order of monuments . . . ?

Borges: You see, what's important in a writer, as perhaps in a man, is the new voice, a new intonation. I suppose that they tell the same stories over and over again, but they tell it with a difference. Firstly, you're using a language; that language is in a certain tradition. Joyce, for example, invented a new language. But that new language, the language of *Finnegan's Wake,* is based on English. So it's not really a new language. I remember Joyce's lines—

> The rivering waters of . . .
> The hither and thithering waters of night;

That's a very fine line, no? At the same time, I would allow the fact that "rivering" comes from "river," that "hither and thithering" comes from "hither and thither" and the word "night" stands for "night." So really, I wonder if one can work outside a tradition, and every language is a tradition. I don't think I care greatly for Spanish as a language, but I know that the Spanish language is my destiny, my tradition. I can't go beyond it and I shouldn't try to do so.

Question: You said that before and I wondered what you meant by that. In what sense is it your destiny?

Borges: Having been born in Buenos Aires and writing in Spanish should mean something. I don't think I can become an English writer, but in the case of Spanish, I think I know the rules of the game. I have some knowledge of, well, grammar and so on.

Question: Are there Spanish virtues that are not present in English?

Borges: I wonder if there are any Spanish virtues? Of course, as English is to me a delight and not a task, I think of it in a different way. But I have to grapple with Spanish so I know all its difficulties. If you see something written by somebody else, that will be the result of a long struggle; he may have gone through many rough drafts, and you're made to feel that. You feel the page itself, and you don't know what the writer intended to say. But the writer knows only too well what he intended to say. For example, he knows that he has failed, he knows that certain words are not the right words, he knows that certain kinds of words are put in as mere links, in other words fat; he knows all of the weaknesses of what he writes. Now suppose the same case with different languages. I know how difficult it is to write in Spanish, because I have been attempting Spanish for the last fifty years, perhaps failing many times over. Now, when I read something in Spanish, I can see where a writer has failed, I can see where a word has been worked in because he couldn't find a better one. But in the case of English, of course, I'm blind to those things. I just accept everything.

Question: Are there things one can say in Spanish that one can't say in English?

Borges: No. But there are many things that you can say in English that you can't say in Spanish.

Question: What types of things is what I had in mind?

Borges: I'm thinking of all those cases where you have a verb and preposition, "explain" and "explain away." You can't say "explain away" in Spanish. "Loom" and "loom over," that perhaps might be done. But, even such a ... well ... a bad phrase as "he kissed away her tears." That's ridiculous. You can't say it in Spanish. You can't say "kiss away." You might say "he kissed her until she left off crying." That would have been still worse, I presume. Or "live up to" or "live down something." Those things may be said, I suppose, in Germanic languages. They cannot be said, as far as I know, in Spanish or in French. You have to look for a roundabout way.

Then there are all those words that stand, let's say, for a feeling, for a presence of feeling. For example, the words "eerie," and "uncanny." There are no such words in Spanish. Because the Spanish never felt that. In German you have "unheimlich." That would be exactly the sense of the Scottish "uncanny." "Weird" doesn't exist. "Wistful" doesn't exist. "Grim." I don't think it exists. Of course, English has been worked for centuries, and as a language it is inescapable. But, take for example, Joyce's sentence "The rivering waters of . . . The hither and thithering waters of night." I couldn't say it in Spanish. It would be awkward, really. It would be heavy-handed.

Question: I was wondering if I could take up something we were talking about earlier—your interest in narratives and storytelling. I wonder why you said recently "I can't accept a novel because I won't be able to do it and because I'm not interested in it." Now, I can see how the short story might be the most useful vehicle for parables. On the other hand, you said you were writing more straightforward stories now . . .

Borges: A novel needs more than storytelling. You need character; you must give the appearance of being slower. I feel the same way Poe felt when he said that there is no such thing as a long poem. A long poem is merely a succession of short poems. When Poe was writing a story he meant it to be packed. I think the last stories that Kipling wrote are quite as fully packed as any novel. For example, I think that "Children of Antioch" is one of the latest stories he wrote. It is as packed as any novel, but it is not more than twenty or thirty pages long. Conrad, of course, wrote what anyone would think is a short story, and what we're reading these days falls under the spell of *Heart of Darkness*—a very fine novel, no? And then in the beginning of *Heart of Darkness,* I found that Kafka had been anticipated. I found all the virtues of Kafka in those first ten or fifteen pages. The idea of making things awful, not for example, by *trying* to make them real, but by *insisting* that they were real. For the man of the novel fights his way into Africa. Remember? He goes up the river, then he sees that French gunboat, or Belgian gunboat, firing into the continent. He insists all the time that those things were unreal; that people there seem to him to be made, let's say, of thin paper, that he can poke his finger through them. Well, that's very uncanny, because Kafka was to do so twenty years afterwards.

Yates: This follows so perfectly with your essay on Kafka and his precursors. One of the reasons for remembering Conrad is that he is a precursor of Kafka. You can go back to the whole series; you can look at Kafka as helping to keep those people alive because they remind us of Kafka.

Borges: In the case of Conrad, I don't think he needs Kafka.

Question: It seems you are dealing with Plato's notion of the universe and man's attempt to deal with the instability of appearances.

Borges: I'm quite unaware of it. I mean, I'm doing it instinctively.

Question: Is there any part of Plato you're particularly interested in?

Borges: With Plato, you feel that he would reason in an abstract way and would also use myth. He would do those two things at the same time. But now we seem to have lost that gift. I mean, you have gone from the myth to abstract thinking. But Plato could do both at the same time. I think we are made to feel that very keenly in "The Last Day of Socrates." When Socrates still wants something very near to him—the immortality of the soul—he's just about to drink the hemlock—he talks about it sometimes; he discusses the probabilities; he uses arguments in his belief in the soul being deathless, and sometimes he falls back on myth, and he seems peculiarly unaware of the difference between the two things. I suppose at that time it could be done. But nowadays those things seem to be in watertight compartments. Either we are thinking or we are dreaming. But Plato and Socrates could do both; or perhaps Shakespeare also. Shakespeare, for example, would make a statement—he would be using metaphors and symbols—and at the same time, he might say, for example, "Ripeness is all." Here, I do not know whether this is abstract or whether this is symbol. It seems abstract rather, but he can do both things at the same time. But *we* are either abstract thinkers, we're either Kant, or we are dreamers. But, of course, Poe wanted to be a thinker, but I think that he was really a dreamer, at least in his best stories.

Question: You have spoken a couple of times about respect for your reader and how the reader plays a creative role when he reads your stories; I often feel with your short stories that I'm being more drawn into the environment or to a feeling, and I feel less than creative. Sometimes more as if I'm being drawn in rather than participating.

Borges: Well, then you should be. If you're not participating in the book, why read it? If you're not sharing the book with the writer . . .

Question: You say that the reader should be creative and yet I feel—and I've heard other people say—that one is drawn into the environment of your stories, into a world that is pre-existing.

Borges: Would you think that those two ideas cancel each other out, that you can't have them both? I mean, I talk of sharing something, and then *you* talk of being drawn into it. Those are different metaphors for the same thing, I should say. At least, that's the way I feel. I wonder what you make of it?

Yates: I think she's expressing a feeling that many of your readers have— that they are "intimidated" or at least made to feel uneasy and not on familiar ground . . .

Question: Exactly.

Yates: . . . which I think may be something that perhaps unconsciously, Borges, you intend with everything you write—to disconcert the reader.
Borges: If I do that, then I beg the reader's pardon. I don't want to do that.

Yates: But if you beg our pardon for that, you are begging our pardon for a large amount of everything you have written.

Question: I feel sometimes more an impression of atmosphere in the sto- ries—not exactly intimidating but . . .

Yates: You don't find it intellectual, it's more emotional?
Borges: It *is* emotional. A story that is not emotional is merely intellectual.

Yates: We've already had a question saying that the emotional effect of your stories was perhaps more apparent than their plotting and narrative and dramatic qualities. I don't necessarily agree, but I know that observation has been made already tonight.
Borges: But I thanked him for that observation. You think of me as a cold fish, and I am not really.

Yates: I think that you intend in your heart of hearts, in the very center of your creative being, to disturb your reader and not to leave him the way he was before he read your story or your poem, Borges. It seems to me . . .

Borges: Perhaps I do so, but it is unconscious.

Yates: Well, fine. I'm sorry I mentioned it because it shouldn't be, I don't think.

Borges: No, no. Well, if you think that if I act in that way, then I am doing wrong.

Yates: No, I'm not saying that at all . . .

Borges: That the police should be called in. (laughter)

Yates: Now what action will you take against this man?

Question: I'd like him to comment on how that relates to the creative aspects of the reader, that he brings to his reading of Borges. I feel sometimes as though . . .

Borges: Well, how is the case of Borges different from the case of any other writer? When you are reading a book, if you don't find your way inside it, then everything is useless. The problem with *Lord of the Rings* is you're left outside the book, no? That has happened to most of us. In that case, that book is not meant for us . . .

Yates: In Chicago, last night and here before and every place else, people come to Borges eager to find out his opinion on Tolkien.

Borges: Well I could never . . . I wish somebody would explain it to me or somehow convey what the book's good for. Those people say if I like Lewis Carroll, I should like Tolkien. I am very fond of Lewis Carroll, but I am disconcerted by Tolkien.

Yates: Last night you mentioned the difference between Tolkien and Lewis Carroll. You said Lewis Carroll is authentic fantasy and Tolkien is just going on and on and on.

Borges: Maybe I'm being unjust to Tolkien but, yes, I think of him as rambling on and on.

Question: Perhaps one more question that was on my mind tonight. We've been talking about your work mainly in relation to English literature, but at the same time, we heard earlier that you said that the Spanish language is your destiny. We have heard very little about the Spanish tradition which may have influenced your work. We have been talking about English literature.

Borges: I think that can be explained, I'm sorry to say, politically. We had a revolution in 1810. We were, of course, Spaniards, but we tried to be something different. We thought, well, we'll be Argentines. In other words, we bore no meaning whatever at that time. We merely stood for a political fact. We thought since Spain was the king and the country with the greater tradition, we had to find some other. And then we looked for it in France, as is only natural, and afterwards, we looked for it in England. So I wonder if I feel indebted to the Spanish tradition except in the sense that I am using the Spanish language, which of course *is* a strong tradition. I do not feel that I am essentially akin to Spanish writers. I remember talking that over with Reyes who said to me—and what he said was very fine—"Yes," he said, "we accept England and France because they are quite different, and we know that they are different. But in the case of Spain, what we feel is the fact that we are like Spain, but at the same time, there is a difference. And that is what disconcerts us." I think that is an intelligent observation on Reyes' part. In the case of other countries, well, perhaps, they're different, but in our case, we feel that at any moment, we may stumble back into being Spaniards and we try to avoid that. But all the same things happened here, too. In America, they have done their best not to be Englishmen. I don't think that Walt Whitman intended to be an Englishman and so he wasn't. I don't think Emerson intended to be an Englishman. When he went to see Wordsworth, he said that Wordsworth had a narrow British mind. We don't think of Walt Whitman as an Englishman. But I must say a word against Cervantes. Cervantes wrote thousands of words. At the same time, I wonder if I am especially indebted to Cervantes or if I delight in him the way I delight, for example, in Stevenson, Sir Thomas Browne, Emerson, and other writers I could name. But I have no wish to demolish Cervantes—that would be insane—and quite meaningless. Besides why should I do such things anyway?

Now I Am More or Less Who I Am

Miguel Enguídanos, John Dyson, Russell Salmon,
Luis Dávila, José Miguel Oviedo,
Nancy Newton / 1976

From Indiana University, April 1976. Published in *Boulevard* Magazine 1998; interview transcribed and translated by Willis Barnstone. Reprinted by permission of Willis Barnstone and *Boulevard* Magazine.

Miguel Enguídanos: I have always defended the notion that Borges is fundamentally a poet. Yet we must recognize that his great poems, that is, those poems that have given him fame, are stories. For better or for worse, they are great stories and, poetic or not, they are obviously still stories.

Borges: I don't know if there is any essential difference between my stories and poems. I believe there is none. Of course there is a formal difference. As you note, I am a very timid man. In Buenos Aires people had accepted and tolerated me as a poet. I knew that if I published stories, they would see me as an intruder. Then I published some of the first stories. For "Man from the Slums" I used the name of some kind of great-great-great grandfather, Francisco Bustos, and published it pseudonymously under his name. And then I became adventurous and I went on, shall we say, to intermediary tests, to what we might call a mystification, or a hoax, as for example, "Pierre Menard, Author of *Don Quijote*" or "The Approach to Almotasim." Then I turned to writing stories. And now people think if I publish poetry I am an intruder for writing poetry. So I do both things and I laugh a bit at what a friend might say.

Enguídanos: Many thanks. But as usual, you keep avoiding my question. Tell me something about the essays. Why do you say that you don't wish to write essays and then go on writing them? What is the essay for you?

Borges: I know that an essay requires a great deal of preparation. For example, if I write about an author, I have to refer to the author. I have to read something about him, I must be certain of my opinions, I must distinguish between my personal preferences and critical arguments for and against. Now that I am blind, now that in my idleness I can resort to blindness, I can believe that there is no reason to yield to this work. So I have given up writing essays, since essays demand not only substantial preparation but objectivity and not merely sounding forth. As for a story, a poem, they do not demand that objective work. Essays are read in another way, a critical way. But one who reads a story or a poem reads them for happiness (an ambitious word), for the personal emotion of the moment. A person who reads a study of an author is in some way arguing with the essayist. I now have the difficulty of not being able to go over texts properly. I was preparing a few books. I remember that the last time I was with my excellent friend Enguídanos, I spoke to him of a book about Spinoza. Then I gathered materials for it, gathered so many materials that I concluded that I couldn't write the book. Now I am thinking of doing another book about the Swedish mystic Swedenborg, which possibly I may not write, perhaps for having read too much about him and proving to myself that I can't add anything to the good and many works already written about him.

But a poem, a story, is an effusion. They are personal improvisations to be read differently. The distinction between the genres may not be an intrinsic difference but a difference in the way in which a work is read. For a long time I thought that much of the free verse you see published is simply typographically disguised prose placed in irregular lines. Although they are really lines of prose, the disguise lets the reader know that the piece must be read as a poem—that emotion, not simply information or dialectic, should be sought.

Essays are always read objectively. Although I write essays, if I compose a poem, I offer the passion of an emotion. Nothing else. It is an easier task for me.

John Dyson: Señor Borges, yesterday you said you valued friendship above other things because it did not call for the annoying and irrational demands of love. In that context, what characters in your stories bother you the most?

Borges: I don't know to what extent I have created characters. I think all my characters are hypostatic, to use a pedantic word. (I can't think of another.) I think I have created only one character and that is me. I imagine myself in different situations. If I allude to a friend satirically, it's most unusual.

Let us consider some notorious cases. If I think of Gustavo Adolfo Bécquer, if I think and think of Shakespeare, I think of a multitude. But if I think of myself, apart from the essential difference that they were genuine writers and I doubt that I am more than an amateur, the difference is that what I have written, what I have dreamt up, exists in several mirrors, in several of my own shadows. But I've created no figures who live on their own. I did so in the works written in collaboration with Brice Echeniaque and in books with Adolfo Bioy-Casares signed as Bustos Domecq. Those works have real characters. I go on always imagining things but there is one personage behind everything I have written, and for the purpose of better identification we may call him *me*.

Enguídanos: Which means, Borges, that you've been a "Man from the Slums" only in fragments.

Borges: Yes, since that "Man from the Slums" in fragments is a metaphor of the long insomnias I've endured, or are you referring to "Funes the Immemorious." That story turns out to be a parable or metaphor for insomnia. When I suffered from insomnia I tried to forget myself, to forget my body, the position of my body, the bed, the furniture, the three gardens of the hotel, the eucalyptus tree, the books on the shelf, all the streets of the village, the station, the farmhouses. And since I couldn't forget, I kept on being conscious and couldn't fall asleep. Then I said to myself, let us suppose there was a person who couldn't forget anything he had perceived, and it's well known that this happened to James Joyce, who in the course of a single day could have brought out *Ulysses*, a day in which thousands of things happened. I thought of someone who couldn't forget those events and who in the end dies swept away by his infinite memory. In a word that fragmentary hoodlum is me, or is an image I stole for literary purposes but which corresponds to my own insomnia. Each time I suffer from insomnia, I can free myself from memory because this book contains it all, and I can sleep.

There is an expression that may or may not be used in Spain and which is no longer used in Buenos Aires. It is "remember" me for "wake me." "Tomorrow remember me early." I thought of the metaphysical sense of that psychological phrase, "Tomorrow remember me early." That is, "I will be sleeping, I will be nobody, I will be everybody. And then they will wake me and I will remember who I am: somebody or other, who was born in such and such a period, who lived in such and such a place, who has such and such a past, who was afraid of such and such person, who has read such and such books, all that is there in "Remember me tomorrow" as opposed to "Wake me tomorrow." The word "to remember" is significant here. Of course when it's used, no one thinks of its psychological import. But of course it has such an import. So I might answer saying I have been a hoodlum in fragments, and if you read this story you can see what I was before I was born. The genesis of this story is before my birth, and the protagonist dies before my birth. So if the transmigration is certain, I am another hoodlum.

Russell Salmon: I am very interested in the magnificent literary history of the Rio de la Plata area. Can you speak or comment on the literary affinity between Horacio Quiroga, Leopoldo Lugones and Ricardo Güiraldes and your own literary work?

Borges: In the case of Horacio Quiroga, I can't say anything, because I am not familiar with his work. I knew him personally, but I never read anything by him. Or more accurately, I started to read him but I never felt attracted by it. In the case of Lugones, I remember that my generation believed, erroneously of course, that to write well was to write in the manner of Lugones. We all felt the magnet of Lugones, and we were in a paradoxical situation, since we had founded a secret sect. The whole matter might have been limited to that evolution of faith, which was that the essence of literature was the metaphor. Unfortunately, or happily, for us, Lugones had said the same thing ten or fifteen years earlier. We thought we were combating Lugones and we were struggling against him with the very literary notions that he himself had discarded. So in regard to Lugones, I recognize myself as a disciple and now that I write rather differently and profess a different aesthetic, I always suspect that I am writing something in secret for Lugones.

As for Güiraldes, I cannot conceive of Güiraldes without Lugones. The style of Guiraldes' *The Glass Ashtray* and *Don Segundo Sombra*, as well as his poems, is also the style of Lugones. There is a book by Lugones, *El Payador*, and in this book there is a chapter which ends speaking of the *gaucho* who is lost in the plains, who is lost in the time of oblivion, which verbally is almost the same as the last page of *Don Segundo Sombra* that ends, "I went away like someone who is bleeding."

Güiraldes was the disciple, though a rebellious disciple, of Lugones, and I have been a rebellious disciple, yet now I don't know whether I should use the word "rebellious." Of course I owe much to Lugones, and I'm honored by that, though I'd rather resemble Paul Groussac than Lugones. But I'm probably more like Lugones, which doesn't entirely please me. Everyone is marked by a generation, by a period. We all felt the attraction of Leopoldo Lugones, and happily it was before 1938, the year of his suicide.

I remember that González Lanusse and I used to play at speaking poorly

of Lugones. Yet when we went out to walk about the outskirts of Buenos
Aires and saw the sunset, we said to each other, "Let the eternal sun die like
a tiger." So our memory was full of lines from Lugones. Especially the moon
was like a Lugones invention. Güiraldes owed a good part of his fame to
Lugones. If Lugones had not written that congratulatory article in *La Nación*,
people would not have read *Don Segundo Sombra*. Of course I knew his book
El Payador, since Güiraldes had urged me to read it. I recall that we had a
small group, consisting of my cousin Guillermo Ocón Borges, Roberto Artile
Ortele, Nora Light, Tello Pinero (who died), González Lanusse and myself.
We went to see Lugones. We were going to get him, but Lugones knew that
our attacks did not correspond to the truth, to our true feelings. We did it
because we had to be ourselves and we were already too much in Lugones'
shadow. We had, in some way or other, to free ourselves from him.

Now I feel quite far from Lugones, but in a general way he has an influence
on me. For example, I did not really write that phrase "the unanimous night,"
which is in the first lines of "The Circular Ruins." I said it with the desire of
finding myself reflected in the group hanging around Lugones. Now each
time I think of a metaphor, and I try not to think of too many, I have a
particular notion that I've read that metaphor in Lugones' work, which is
itself derived from Baudelaire's *Les Fleurs du Mal* and especially from Victor Hugo. I confess, and I'm not troubled by the confession, that for a certain
period I was a son of Lugones. My entire generation was, although it might
deny it for polemical reasons or above all because we didn't wish to be sons
of Lugones. We wanted to be something else. But we were perhaps his prog-
eny and after a while one cannot deny one's literary father.

Enguídanos: Once you told me that you denied Lugones in order to be
able to breathe.

Borges: Yes, that's exactly right. I couldn't find the phrase. To be able to
breathe. Drawn to Lugones we absurdly believed that he was literature. Of
course that's false. Lugones represented a moment of *Modernismo* and nothing more. And nothing less.

Nancy Newton: I'd like to change the subject a bit.

Borges: Let's change it as much as you want. My true name is Proteus.

Newton: In the prologue to *In Praise of Shadow*, you refer to ethics as one
of the themes of that book, and add that among the virtues which you prefer
in Protestant as compared to Catholic countries is the question of ethics. Do

you believe that literature has an important ethical function? And can or should it exercise moral power?

Borges: I think so, but perhaps the writer should not do it in a conscious way. Everything doesn't have to be Aesop, but it may finally come to be Aesop. Paul Marchand's work certainly has an ethical function and I would say that all literary works have an ethical function. Now that doesn't mean that an author must be a preacher or a moralist, since, then, he or she would not be a writer. Nor a poet. Poetry has an ethical purpose in the same way that it has an aesthetic dimension, which is the essential one.

Luis Dávila: I would like to ask you to elaborate on those tigers and that gold that come up in your poetry and stories. Despite having the geographical elements which you have recounted many times in interviews of having an uncle who knew some tiger hunters. . . .

Borges: My father.

Davila: What would you recommend to a young person who as a reader admires you and who at the same time would like to escape from your shadow and that of Lugones? How should one approach those tigers and those other images, Borges?

Borges: Well, let's begin with the tigers. The tiger I remember was one of the first things I saw in my life. I remember that I was going to the zoo, that I didn't see other animals, I remember that later on I saw a bison but at the beginning I saw only the tiger. Years afterward I found a phrase by Chesterton (I'm always citing Chesterton) who called the tiger, "an emblem of woeful elegance." Then there is that other famous literary tiger of Blake, "Tyger! Tyger! burning bright/In the forests of the night." Blake uses the tiger as a symbol of evil. He uses it for the problem of how an omnipotent God could create the tiger and the lamb. "Did he who made the Lamb make thee?" I felt drawn to tigers, those first things I saw in life. Later came years of myopia, years of blindness, but there was one color that survived. It was the color yellow. And that's why I entitled a book, *The Gold of the Tigers*. Since my first vision was the gold of tigers, the color yellow is the color that stands out. It was the last color that my declining eyes could see as they became lost in a gray mist. I can say that in the course of my life I have felt attracted to the tiger because I felt attracted to the tiger as a child.

I remember that my parents gave me an admirable book, *The Jungle Book*, the *Second Jungle Book* of Kipling. What reconciled me to the book was a confusion: the fact that the tiger Shere Khan (in the story "Tiger! Tiger!")

was lame. The good animals are the bear, the panther, and there is the boy hero they call Mowgli, which means little frog. I didn't like it that the tiger represented evil. Nevertheless, I have argued that the tiger is the enemy in the work.

As for reasons for my admiration for the tiger, I think it is something very profound and psychological. Psychoanalysts who can explain everything can explain this also, but their explanation is worth absolutely nothing. But my admiration exists and I go on feeling something for a tiger that I do not feel for leopards, jaguars and other animals that people also fear. I have a story entitled "The God." It has a jaguar, which is the South American tiger—my personal preference—and I myself don't know the root of it. Simply, when I was a child I already saw very little and then I saw yellow and saw it in the tiger and I saw it more than other colors, and so came my idea of evil, of the ferocity of the tiger, which probably gave me the idea that I was not more evil than those animals. And I liked looking upon them in such a way. I have never had any designs on lions. I don't know if I can explain this personal preference.

José Miguel Oviedo: Borges, all readers and critics, and I am referring to professional readers, have noted that in your stories there is a great verbal precision, a great exactitude, almost mathematical or algebraic, with an almost scientific rigor in your use of adjectives in plot development, and in the way you form and develop the outcome of your stories. And as one goes over the texts many times—and it is your fault since one rereads your texts many times—periodically one keeps discovering things one did not see earlier. In one of my multiple readings of one of your texts, I found two things (I refer to them in this absolutely vague way) which I'm not up to calling errors but which I want to reveal to you. They are two types of "intentional" errors that I believe are apparent, tricky, calculated by you to be just as they are, dispersed in the text for some motive I cannot fathom.

Borges: I am very curious. There must be more than two.

Oviedo: In *Tlon, Uqbar, Orbis Tertius* you speak of the language of Tlon, and say, "There are no nouns in Tlon's conjectural *Ursprache* from which come the present languages and dialects." (The "there are no nouns" is important.) "There are impersonal verbs modified by monosyllabic suffixes (or prefixes with an adverbial value). For example there is no word corresponding to the word "moon," but there is a verb which in English would be to "moo-

nate" or to "moon." "The moon rose above the river" is *hlor u fang axax-axas mlo*. I don't know if my pronunciation is correct.
Borges: It is correct.

Oviedo: And a little further on it says, "The noun is formed by an accumulation of adjectives. They do not say "moon," but you use the same example. They say, "round airy-light" or "pale orange of the sky." Now sky is a noun.
Borges: But since it is not celestial, we are on the other side.

Oviedo: Yes, but did you not think of this detail in going over the story? Didn't you think that you were using a noun although you were claiming that in the Tlonic language there are no nouns?
Borges: No. I didn't realize it, but I did feel that if I put in another adjective, the phrase would be unwieldy. I think I used "of the sky" because I supposed it would produce an adverbial phrase.

Enguídanos: "Of the sky" is not an adverbial phrase. A noun preceded by a preposition is not an adverbial phrase.

Oviedo: But then you went out of your way to come upon "airy" and not "of the air" when you could have used "celestial," a very poetic word at that.
Borges: In the next edition I will use "celestial." I will note: "Adjective donated by Oviedo."

Oviedo: The other question refers to "an error" only in parenthesis, and much less important. It refers to a certain attitude of disdain for grammatical demands, which in your case occurs frequently.
Borges: About grammar, I am highly ignorant.

Oviedo: Very well.
Borges: I don't know grammar. A little bit of Latin grammar.

Oviedo: In the prologue to "The Gold of the Tigers," you speak of the members of the Royal Academy. Here is the phrase, let me quote it: "Emma Zunz's manner was also true, her embarrassment was true, her hatred was true. Also true was the outrage she had suffered. Only false were the circumstances, the time, and one or two proper nouns." The normal grammar here for "false," *falsas*, would be masculine (since it agrees with a series of nouns the last of which is masculine).
Borges: Yes, but my ear told me that after "false" (*falsas*), since there

were two feminine words (*circunstancias* and *hora*), it was better to have the agreement be immediate, with the first words. It would be strange to put "solo eran falsos la hora" (using a masculine "false" with a feminine "time.") So my ear accepted the feminine. Grammatically it's wrong, but I let myself be carried away by my ear. It still sounds better to me. But to say "eran falsos la hora . . ."

Oviedo: Clearly. That's correct but ugly.

Enguídanos: Fifteen minutes now for questions from the gallery. "From the courtyard of the musketeers," as Borges says.

Audience: Which of the following three categories do you consider most difficult to define: human being, citizen of the world or artist?

Borges: I was unhappy during my adolescence, but the truth is that I wanted to be unhappy. I wanted to be a Prince Hamlet, a Raskolnikov, I even wanted to be a Werther, and possibly did become one, but now I realize that I was acting a bit, as young romantics act, as do all "angry young men." These are romantic games, vain, and I would say unimportant. Now I don't know whether I feel resigned or not, but I feel relatively happy. Perhaps because now I am more or less who I am. I know my limits, I know that there are many things that I should not try to do, I believe I know what I should write, or rather what I can write. When I was young I knew that I was going to be a writer. At the same time I felt limited and didn't know what kind of writer I was going to be. I wanted to be, naturally, Kipling, Dostoyevski, Conrad, Walt Whitman. It's hard to be one of them. I've come to be more or less who I am. As for being a citizen of the world, at this time to feel oneself a citizen of the world is a rather unhappy fate. Just being a citizen of Argentina, I already feel rather miserable.

Audience: Maestro, what influence has music and the other arts had in your own work? And in your personal life?

Borges: Unfortunately very slight. Often I have a strong feeling for language, for several languages. I have felt words, and what words mean, and the perplexities we may call metaphysical. But the other arts have existed only very slightly for me. I should confess that I have been able to live in a world without music, without painting, without sculpture. That is my poverty and I recommend it to nobody. It is something to be confessed. Often I have felt moved by music, yet I listen to completely incompatible pieces. I have felt moved by Brahms, at the same time by blues and the fast tango *milongas*.

So I don't know whether these tastes mean anything. It's like my taste for coffee, which I never think of reasoning out, or a taste I have for chess, though I am the worst player.

As for painting, when I could see I liked to look at reproductions of Rembrandt and Turner, of Velázquez and Klee, and I know that other painters didn't affect me particularly. But these preferences are of no value—nor are my aversions, which are almost infinite. I would say that I am a writer, not in the sense that I write well but in the sense of being a man who feels poetry, who feels philosophy, and who does not feel the other arts. In sculpture, for example, I am very poor.

Audience: Maestro, I am very interested in several Spanish writers, especially of the Generation of 1898. I'd like to know your thoughts on this period.

Borges: For me there is one name. I don't know whether it corresponds exactly to the Generation of '98. For me there is one man, and he is Miguel de Unamuno. He is the one who interests me. I think of other writers, I think of the poetry of the period. I very much like a poet whom the world censures, Manuel Machado, which doesn't mean that I don't like Antonio Machado. But I also like Manuel. Of course one must speak poorly about Manuel Machado. It's a kind of duty. I recall other names. Formerly, I read many works by Pío Baroja. Now I don't know whether I would care to read him. Other writers, I simply have not liked. For example I don't care for Ramón de Valle-Inclán.

Audience: Maestro, I wonder if I could have the honor of hearing you recite by heart one of your sonnets that has most impressed me, that is the sonnet entitled "Spinoza." I would like to ask you about God, if he exists, and specifically about the reference in the last line of the sonnet to "That one who is all the stars." Could you elaborate that line?

Spinoza

Here in the twilight the translucent hands
Of the Jew polishing the crystal glass.
The dying afternoon is cold with bands
Of fear. Each day the afternoons all pass
The same. The hands and space of hyacinth
Paling in the confines of the Ghetto walls
Barely exist for the quiet man who stalls

There, dreaming up a brilliant labyrinth.
Fame does not disturb him (that reflection of
Dreams in the dream of another mirror), nor love,
The timid love of women. Gone the bars,
He's free, from metaphor and myth, to sit
Polishing a stubborn lens: the infinite
Map of the One who now is all His stars.

Borges: In that last line I refer to Spinoza's pantheist God. God, therefore, is all his stars. But that does not mean that I believe there is a divinity who is all the stars and who is all of us. That may or may not be the case, but no, I affirm nothing.

There is a very attractive phrase by George Benard Shaw that might clarify what we are talking about when he says "God is in the making," God is something we are always creating. Then we would all be helping him to exist. If not objectively, at least unconsciously, and that's already crucial. There are many who without knowing it, without intending to, are collaborating to make "that God in the making" exist: philosophers, poets, all those who pray, all those who feel that there is possibly a secret will behind the most diverse events. Personally I don't believe, at least not now, in a personal God. And neither have I given up believing. I don't understand, for example, when Unamuno says that God is the producer of immortality. I cannot support this view, because I have no desire for immortality, which for me would be a nightmare. I cannot desire a producer of immortality, since he would be my enemy. I do not want to be immortal. I want to die completely and I would prefer that after my death no one remember me, that everything cease. Which does not mean that everything will cease. In that sonnet, I refer specifically to the philosopher Spinoza. He is polishing crystal lenses and is polishing a rather vast crystal philosophy of the universe. I think we might consider those tasks parallel. Spinoza is polishing his lenses, Spinoza is polishing vast diamonds, his ethics. I made a sonnet out of this subject and I think it turned out rather well. But that sonnet doesn't accord with what I think. It accords with what I have detected, with what I have been able to feel, that Baruch Spinoza of Holland might have thought and felt.

Audience: Señor Borges, I would like you to comment on your attitude toward the professional reader, on the literary critic, and what differences there are for you between the reader and the critic when you conceive your works.

Borges: I suspect that if the professional reader is not a reader who feels things, that reader is not a good reader. I suspect that a critic must also feel things. The best would be for us to impose a *sine qua non* condition: critics should feel things. If not, why write about a work that is unfelt. It seems insane to me. But when I write I don't think about readers. Perhaps when I write I try to write in a clear and more or less grammatical way. (Clearly *less*, as I've just discovered.) I don't think about readers, nor about the sale of my work. When people ask me how many copies have come out, I send them to book store owners and to editors, since they know about those things. Not I. I am simply a writer. Once I've written something, I let it have its own life and I don't care much about its destiny—though if it goes well it pleases me. It pleases me because it is like a son or daughter, my own production.

Audience: What difference is there between Buenos Aires of the past and Buenos Aires today?

Borges: The Buenos Aires of the past was an honorable city, in sum, a city in which there were values. Among the most humble people, for example, there was the cult of courage. This phrase comes from a neighbor, the poet of Palermo [a *barrio* of Buenos Aires], Carriego. And besides it was a country that had great curiosity, a country open to all the countries of the world, that in some way felt itself the inheritor of all Western culture and of what could be drawn from Oriental culture as well.

Presently, we are—and this I say with sadness—a poor misled and anarchic country. I know that someone will say I should not say these things, but I believe that I am speaking to you, to friends, and to denounce what is happening now is not to reveal any secret. I am revealing what you know. I have tried not to hide what is ridiculous. But I want to add that I go on believing in my nation more than ever, perhaps precisely because it is a misled nation.

Thirteen Questions: A Dialogue with Jorge Luis Borges

Willis Barnstone / 1980

From *Chicago Review*, The University of Chicago, Vol. 31, No. 3, Winter 1980, pp. 11–28. Reprinted by permission.

Willis Barnstone: In case you want a hardboiled egg?
Jorge Luis Borges: Why of course.

WB: And I'll crack it for you.
JLB: Look here, if not. I can't break a hardboiled egg. Not a hardboiled one!

WB: It's good to bring hardboiled eggs into radio stations, no?
JLB: A fine combination I feel. Hardboiled eggs and radio stations!

WB: Borges, would you put them in a poem?
JLB: No, I wouldn't. Yet I suppose all things are right for a poem. All words are right. In fact all things are. Anything can be done, you know, but very few things can be talked about.

WB: I have some questions. Maybe wordy but your answers won't be.
JLB: They will be laconic, yes?

1. WB: We know that consciousness resides in every other human being, yet we possess an awareness of only our own mind. At times we wake, as it were, to a puzzling knowledge of the mind's separate existence.
JLB: Well, but this is a question on the nature of solipsism, no? Now I don't believe in solipsism, because if I did I'd go mad. But of course it is a curious fact that we exist.

At the same time I feel I am not dreaming you, or, let's put it the other way, that you are not dreaming me. But this fact of wondering at life may stand for the essence of poetry. All poetry consists in feeling things as being strange, while all rhetoric consists in thinking of them as quite common, as very obvious. Of course I *am* puzzled at the fact of my existing, of my existing in a human body, of my looking through eyes, hearing through ears, and so on. And maybe everything I have written is a mere metaphor, a mere

176

variation on that central theme of being puzzled by things. In that case, I suppose, there's no essential difference between philosophy and poetry, since both stand for that same kind of puzzlement. Except that in the case of philosophy, the answer is given in a logical way, and in the case of poetry you use metaphor. If you use language, you have to use metaphors all the time. Since you know my works (well, let the word go at that. I don't think of them as *works*, really), since you know my *exercises*, I suppose you have felt that I was being puzzled all the time, and I was trying to find a foundation for my puzzlement.

2. *WB: In Cincinnati when an admirer said "May you live one thousand years," you answered, "I look forward happily to my death." What did you mean by that?*

JLB: I mean that when I'm unhappy, and that happens quite often to all of us, I find a real consolation in the thought that in a few years, or maybe in a few days, I'll be dead and then all this won't matter. I look forward to being blotted out. But if I thought that my death was a mere illusion, that after death I would go on, then I would feel very, very unhappy. For really, I'm sick and tired of myself. Now, of course if I go on and I have no personal memory of having ever been Borges, then in that case, it won't matter to me; because I may have been hundreds of odd people before I was born, but those things won't worry me, since I will have forgotten them. When I think of mortality, of death, I think of those things in a hopeful way, in an expectant way. I should say I am greedy for death, that I want to stop waking up every morning, finding: "Well, here I am, I have to go back to Borges."

There's a word in Spanish, I suppose you know. I wonder if it's any longer in use. Instead of saying "to wake up," you say "*recordarse*," that is, to record yourself, to remember yourself. My mother used to say "Que me recuerde a las ocho," I want to be recorded to myself at eight. Every morning I get that feeling, because I am more or less non-existent. Then when I wake up, I always feel I'm being let down. Because, well, here I am. Here's the same old stupid game going on. I have to be somebody. I have to be exactly that somebody. I have certain commitments. One of the commitments is to live through the whole day. Then I see all that routine before me, and all things naturally make me tired. Of course, when you're young, you don't feel that way. You feel, well, I am so glad I'm back in this marvelous world. But I don't think I ever felt that way. Even when I was young. Especially when I was young. Now, I have resignation. Now, I wake up and I say: I have to face another day. I let it go at that. I suppose that people feel in different ways, because many people think of immortality as a kind of happiness, perhaps because they don't realize it.

WB: They don't realize what?
JLB: The fact that going on and on would be, let's say, awful.

WB: Would be another Hell, as you say in one of your stories.
JLB: Yes, it would be, yes. Since this life is already Hell, why go in for more and more Hell, for larger and larger doses!

WB: For two hundred years?
JLB: Yes. Well, of course, you might say that those two hundred years don't exist. For what really exists is the present moment. The present moment is being weighted down by the past and by the fear of the future. Really, when do we speak of the present moment? For the present moment is as much an abstraction as the past or the future. In the present moment, you always have some kind of past and some kind of future also. You are slipping all the time from one to the other.

WB: But obviously you have great moments of pleasure during your life.
JLB: Yes, I suppose everybody has. But I wonder. I suppose those moments are perhaps finer when you remember them. Because when you're happy, you're hardly conscious of things. The fact of being conscious makes for unhappiness.

WB: To be conscious of happiness often lets in an intrusion of doubt.
JLB: But I think I have known moments of happiness. I suppose all men have. There are moments, let's say, love, riding, swimming, talking to a friend, let's say, conversation, reading, even *writing*, or rather, not writing but inventing something. When you sit down to write it, then you are no longer happy because you're worried by technical problems. But when you think out something, then I suppose you may be allowed to be happy. And there are moments when you're slipping into sleep, and then you feel happy, or at least I do. I remember the first time I had sleeping pills. (They were efficient of course, since they were new to me.) I used to say to myself, "Now hearing that tramway turn around the corner, I won't be able to hear the end of the noise it makes, the rumble, because I'll be asleep." Then, I felt very, very happy. I thought of unconsciousness.

3. WB: Do you care about literary recognition? Do you want fame?

JLB: No. No! Those things are non-existent. At the same time, when it comes to me, and it may have come to me, I feel that I should be grateful. I mean if people take me seriously, I think, well, they are wrong. At the same time I should be thankful to them.

4. WB: I wanted to ask do you live for the next poem, story, or essay or conversation?

JLB: Yes, Yes, I do.

WB: It seems to me that you're a lucky man to have unending obsessions to create and to record. Do you know why you had that destiny of being a writer? That destiny or that obsession?

JLB: The only thing I know is that I need those obsessions. Because if not, why should I go on living? Of course, I wouldn't commit suicide. But I should feel very unjustified. This doesn't mean I think very much of what I write. It means that I *have* to write. Because if I don't write something and keep on being obsessed by it, then I have to write it and be rid of it.

5. WB: In the Republic, Plato spends much time seeking a definition of justice, a kind of public definition. Is this notion valid to us personally? Is your life, which ends in death, a just experiment in life, or is it a biological double-cross against both the mind and the body? Plato speaks about public justice. Given the fact of death, do you believe in private justice?

JLB: I think that the only justice is private justice, because as to a public justice, I wonder if that really exists.

WB: Do you believe private justice exists? How do we consider morality and doomsday?

JLB: At the very moment of our lives we know whether we're acting the right way or the wrong way. We might say that doomsday is going on all the time, that every moment of our lives we're acting wrongly or rightly. Doomsday is not something that comes at the end. It's going on all the time. And we know, through some instinct, when we have acted rightly or wrongly.

WB: Is there a biological treason in life because of death?

JLB: I don't understand what you mean by biological doublecross. Biology sounds so dim to me, I wonder if I can take that word in, no?

WB: Physical, then.

JLB: Well, *physical*, yes. I think I can understand that. I am a very simple-minded man. If you go in for those long fancy words, *biology* and *psychology*!

WB: We get into language that your father might have used, right?

JLB: Yes, he might have used it, but he rarely did so, being a professor of psychology, a skeptic also.

6. *WB: I spent one year of my life, when I was a student, seeking the center of consciousness. I never found it.*

JLB: I don't think you can. It keeps eluding you all the time.

WB: But I did discover that seeking oneself was fascinating and intolerable.

JLB: Yes, it is. Of course, since I am blind, I have to do that, more or less all the time. Before I went blind, I was always finding refuge in watching things, seeing things, in reading, while now I have to go in for thinking or, since my thinking capacity isn't too good, let's say for dreaming, and in a sense for dreaming away my life. That's the only thing I can do. Then of course I have to go in for long spells of loneliness, but I don't mind that. Before I couldn't. Before, I remember I lived in a town called Adrueto south of Buenos Aires; when I went on a half hour's journey and I had no book with me I felt very unhappy. But now I can spend hours and hours on end, with no books, because I don't read them. And so I don't think of loneliness as being necessarily unhappy. Or for example if I get a spell of insomnia, I don't mind about it because time slips down. It's like an easy slope, no? So I just let myself go on living. Now when I was not blind, I always had to be furnishing my time with different things. Now I don't. I just let myself go.

WB: Yet you do very much enjoy all the times you are with others.

JLB: But of course, I live in memory. And I suppose a poet should live in memory, because after all, what is imagination? Imagination, I should say, is made of memory and of oblivion. It is a kind of blending of the two things.

WB: You manage with time?

JLB: Oh yes. Everybody who goes blind gets a kind of reward: a different sense of time. Time is no longer to be filled in at every moment by something. No. You know that you have just to live on, to let time live you. That makes for a certain comfort. I think it is a great comfort or perhaps a great reward.

A gift of blindness is that you feel time in a different way from most people, no? You have to remember and you have to forget. You shouldn't remember everything because, well, the character I wrote about, Funes, goes made because his memory is endless. Of course if you forgot everything, you would no longer exist. Because you exist in your past. Otherwise you wouldn't even know who you were, what your name was. You should go in for a blending of the two elements, no? Memory and oblivion, and we call that imagination. That's a high-sounding name.

WB: I know you don't go in for high-sounding words because you're a literary man.

JLB: No, because I am too skeptical about words. A literary man hardly believes in words.

WB: To return to my original question, as I attempted to discover myself, it was fascinating and intolerable, because the more profoundly I thought I had gone into myself, the more I disappeared until I was uncertain of everything, even of my own existence.

JLB: Well, I think Hume said, when I've looked for myself I have never found anybody at home. That's the way the world is.

WB: One goes from reverie to nightmare.

JLB: I have a nightmare almost every night. I had one this morning. But it wasn't a real nightmare.

WB: What was it?

JLB: It was this. I found myself in a very large building. It was a brick building. Many empty rooms. Large empty rooms. Brick rooms. Then I went from one to the other, and there seemed to be no doors. I was always finding my way into courtyards. Then after a time I was going up and down, I was calling out, and there was nobody. That large and unimaginative building was empty, and I said to myself, why, of course, this is the dream of the maze. So I won't find any door, so I'll just have to sit down in one of the rooms and then wait: and sometimes I wake up. And that actually happened. When I realized it and said, this is the nightmare of the maze, and since I knew all about it, I wasn't taken in by the maze. I merely sat down on the floor.

WB: And waited it out.

JLB: I waited a moment and woke up.

WB: You have other recurrent nightmares? What are they?

JLB: I have two or three. At this moment I think the maze is the one that comes back to me. Then I have another one and that came out of my blindness. That is a nightmare of trying to read and of being unable to because the characters become alive, because every letter turns into other letters, and then the words at the beginning are short when I try to make them out. They are long Dutch words with repeated vowels. Or, if not, the spaces between the lines widen out, and then the letters are branching out, and all that is done in black or red characters, on very glossy paper, and so large as to be intolerable. And when I wake up, those characters keep me company for some time. Then for a wild moment I think, I'll never be able to forget them and I'll go mad. That seems to be happening all the time. Especially after I lost my sight, I was having that dream of reading, of being unable to read because of the characters becoming alive. That is one of the dreams I have. And the others are dreams about mirrors, about masked people. I suppose I have three essential nightmares: the maze, the writing, and the mirrors. And then there are others, that are more or less common to everybody, but those are my three recurrent nightmares. I have them almost every night. They stay with me for a minute or so after I'm awake. Sometimes they come before I'm quite asleep. Most people dream before going to sleep and then they keep on dreaming a moment after they awake. They are in a kind of half-way house, no? Between waking and sleeping.

WB: It's also a place from which you gather much material for your writing, isn't it?

JLB: Yes, it is. De Quincey and so on. There is a fine literary tradition to that. De Quincey must have worked out his nightmares when he wrote them down, no? Because they're so fine. Besides, they depend on words also. While nightmares, generally, don't depend on words. What's difficult about writing a nightmare is that the nightmare feeling does not come from the images. Rather, as Coleridge said, the feeling gives you the images.

WB: That's a major distinction, because most people think the opposite. They don't think it all through.

JLB: When you write down the images, those images may not mean anything to you. It's what you get in the case of Poe and of Lovecraft. The images are awful but the feeling isn't awful.

WB: And I suppose a good writer is one who comes up with the right images to correspond to the feeling.

JLB: To a feeling, yes. Or who may give you the nightmare feeling with common objects or things. I remember how I found a proof of that in Chesterton. He says that we might think that at the end of the world there is a tree whose very shape is evil. Now that's a fine word, and I think that stands for that kind of feeling, no? Now that tree could hardly be described. While, if you think of a tree, for example, made of skulls, of ghosts, that would be quite silly. But what we said, a tree *whose very shape* is evil. That shows he really had a nightmare about that tree. No? If not, how would he know about that tree?

WB: I've always been puzzled why my tongue moves, why words come out of my mouth or from in my head. These words are like seconds of a clock, happening, sounding almost by themselves.

JLB: But I think that before going to sleep you begin, at least I begin, to mumble meaningless sentences. And then I know that I am going to sleep. When I hear myself, when I overhear myself saying something meaningless, it's a good sign that I'll be asleep in a moment.

WB: Well, I was going to ask you, about the words happening, forming in our mouths. As long as time exists, the words come. Hence, also the thoughts. But I don't will those words, or even will to will them. They possess me.

JLB: I don't think those words stand for any meaning. At least you don't know the meaning.

WB: I don't mean the words before one sleeps. I mean all the words that are coming to you right this moment or to me. In other words, I don't know why words are coming out of my mouth right now. Some force is letting them out. I am never there manipulating them. I don't understand that. It's a kind of fundamental mystery to me.

JLB: But I suppose those words go with certain thoughts. But otherwise they would be meaningless or irrelevant.

WB: But I feel like a clock wound up in which the seconds tick, in which words come out of my mouth. I have no idea why I'm speaking to you in any half logical way now. Or why you're answering me. It's a tremendous puzzle to me.

JLB: Yes. I think you should accept that.

WB: I do accept it or I'd go mad.

JLB: Yes, that's it. You might even say that if you try to think, you go mad.

WB: Yes.

JLB: Thought should be carefully avoided, right?

WB: Well, I think if you try to think why you think, you can't think that. Yet sometimes I walk down the street and say: not who is this walking down the street, but who is this thinking he's walking down the street, and then I'm really puzzled.

JLB: Yes, and then you go to thinking: who is this thinking he's thinking he's thinking, no? I don't think that stands for anything. That's merely grammatical, they are only words.

WB: It sounds like a mirror.

JLB: You might go into a second category. You may feel a very strong physical pain. For example, you may get it through electricity or through a toothache. Then when you feel that pain, you won't feel the pain. Then, after that, you say, well, this is a toothache, and then you know that you felt the pain. Then after that you might go for a third time and say, well, I knew that I knew. But after that I don't think you can go on. You can do it successfully within the same game, because you keep on thinking the same thing over and over again. But I don't think you could do that any more than three times over. If you say, I think that I think that I think that I think that I think that I think, all of that is quite unreal after the second term, perhaps. I read a book, by John William Dunne, *Experience with Time*, in which he said that since, if you know something, you know that you know it, and you know that you know that you know, and you know that you know that you know that you know it, then there is an infinity of selves in every man, but I don't think that can be proved.

WB: What do you think of that momentary wakening, which is both exhilarating and frightening, of wondering how our minds happen to be thinking and talking? I always wake to the astonishment that I exist, that I am.

JLB: When I wake up, I wake to something worse. It's the astonishment of being myself. So and so born in Buenos Aires in 1899, somebody who was in Geneva.

WB: Why aren't you the Peking Man, or someone who's going to live in five million years from now?

JLB: Well, once I thought out a kind of fantasy, which was for literary purposes. This is that at any moment we all change into somebody else. Now since you are changed into someone else, you are not aware of it. For example, at some moment I will be changed into you. You will be changed into me; but since the change, the shift, is complete, you have no memories, you don't know that you are changing. You're changing all the time, you may be the man in the moon, yet will not know about it, since when you became the man in the moon, you become the man in the moon with *his* past, with his memories, with his fears, with his hopes, and so on.

WB: The past self is obliterated.

JLB: Yes, you may be changed into somebody else all the time, and nobody would know. Maybe that kind of thing is happening. It would be meaningless, of course. It reminds me of a story, only a story, but things are only good for literary purposes! But for not too good literary purposes, for trick stories.

7. *WB: This is a question I hadn't intended to ask. There is a powerful force, always in us, to move out from ourselves to reach the world. It shows itself in all ways: sexually, by writing, by talking, by touching. . . .*

JLB: Well, living.

WB: By living. We are only ourselves and yet there exists the strongest impulse to destroy our solitude by including more in it. Sappho has a fragment where she sums it up. She says, "I could not hope/to touch the sky/with my two arms." Her thought represents that compelling life force to reach out.

JLB: If I understand you, you say that we're running away from ourselves all the time, and that we have to do so.

WB: We're trying to expand to be more, to reach, to touch outside our own circle.

JLB: I suppose we are. But I don't think you should worry about that. You should not feel unhappy about that. Though, you know we can't do it, or we can't do it utterly, only in an imperfect way.

WB: We cannot do it, but part of the art of living is to go through the motions of doing it, and it makes for writing, it makes for love, it makes for all the things that bind people together.

JLB: Since we're given, what? threescore years and ten, and we have to furnish them somehow, why not attempt those things? And after all, we have a life span. If not, you'd be utterly bored.

8. *WB: Let me ask you. You obviously value your future work as more important than earlier achievements.*

JLB: Well, I have to.

WB: Anything less would be fatal. Yet, I'm surprised that you seem to consider your recent books of poems as less important than earlier books of poems.

JLB: I know them only too well.

WB: I'm convinced that your new poems are your most powerful, both in their intelligence and passion; the latter is often expressed in a personal despair you don't allow in your stories or essays.

JLB: No, I think that you are wrong. You think of my poems as being good. You read them through the light of the early poems, but had these poems come to your notice as being the work of an unknown poet, you'd toss them away. Don't you think so? When you read something written by a writer whose work you know, then you read those last pieces as the last pages in a long novel, but those pages would make no sense without the pages that came before them. When you think of a poet, you always tend to think of his last poem as a fine poem; but taken by itself, it may not be.

WB: Yes, but the last poems also help the early poems, because they contribute to the cumulative personality of the voice. Without those last poems your earlier poems would be heard less fully.

JLB: Well, I suppose they are helping each other.

WB: Because they create one total voice. When Blake says something amusing, it's partly amusing because usually he doesn't say anything amusing, and therefore we say, "Ah, there's Blake being witty in an epigram."

JLB: He's generally long-winded and ponderous!

WB: To continue this question, to me your new poems are your most powerful in terms of intellect and passion.

JLB: Let's hope so. I don't think of them in that way. They are mere exercises. Besides, as I feel lonely for something, I feel homesick, those poems are merely experiments in being back in Buenos Aires or in running away from things. They are merely meant to be used for padding the new book I'm writing. But I do hope you're right.

WB: As you stand before a mirror or record a dream in the poems, your precise delineation of pathos is a quality lost to modern poetry. It is well that you do not overesteem your recent poems, but you should know that you're probably wrong in your judgment.

JLB: But I hope I'm wrong! I'm glad to be convinced by you, only I can't.

I don't want to be right. Why should I be right? Why should I insist on the fact that I'm writing very poor stuff?

9. WB: Is there a poem usually lurking in your mind that you stumble on? Is it an act of recognition of a common thing, as when you suddenly remember that you love your mother or father? Is it that you fall upon a poem, or does the poem fall on you?

JLB: I would say the poem falls on me, and even more in the case of a short story. Then I am possessed. Then I have to get rid of it, and the only way to get rid of it is to write it down. There is no other way of doing so, or else it keeps on.

WB: You say your poems are mere exercises, but what are they exercises in?

JLB: I suppose they are exercises in language. They are exercises in the Spanish language, in the euphony of verse, exercises in rhyming also. Since I'm not too good a rhymer, I try to get away with it. And they are also exercises in imagination. In the case of a story, I know that I must think out a story, clearly and coherently, and then I can write it down. If not, I can't. If not, the whole thing would be a jumble of words. It should be more than that. A story should mean not only the words, but something behind the words. I remember reading—maybe it was one of Stevenson's essays: "What is a character in a book? A character in a book is merely a string of words," he said. Now I think that's wrong. He may be a string of words, but he should not leave us the impression of being a string of words. Because when we think of Macbeth or Lord Jim or Captain Ahab, we think of those characters as existing beyond the written words. We are not told everything about them, but there are many things that have happened to them that surely existed. For example, we are told about a character doing such and such a thing. Then the next day he does another thing. Now the writer doesn't say anything about it. We feel that he had his nights of sleep, that he has had his dreams, that things happened to him that we are not being told about. We think of Don Quixote as having been a child, though there is not a word concerning Don Quixote's childhood in the book as far as I remember. So the character should be more than a string of words. And if he is not more than words, he would not be a real character. You wouldn't be interested in him. Even in the case of a character who exists, let's say, within ten lines. "Alas, poor Yorick, I knew him well, Horatio." That character exists by himself. Yet he only exists as a strong of words within ten lines, or perhaps even less.

WB: And in someone else's mouth. He never even presents himself on stage.

JLB: Yes, in someone else's mouth, and yet you think of him as having been a real man.

WB: And feel compassion for him.

JLB: And feel compassion for him. Shakespeare had Hamlet in a grave-yard. He thought that making him handle a skull, a white skull, Hamlet was in black, all that would have made a quite effective picture. But since he couldn't be holding the skull and not saying a word, he had to say something. And so, Yorick came into being through that technical necessity of Shake-speare's. And he came into being forever. In that sense, Yorick is far more than a string of words. I suppose Stevenson knew all that, since he was a writer, since he created many characters, and those characters were far more than a string of words.

WB: And in ten words, he outsmarts time forever.

JLB: Yes, that's very strange, eh?

WB: I have a very personal question.

JLB: The only interesting questions are personal questions. Not those of the future of the Republic, the future of America, the future of the cosmos! These things are meaningless.

WB: I think these questions have all been rather personal.

JLB: They should be personal.

10. *WB: Do you have paternal feelings toward your friends? Or is this word paternal completely irrelevant?*

JLB: No, they're not paternal . . .

WB: Everyone is an equal?

JLB: Brotherly, fraternal, rather than paternal. Of course, being an old man I'm expected to be paternal, but really I'm not. Because, after all, I think it is rather sad. Now, Macedonio Fernández thought that paternal feelings were wrong. He said to me: "What do I have in common with my son? We belong to different generations. I'm fond of him, but that's my mistake. He's fond of me, that's his mistake. We shouldn't really care for each other." Then I said to him, yes, that doesn't depend on the rule. You may care for him in spite of those arguments. And suppose that your arguments are made because you think that you are worrying too much over him, or you feel that you haven't done right by him. There's quite a lot of nonsense about fathers not being allowed to love their sons and sons not being allowed to love their fathers.

WB: Go on.

JLB: Of course he had abandoned his family. There's a very obvious explanation: the fact that he had left them to live his own life.

11. WB: To go from fathers to reverie, you speak much of dream. What do you mean by dream? How is a dream different from any other state of wakefulness?

JLB: Because a dream is a creation. Of course, wakefulness may be a creation: part of our solipsism and so on. But you don't think of it in that way. In the case of a dream, you know that all that comes from yourself, whereas, in the case of a waking experience, many things may come to you that don't come out of yourself, unless you believe in solipsism. Then you are the dreamer all the time, whether waking or sleeping. I don't believe in solipsism. I don't suppose anybody really does. The essential difference between the waking experience and the sleeping or dreaming experience must lie in the fact that the dreaming experience is something that can be begotten by you, created by you, evolved out of you.

WB: But not necessarily in sleep.

JLB: No, no, not necessarily in sleep. When you're thinking out a poem, there is little difference between the fact of being asleep or awake, no? And so they stand for the same thing. If you're thinking, if you're inventing, or if you're dreaming, then the dream may correspond to vision or to sleep. That hardly matters.

12. WB: I have two more questions, Borges. Like all of us, you are a selfish man. You have dwelled on yourself, have explored and exploited your own mind and transmitted your observations to others.

JLB: Well, what else can I do? I shouldn't be blamed, I shouldn't be held to blame for that.

WB: Because you have transmitted your self-observations to others, you are surely not selfless. Yet the fact of giving your work to others, as you also offer a kind of Socratic conversation to others, is an act of generosity of a curiously rare ethical breed.

JLB: I think I need it, because I'm enjoying it also.

WB: Yet I fear that this breed of ethical generosity is becoming extinct, and that one like you, protected by blindness and loyalty to earlier authors, may not appear again. Then I worry a bit more and become optimistic and think that this ethical man and artist will occur again.
JLB: He or she will be lost forever and ever!

WB: Are you an ethical man?
JLB: Yes, I am essentially ethical. I always think of things in terms of right and wrong. I think that many people in my country, for example, have little feeling for ethics. I suppose in America people are more ethical than in my country. People here, for example, generally think of a thing as being right or wrong, the war in Viet Nam, and so on. But in my country you think of something as being profitable or unprofitable. That may be the difference. But here Puritanism, Protestantism, all that makes for ethical considerations; while the Catholic religion makes for pomp and circumstance only, that is, for essential atheism.

WB: Before my last question, I want to throw in this. There's a lot of fun in you, Borges, you're very childlike, you enjoy things, you have a tremendous humor.
JLB: Well, I should, after all. I wonder if I'm really grown up. I don't suppose anybody is.

13. WB: No, none of us is. My last question. When I was unhappy in the past, in love, some foolish things like that. . . .
JLB: No, not foolish. Those things are a part of every human experience. I mean the fact of loving and not being loved, that is a part of every biography, no? But if you came to me and said, I am in love with so-and-so. She's rejected me. I think that every human being can say that. Everyone has been rejected, and has rejected also. Both things stand out in everyone's life. Someone is turning down someone or being turned down. It's happening all the time. Of course, when it happens to us, as Heine said, then we're very unhappy.

WB: Sometimes when I was unhappy I wanted to die, but I knew that this was just a sign that I wanted to live.
JLB: I have thought of suicide many times, but I've always put it off. I say,

why should I worry, since I have that very powerful weapon, suicide, and at the same time I never used it, at least I don't think I ever used it!

WB: Well, you've almost answered my question. I wanted to say that the thought of suicide was merely a sign of wanting to live, that even the false suicide I often conceived was a desperate wish to live, more fully, better.

JLB: When people think of suicide, they only think of what people will think about them knowing that they committed suicide. So in a sense they go on living. They do it out of revenge, generally speaking. Many people commit suicide because they are angry. It is a way of showing their anger and revenge. To make someone else guilty for what you do, which is remarkably wrong.

WB: Suicide is largely a young man's romance, a false door young people sometimes step into. But what about the converse? Why the passion to live? Why that passion that drives the young to death and the writer to his pen? Why the consuming passion to live?

JLB: If I could answer that, I could explain the riddle of the universe, and I don't think I can, no? Since everybody else has failed. I've known many suicides. Many of my friends have committed suicide. In fact, among literary men in my country, suicide is fairly common, perhaps more than in this country. But I think that most of them have done it out of a desire to spite somebody, to make somebody guilty of their own death. In most cases that is the motivation. In the case of Leopoldo Lugones, I think he was trying to turn somebody else into a murderer.

WB: Sometimes there's a weariness, a desire to be released, when people are very sick.

JLB: Of course, there's another kind of suicide. When a friend of mine knew he had a cancer, he committed suicide, which was a reasonable thing to do. I wouldn't hold that against anybody. I think that it was right.

WB: I don't have any more questions unless you have a question you'd like to ask me.

JLB: No, I would like to thank you for your kindness and for this very pleasant conversation, because I thought of it as an ordeal, and it hasn't been an ordeal. On the contrary, it has been a very pleasant experience. You were very generous to be feeding me, giving me your own thoughts, pretending that I really thought them out. You've done everything, been handling me very deftly all the time, and I'm very grateful to you. Thank you, Barnstone.

WB: Thank you, Borges.

Borges: Philosopher? Poet? Revolutionary?

Donald Yates / 1982

From *Simply a Man of Letters: Panel Discussions and Paper from the proceedings of a Symposium on Jorge Luis Borges at the University of Maine at Orono*, The University of Maine at Orono Press, 1982, pp. 17–24. Reprinted by permission.

Q: What obligation does a writer have to respect literary conventions—words and what words should mean, story and what story form should mean, and so forth?

A: I think conventions help. Conventions make things easier. For example regular verse makes for easiness. There is no obligation. You have to accept certain things. If you refuse the language, you refuse the writing. Besides, I don't think what a man can do with the language is very important. Even in the case of such a fine writer, of such a renewer of the language as James Joyce. Let us take this sentence, one of his finest sentences; "The rivering waters of, the hither-and-thithering waters of night." That is very fine, but you have to accept the fact that "river" means "river" and "night" means "night," that "hither" and "thither" mean "hither" and "thither." It can't be done otherwise. Why not accept the conventions, since, after all, conventions are helpful? They are not all false; since we accept them, there is no reason why we should shy at them. But, of course, if you want to invent a fancy language of your own, then I suppose you will be a kind of Robinson Crusoe, no? You will lead a very lonely life.

Yates: But how about the convention which says that when you write a book review, the book that you are writing your review about should exist?

A: (Laughter) Well, I suppose you have me there. But still I remember a very fine book, *Sartor Resartus* by Carlyle, where he reviews a certain German philosophical non-existent book called *Die Kleider, ihr Werden und Wirken*. And then he wrote the book called *Sartor Resartus* or "The Tailor Patched"; so that review was also a convention.

Yates: You were following the convention then of the literary hoax.

A: The convention of the convention.

192

Q: The first part of the question: is writing pleasurable for you? And the second part: when you are writing the middle of your story which you can't find, is it groping or does it come clear to you?

A: Writing should be a pleasure. All things should be a pleasure, even a toothache, I suppose, if taken the right way. Now as to groping our way, that is a pleasure also. There is a pleasure in groping; a pleasure in hesitating— why not? Those are parts of the game. I accept them. Yes, I always think of writing as a pleasure. If it's not done for pleasure, it can't be done. It's not compulsory.

Yates: The answer to the second part is that you do grope in the middle for what is going to be the story?

A: Yes. I enjoy the groping.

Yates: In one story that you wrote, "The Circular Ruins," your groping became part of the story since the magician or the stranger—whoever—was trying to find a way to imagine or dream or create another person, and he tried several things that didn't work. These were your attempts to write the story. Is that right?

A: Yes, of course I was. I am sure I was very clever to have woven them into a story.

Q: First, do you accept the linking of your name with Kafka, and second, do you enjoy being linked with Kafka?

A: I think Kafka taught me the way to write two quite bad stories: "The Library of Babel" and "The Lottery of Babylon." Of course, I owe a debt to Kafka. Naturally. I enjoyed that. At the same time, I couldn't go on reading Kafka all the time so I left it at that. I only wrote two stories following the pattern and then I left off. Of course I owe much to Kafka. I admire him, as I suppose all reasonable men do.

Yates: In the "Library of Babel" you insert a word spelled thusly: Qaphqa. I think the only way to pronounce that is Kafka. Did you put that in there to show that you were aware that you were writing like Kafka?

A: Yes. Of course I did.

[To a question on the influence on Borges of contemporary Latin-American writers.]

A: I am not a futurist. I was not aware of García Márquez and Cortázar, who came after.

Yates: The response is that Borges went blind for reading purposes in 1955 and simply hasn't read Cortázar and hasn't read Paz.

A: They came after me. I am not a prophet. I was not affected by them. They are in the future. We are not affected by the future.

Yates: Part of the question was: you have been credited with influencing them. In what way do you think you might have influenced them? Where do you think Latin American literature is going in their charge?

A: I hope Latin American literature has escaped my influence.

Yates: In 1955, you left off writing longish narratives and when the time came in 1960, when Carlos Frías, your editor at Emecé, asked you for a book, you said, "I have no book." And he said, "Every writer has a book if he digs around in his drawers and his files and his cabinets, and so forth," so you looked around and came up with a book called *El Hacedor—Dreamtigers*. They are all short pieces—apparently short pieces you had written since 1955 when you had lost your sight and couldn't write anymore in the old way. In 1966, after not having written a long story since "El Fin" in 1953—that's some 13 years—suddenly you wrote a long story, "La Intrusa." What was behind your change of mind about giving up writing just short pieces like those of *El Hacedor* and writing a long story like "La Intrusa"?

A: I had been rereading my Kipling. I reread *Plain Tales from the Hills*, and I thought that what a young man of genius like Kipling did (he was twenty-odd when he wrote *Plain Tales from the Hills*), perhaps an old experienced hand, who is certainly not a man of genius, may be able to do somehow. I put it down in a way that had nothing to do with Kafka or Henry James or Melville but that might perhaps have pleased Kipling, though the setting, of course, was quite different. So I dictated that story to my mother, who wrote it down. I think it is one of my best stories, perhaps my best, because it is hardly like me. It is good enough to have been written by somebody else.

[In a question phrased in Spanish, Borges was asked about the theme of his poem "Lucas XXIII," and whether he might write another poem like it. He answered in Spanish to this effect:]

I would write another such poem if I could, because I consider it rather good. The poem's theme seems obvious to me: that the impulse which led the Good Thief to be a thief was the same one which led him to accept the extraordinary fact that the other person being crucified was God. I think that is the theme; and I would like to write another poem as direct as that one,

especially that line which runs: *"De aquella tarde en que los dos murieron."*
I find it a line charged with feeling, although I should not say so because I
wrote it. But after all, since I have written nothing, since everything has been
given to me mysteriously, I can say that I like it—that I like that poem; and
you are perhaps the first person who has noticed that poem, except for Dr.
Cortinez, who seems to have noticed it because he recited it [in his introduction to Borges' talk]. At this point I have two readers, and I am grateful.

Yates: Professor Alazraki observes that in your fiction you have developed
metaphors to disguise the autobiographical content or personal feeling behind
your stories. You have done the same, he suggests, in your poetry. Then
suddenly, in a new vein of poetry—he cites the poem "Remorse"—you have
thrown away the mask and bare yourself—your personal self, your most intimate self—to us. What is behind your change in attitude towards hiding from
the reader your most intimate feelings?

A: I suppose I was more inventive and now I have to fall back on saying
simple things. It may be a failing for all I know. That might be a reason. I
suppose that when I was a younger man, I was happy in inventions, and now
I feel that I no longer need inventions, or maybe I am not getting them. I am
unworthy of inventions. And so I fall back on merely stating my emotions or
hinting at them, and that perhaps may prove sufficient, for all I know.

Yates: Do you feel that this new ability or need to express things simply
and in a straightforward manner is an impoverishment of what you had before, or is it finding your voice at this stage in your life?

A: It may be an impoverishment, but I don't have to think of it in that way;
that would be discouraging. I'd rather think of it as something new in order
to go on.

Q: In respect to your relationship with the literature that you used to be
able to read, that you can no longer read. Does someone read to you, and if
that is the case, do you feel a different relationship now with what you used
to be able to read before, and that is now just read to you?

A: Things are very generously read to me, but of course it is not quite the
same thing. I cannot browse over a book. I merely have to hear what is being
read to me. It is a pleasurable experience though not exactly the same. At the
same time, having things read to me means knowing them better. When I had
my sight, I used to read in a very superficial way, since I knew the book was
there and I could look things up in it at any moment. But now I know that

since readers are not available all the time, I have to remember what I have been read. And so that may have made my memory better, for all I know. Still, after all, the only thing I can do is to have things read to me, and having things read to me is a pleasure. Not the same kind of pleasure I had got before, but a different kind of pleasure, a pleasure one should be thankful for.

Q: What books do you have read to you now?

A: Except for the purposes of Old English or of Old Norse, I am more or less rereading. I prefer rereading to reading, since when you reread, you are delving down; but when you read, the thing is done in a very perfunctory and superficial way. So I am always going back to such writers as I read when I had my eyesight. I am always going back to Robert Louis Stevenson, to Edgar Allan Poe. . . .

Q: In what ways has Poe influenced you?

A: Well, I suppose Poe taught me how to use my imagination. He taught me—though I was unaware of it, but I must have felt it strongly—that one may not be tied down by mere everyday circumstances; that being tied down to everyday circumstances stood for poverty, stood for dullness. I could be everywhere, and I could be, let's say, in eternity. And I suppose Poe taught me that. He taught me the width, the vastness of freedom. Those were taught to me in the first stories of his I read, *The Tales of the Grotesque and the Arabesque*. Though my style, of course, is far different from Poe, since Poe wrote in what we may call a pompous style, and I write in a rather grey, everyday style. But I suppose I should be thankful to him for his teaching me that writing could transcend personal experience—or rather, could be woven out of personal experience transmuted in some strange way. One should be thankful to Poe; and besides, why not be thankful to a man who gave us *The Adventures of Arthur Gordon Pym*, and who created a genre, something nobody else has done—who has given us all the many detective books written since his time? They all came out of Poe; they were all begotten by Poe, when he wrote those three stories that you all know. So, I think I should be thankful to Poe, though I think of him as a prose writer. I do not like him as a poet. As for what was wrong with his poetry, I remember Emerson's joke about him. Somebody spoke to Emerson, that cold intellectual poet, about Poe, and he said, "Ah, Mr. Poe, the jingle man."

Q: What do you admire especially in Stevenson?

A: I admire everything in Stevenson. I admire the man, I admire the work,

I admire his courage. I don't think he wrote a single indifferent or despicable line. Every line of Stevenson is fine. And then there is another writer I greatly admire: Chesterton. And yet Chesterton would not have been what he was had it not been for Stevenson. For example, if we read Chesterton's Father Brown saga, or *The Man Who Was Thursday*, or "Man Alive," we get the same fairy London that was invented or was dreamt by Stevenson in his *New Arabian Nights*. I suppose I should be thankful to Stevenson. I suppose we should all be thankful to Stevenson. I hardly see why you ask me that. The thing is as obvious as the sun in heaven.

Q: Why are mirrors a recurring symbol in your writing?

A: Because mirrors are very strange things. Mirrors give you the sense of the double. They give the Scottish wraith. When a man sees himself, according to Scottish superstition, he is about to die. His real self comes to fetch him back. Then you have in German the Doppelgänger, the man who walks at our side and with ourselves. Those things, of course, are given to us by the mirror. Then you have (I only know the Latin, I don't know Greek) the *alter ego*, the other I. Those things also were suggested by the mirror. There is something strange in the fact of the visual world being reproduced in every detail in a piece of glass, in a crystal. When I was a child I was amazed at it. I find it very strange that there should be in the world such things as mirrors.

Yates: Can you explain the perception that you have of two Borgeses? The two Borgeses that you write of in "Borges y yo"?

A: I suppose the perception came originally from the mirror. Because when you look into a mirror, well, there you are, there you are yourself looking at it, and the image looking at you. As for two Borges, I have been made keenly aware of the fact that there are two, because when I think of myself, I think, let us say, of a rather secret, of a rather hesitant, groping man. Somehow, this can hardly be reconciled to the fact that I seem to be giving lectures all the time and traveling all over the world. So I think of those two men as being different: the private man and the public man. Or, if you prefer it, why not speak of the private man, the shy man, the man still wondering at things even as he did when he was a boy, and the man who publishes books, whose books are analyzed, who has symposiums and that kind of thing happening to him—why not think of those two as being different? I do.

Yates: In your poem, "The Sentinel," "El centinela," do you give a chance for the other Borges to speak, the one whose voice was not heard in "Borges and I"?

A: [Affirmative.]

Q: What things are taken into account when you decide whether what you're going to write is poetry or prose?
A: I suppose if I feel very lazy, it's poetry. If I feel very active it's prose.

Q: You begin by reminding us that all things lead to a book. I wonder what, in your judgment, a book leads to.
A: It should lead to happiness. If not, if a book does not lead to happiness, or, let us say, to emotion, then that book doesn't really exist. I don't think in terms of compulsory reading. Books are meant to stand for experiences. For fine experiences. For real experiences.

An Interview with Jorge Luis Borges
John Biguenet and Tom Whalen / 1982

From *New Orleans Review*, Fall 1982, pp. 5–14. Reprinted by permission.

Jorge Luis Borges, the distinguished Argentine author of short fiction, poetry and essays and the winner of the International Publishers Prize, was interviewed by the *NOR* on a recent trip to New Orleans to receive various civic and academic honors. His most recent collections in English include *Borges: A Reader, The Book of Sand*, and *The Gold of the Tigers*. For an excellent appreciation of Borges' work, see John Updike's "Borges Warmed Over" in the May 24, 1982, *New Yorker*. The interview was conducted in English on January 27, 1982.

In your work, your devotion to Buenos Aires is obvious.

Yes, I don't know why for such a drab city, and yet ten million people, it sprawls all over. Of course since I was born there, the city has really changed. Now there are tall buildings. When I was a boy, tall buildings had two stories, not more than that. The houses had flat roofs, patios, cisterns; that was not just the downtown, the whole city was like that. And we had apartments; that was all the way back in 1899. And the first apartment house for rent—I think it was erected in 1910 or so. The whole city was different. Of course it was a small city, but a growing city, often very elated. Today we're rather, in a quiet way, hopeless-in a quite way.

That sounds like New Orleans

No. I think of New Orleans as brimming over with music and jazz. They speak of the tango. But you may spend several years in Buenos Aires and not hear a single tango. Usually you can spend a long time in, well, Brazil and not hear any music, as far as I am aware. But here, the city is brimming over with jazz. You're hearing it all the time and enjoying it and taking it in. But the tango, the tango in Buenos Aires, as most people have written about it, was evolved in the brothel houses about 1880. And the people didn't accept it because they knew whom it came from. When people heard that they were dancing it in Paris, then they took it seriously. They were a nation of snobs. Paris, of course, they took for reality. So then people said, "Ah, the tango."

They all knew it came from the brothel houses and shouldn't be talked about. It wasn't accepted by the people, but when people knew that the right people were dancing it and it was being sung in Paris, the it was taken up by them. When I was a boy, yes, I can remember only two tangos. I was hearing all the time French music, Italian music, now and then perhaps Spanish music— no, that was rare.

When you describe the city, it often sounds like the sort of labyrinth that some of your fiction employs. Is the city a kind of labyrinth for you?

Well, it is today because it's very large. When I was a boy, it wasn't. It was quite small, but, somehow, very hopeful, very proud in 1910. But since then—well, of course, we had that awful scoundrel Perón. But even before Peron things were falling down, falling down. And I was declining and falling. I don't suppose anyone would disagree, the whole thing has gone beyond it. But on the other hand, I don't think anything can be done about it. Elections would be a mistake of course, in which we would have lots of scoundrels like Peron; and the military do their best, but inefficient best I should say, maybe their well-meaning best, as far as I know. I was a conservative, then left the conservative party, and now I'm just a writer and not too conspicuous in my country. They know I'm there and that's that.

As a writer, although you seem very rooted in Argentina and Argentinean history . . .

You shouldn't say *Argentina*. There's no such word. It's *Argentine*. Because you see, *Argentine* means *silvery*. The Rio de la Plàta means the *Silver River*. You don't have to add Argentina, because that's non-sensical. Someone invented it to rhyme with *Bolivian* and *Peruvian*, but *Argentinean*— there's no such word. If you said, "Argentiniano," the Spanish people would laugh at you. No, it's *Argentine*. The Argentine Republic, yes, but the Argentine, not Argentina, wherever that may be.

Despite the fact that you are a citizen deeply rooted to your home, Pablo Neruda, even though he criticized your work, said you are one of the very few universal Latin American writers.

Yes, of course. I'm a kind of world-wide superstition. I don't take myself seriously as all that. I dislike what I write and I like what I read in my other writers, not my own stuff, my own output. I don't like it but I put up with it. I'm 82, too old to attempt new tricks. I just go on writing. Yes, what else can I do? I'm 82. I'm blind. I've been pensioned off with two pensions. From the library, of course, then as a professor of English literature. Then when the time came I had two pensions and royalties, but royalties—you can't make a living in my country from books. Perhaps the book sellers can, but not the writers. And the publishers can't either, because they only get 20 percent for a book sold. They have to pay for the printing, for the propaganda, for sending the book all over. While the writer, whoever writes the book, has no expenses but he may be paid royalties every six months (that's theoretically), but really quite possibly he might not get a cent. And then there are the lectures. I lecture in Buenos Aires. If I lecture, let's say, at a library or a school, then of course I don't charge them anything. But if it's an institution, people pay for hearing me or chatting with me then, of course. They give me something. But who would make a living out of my literature? Nobody can. Even if you condescend to pornography. But even then, you are obscene and still poor, no?

Even someone as widely translated as you doesn't make . . .

No, because it goes through so many hands before it reaches the writer. Yes, I've been widely translated. I don't know why, because there are far better writers than I in my country. Somehow they don't get translated, and I do. I don't know why it is. I never thought in terms of fame or selling or even of finding readers. The only reason was that I felt an inner urge to do so. And my father advised me, "Don't, above all, don't rush into print. Publish as little as you can." I published my first book when I was 24, a book of poems and already I had destroyed three or four books before I published that one. Not a very good book either.

You have said that translations are different perspectives of an object in motion.

Yes, I suppose they are. But every translation is a new version. And every book is really a rough draft. As [Alfonso] Reyes said to me, we publish our books in order not to spend our lifetimes going over rough drafts. We publish a book and then we're rid of it. We can go on to other or perhaps better things. When I publish a book, I let it find its way in the world. I don't worry about it. I haven't read a single line written about me. I haven't read the translations either. I never reread my own work because I'd get very discouraged if I did so. So I go on writing. Because what else can I do? I'm blind. I would like to go on reading, that would be far better than to go on writing. But unhappily that is forbidden me. But I keep on buying books. I don't know why. I like being in a bookish atmosphere. Of course the books, well,

they might as well be in Timbuktu since I don't read them. Friends come and
visit me and then we read, we reread; then generally, we take some history
or philosophy or Schopenhauer or if not, well many favorites of mine. We go
in for poetry; generally we read Browning or Emerson. I love Emerson. He
was somewhat influenced by Whitman.

And Emerson was the only one to see Walt Whitman as a great poet.
    Yes. You know what he called Poe? He said, "Oh, Edgar Allan Poe, the
jingle man." He was thinking of "The Bells," I suppose; it was really a jest.
It was all the same. These things don't have to be right or not. The jingle
man.

*I would like to ask you about a writer that most American readers are still
unaware of and that's the Austrian Gustav Meyrink.*
    Well, they should not be. I taught myself German in order to read Scho-
penhauer (just for reading purposes, I don't speak German). I taught myself
German with this method. I recommend it to everybody. I got hold of Heinrich Heine's *Buch der Lieder* (*Book of Songs*). And then, a German-English
dictionary, since English was the only language they had. And then I began
reading. I was looking all the time in the dictionary. The only German I had
was "Der, die, das, die. Den, die, das, die." Then I began reading. Then after
three or four months, at another moment (it was in Geneva; I must have been
seventeen at the time), I cried because I was reading a poem in an unknown
tongue, in German, "In der Fremde." It went thus:

> Ich hatte einst ein schönes Vaterland.
> Der Eichenbaum
> Wuchs dort so hoch, die Veilchen nickten sanft.
> Es war ein Traum.

> Das Küsste mich auf deutsch and sprach auf deutsch
> (Man glaubt es kaum
> Wie gut es Klang) das Wort: "Ich liebe dich!"
> Es war ein Traum.[1]

And then I cried. Not only was it the beauty of the verses, but I was reading
in German, actually. I had conquered the German language. It's the best

---

[1] "Abroad" by Heinrich Heine: "Once I had a lovely fatherland./ The oak trees/ Grew
high there, the violets nodded gently./ It was a dream./ It kissed me in German and said
in German/ (It's hard to believe/ How good it sounded) the words: 'I love you!'/ It was a
dream." [Trans. by J.B. & T.W.]

method. When you are Spanish speaking, then I think the best writer would be Oscar Wilde because Oscar Wilde writes with many Latin words, where for example Browning or Kipling, no, they use plain Saxon words.

I was wondering if you agreed with a character of yours, Dr. Zimmerman, who says in the story "Guayaquil" that The Golem is the only book by Meyrink worth reading. Didn't you edit a collection of short stories by Meyrink, translated into French?

Yes, I did. A book called *Fledermäuse* [*Bats*]. Then he wrote the story about a wandering Jew. In German it's the everlasting Jew. That book is called *Das grüne Gesicht* [*The Green Face*]. Then a book about English wizards, with a beautiful title *Der Engel vom westlichen Fenster*, *The Angel of the Western Window*. But his book is *The Golem*. It was the first book I read in full in German. After Heine, I went on to prose, and then I found a fascinating book, *Der Golem*. So, it was two Jews who led me to German, Heine and Meyrink. Meyrink was actually called Meyer, but that was too commonplace. He changed his name. Meyrink sounds better, no? Meyer in German is like Smith or Brown or Lopez. Borges is a very common Portuguese name. Every other man is called Borges in Lisbon.

There are many American, European and British writers that you have recommended to us for whom we're grateful. I was wondering if there are some South American writers that you think we should be reading?

Yes, perhaps. But I know very little about them. Still I think we have a pretty fine poet; her name is Silvina Ocampo. She's been done into English now. And, well, I won't go in for any more names because all people notice is the omissions, the exclusions. Someone is left out, he stands out, in a sense. Well, I know very little about those writers. García Márquez is a fine writer. Of course, Alfonso Reyes, I think, wrote the finest Spanish prose ever written on this side of the Atlantic. He was a great writer. A great prose writer. He was my master—well, I had many masters. Lugones, in my country. But Lugones here is an unknown quantity, I should say. You see, you have been in the world so much, and we in the world so little. I mean, what we have done is important to us and to Spain but not to the outside world. Such writers as Edgar Allan Poe, Emerson, Melville, Walt Whitman, Emily Dickinson, Thoreau, Frost, Faulkner—well, you can't think them away. There they are; they influence us all the time. What have we given the world? A few words simply, no? For example, Bolivar, pampas, gaucho, Rio de Janeiro, Montezuma, Cortez, Pizarro, perhaps tango—well, that's that.

Many people would argue that Borges, too, belongs on that list of writers.
Oh, no. Not him. Not him.

What do you think of the young poet Borges who wrote Fervor de Buenos Aires?
Well, he was trying to imitate Walt Whitman and failing, of course. He did his best to be Walt Whitman; he failed miserably. But somehow, people remember him still. No, maybe there are one or two pages that may still be readable. But I don't know since I don't read my own output.

How do you weigh your poetry against your fiction? Do you prefer your poems to your stories?
I suppose they are essentially the same. I like my poems. My friends tell me no, my verses are a mistake. Well I say, maybe my poor friends are also mistaken. I like my poems. Well, of course, if I'm writing in verse about something, I'll write about it. A story, after all, is a kind of verbal object you invent. It's outside you. But poetry should surely be flowing from you. But maybe there's no great difference. After all, you have to fall back on inspiration. I don't think books can be explained. If they're explained, they're explained away. See, you can't say that in Spanish. It can't be said because the language wouldn't allow it. Remember some very fine verses by Rudyard Kipling, the famous "The Ballad of East and West." There you have a British officer, who is pursuing an Afghan horse thief. They're riding. Then Kipling writes, "They have ridden the low moon out of the sky, their hoofs drum up the dawn." Now, you can't ride the moon out of the sky and you can't drum up the dawn in Spanish because the language doesn't allow it. It can't be done.

So the translations in Spanish are infinite, then?
Well, you have to find some way or you fall flat, I suppose. For example, you can say in English, you are dreaming away your life. Well, that can't be said in Spanish or any romance language as far as I know. It might be said perhaps in German or one of the Scandinavian tongues, but not in a romance language. There are many words that have no Spanish or French translations. Somebody in English will say, "Uncanny." That's Scots, I suppose. In German, *unheimlich*. But you can't say it in Spanish, because the Spanish never had that feeling. They had no need of the word.

So does that mean that a Spaniard can't dream his life away because he can't say it?
Yes, he can do it, but he can't say it. He can do it, of course. Just as we

can die even if we don't think of death. But English has another virtue. The virtue of Anglo-Saxon words, they're short. If you say *selini* in Greek, that's far too long—three syllables. In Spanish, *luna* or in Latin, two syllables. In French, just one syllable really, *lune*. But in English that beautiful, lingering word *moon*. It's the right word, no? But in Old English the word is quite ugly, *mona*. *Moon* and *sun*, those two were the right words. Or the difference between sky and heaven. In Spanish, you say *cielo* or for example, well in English you have a difference between weather and time. In Spanish, no, it's *tiempo* and that's that. In French also. Such a beautiful English word as *dim*. You don't have any Spanish equivalent for *dim*. In German, of course, you have *Dämmerung*, the twilight, and *Götterdämmerung*, the twilight of the gods.

When you were speaking about your fiction and your poetry, you spoke of fiction as if it were a perfect little object and poetry as a kind of song?

Yes. I suppose that they both come from the imagination. I mean inspiration comes to you; it may be a story or it may be a poem. I suppose the starting point is the same.

And the experience finds its own way to the right genre?

Yes. And the less you meddle with it, the better. The writer shouldn't allow it, should not try to meddle with his writing. His opinions should not be allowed to find their way into his writing. Since opinions, after all, come and go. Emotions, well, emotions go away.

I was teaching this morning H.G. Well's "The Country of the Blind . . ."

What a fine story, eh? I read that in the *Strand Magazine* when I was a boy. It came with its own pictures, the *Strand Magazine*. In it I read "The Hound of the Baskervilles," also. What a fine story, eh, "The Country of the Blind"?

A beautiful story—it echoes for me your short story "The South." The possibility that Nunez's fall down the mountain is his fall to his death, that Dahlmann's journey south is only a dream on the operating table. Many times when one reads your work, there are echoes from literature, "The Book of Sand" echoing "The Blast of the Book" by Chesterton.

Of course there are. I try to be a good reader even if I am a bad writer. And Wells was a man of genius, of course.

Literature that begets literature—some critics see this as a sign of literature being exhausted.

No, I think that Emerson wrote that poetry comes out of poetry. Whitman thought that poetry came from experience, no? I don't think so. I think Emerson was right. I think Victor Hugo said, "Homer, of course, had his Homer." "Homer avait son Homer." I suppose he had; he lived in a literary tradition. It's like time, really, beginningless.

Maybe that's why you say that you are quite incapable of invention. Why should we invent when we have Wells and Stevenson and Chesterton to draw from?

Yes, because we keep on inventing the same stories, eh?

Many critics come back again and again to the subject of time as your most profound concern.

Yes, it is. I think that time would be the central riddle, no? If we knew what time was, of course we would know ourselves.

The other evening, you spoke of the metaphor, "Time is a river."

Yes, I think that's the real metaphor, no? When you think of time, you think in terms of a river, no? Well, the Mississippi, why not? You think of it as being a river. Yes, I was quoting that verse, that line that Tennyson wrote when he was fourteen. "Time flowing through the middle of the night." A fine line. He wrote it when he was fourteen or fifteen. Then he forgot all about it, and it was somehow dug up by his critics.

Living on the banks of the Mississippi we see things washed past us by the river, but it seems that you're able to swim upstream to get back to Homer and Chesterton.

Well, I do my best, after all. Homer and Chesterton are really desirable goals. I wish I could. Really, I am unworthy. My writing is unworthy of my reading, eh? I'm beginning to see language. You see, at home we spoke English and Spanish. My maternal grandmother was English, spoke both languages. Then I went to Geneva when I was fourteen. There I was taught French, and there I was taught Latin, a very fine language. After all, I spoke Spanish and French, I just said, "Now Latin." I'd just think of it in that way. And then, I taught myself German. And when I went blind, I said to myself, "I won't abound in loud self-pity," quoting Kipling. And then I began studying Old English, Anglo-Saxon. And now I go in for Icelandic, for Old Norse. (I love all things Scandinavian.) Old English is a very beautiful language; it's a large language like modern English. If I give you a piece in Old English, it will be—what do you prefer, elegy or epic? I can tackle both. What do you prefer? Elegy or epic?

Elegy.

> Mæʒ ic be mē sylfum		sōðʒied wrecan,
> sīþas secʒan,		hū ic ʒeswincdaʒum
> earfoðhwīle		oft þrōwade,
> bitre brēostceare		ʒebiden hæbbe,
> ʒecunnad in cēole		cearselda fela,
> atol ȳþa ʒewealc,		pǽr mec oft biʒeat
> nearo nihtwaco		æt nacan stefnan,
> þonne hē be clifum cnossað.

That's Old English with a line of French, I think. And the other verses are the same. That was done into English by Ezra Pound. He wrote, although he was off his head, he wrote "May I for my ownself song's truth reckon." Because he was translating the sounds, when the literal translation is "I can offer a true song about myself." And "to tell my travels" he translated as "journey's jargon" ["The Seafarer," in *Ezra Pound: Translations*].

When you speak of Chesterton and Stevenson and other English writers, you seem most delighted by their styles.

In the case of Chesterton, there are many other things, eh? Of course, Stevenson was a great poet. I mean the plots, the style, the metaphors are overwhelming really. Do you remember, for example, "Marble like solid moonlight, gold like a frozen fire." Those are wonderful metaphors. Or "I shall not be too old to see enormous night arise. A cloud that is larger than the world. And the monster made of eyes." "A monster made of eyes," that's weird, isn't it?

Can you speak about your own style?

Well, when I was a young man, I did my best to be Chesterton, to be Lugones, to be Quevedo, to be Stevenson. Then after that, I said no, I'll just be Borges, and that's that. A very modest ambition. But after all, people like it.

And you think Borges is more plain-spoken than these authors?

Oh, of course he is. I began by being baroque, because all young men are. I tried to astonish, I went in for far-fetched metaphors; now I try to avoid that kind of thing. I like to use, well, easy words that aren't dictionary words.

"Blindness is a confinement," you have written, "but it is also a liberation, a solitude propitious to invention, and an algebra."

Yes, but I was cheating myself. No, really it's not. Well, of course, you're lonely. I mean you have to read. I used to read all the books in my house. I used to read all the books.

So you think blindness is a kind of loneliness?
    It is. One feels lonely. And most of the time. After all, my friends cannot afford to give me all their time. I spend most of my time at home. Most of the contemporaries have died, they're in the cemetery.

You still have your good friend Bioy Casares?
    Yes, he's far younger than I am, but he forgives me for being an old man. We meet, perhaps, once a month. Buenos Aires is far too big a city. Ten million inhabitants. Somehow, we drift apart. The telephones don't work, because they're no good.

Do you think your work has lost something by your being blind?
    Well, I try to think that it has gained. But really I'm cheating myself. But I want to go on.

How has your work changed since your blindness?
    For example, when I had my eyesight, I attempted free verse. But now that I have to make a rough mental draft, of course I go in for sonnets or rhymed verse—those things make the memory easier. You can remember a sonnet. I can remember many sonnets. Both in English and French and Spanish and Italian. But I can't remember free verse to memorize. Even in the case of Walt Whitman, who I've read and reread. I wonder if I can quote a page of Walt Whitman for you. If I may. I might decline and fall at any moment.

> These are the thoughts of all men in all ages and lands—they are not original
>   with me;
> If they are not yours as much as mine, they are nothing, or next to nothing;
> If they are not the riddle, and the untying of the riddle, they are nothing;
> If they are not just as close as they are distant, they are nothing.
> This is the grass that grows wherever the land is, and the water is;
> This is the common air that bathes the globe.

He says at the end: "I love you. I depart from my materials." (That's rather ugly.) "I love you. I depart from my materials, I am as one disembodied, triumphant, dead." The words get shorter and shorter. "I am as one disembodied, triumphant, dead." It rings out, as it should. Whitman was a great poet, of course.

In reading your work, I often feel as if there are many Borgeses, perhaps an infinite number of them.
There should be. Let's be endless.

Which Borges are we talking to?
Well, you pays your money and you takes your chances.

Can you tell about the books you still have to write, your future projects?
I have many future projects. What else can I have but projects at my age? I am translating with María Kodama from the German Angelus Silesius's *Der cherubinishe Wandersmann.* He was a 17th century German mystic. That's about to be printed in Chile. Then I am going to write a book about the great historian and writer, Snorri Sturluson. That will be the first book on him in Spanish. Then I'm also preparing a book of short stories and another book of poems. Then, at this moment, a book of mine has just come out in Madrid *The Cipher,* a book of poems. Then, I have two anthologies. One of the Argentine poet Lugones, selected and with a foreword by me, and the other of the famous Spanish writer Quevedo, also selected and with a foreword by me. That's that at the moment, but I keep on writing.

That's a busy schedule.
Yes.

If you were the headmaster of a school for young poets, what would be your curriculum?
Well, I taught English literature, then I said to my students (I had classes for twenty years, and they were always in Buenos Aires), I said, I can't teach you English literature because I don't know it. But I can teach you the love of English literature. Don't go in for dates or place names; don't go in for bibliography. Try to find a way into the book itself. Some of them fell in love with Old English, others fell in love with Chaucer, others with Dr. Johnson, or else with Shakespeare or Marlowe, or Milton, or Bernard Shaw, or Chesterton, or Edgar Allan Poe, or Emerson, whatever the case might be. They all fell in love with some book or another, and that's the gist, that's the important thing, yes?

I was wondering if you ever thought of the universe as being designed by a divinity in a state of delirium.
No. I think what Bernard Shaw said is true. God is in the making, and we are the making, of course. The whole cosmic process is the making. The

universe is history and so on. I don't think of God as a person or a being at all, except he may be. He may be myself for all I know. I may be one of his many disguises. I believe this is more or less the Buddhist idea. I wrote a small handbook on Buddhism and that was done into Japanese. When I went to Japan I saw the book on Buddhism. Of course they know far more about it than I do. Buddhism is one of the two or three religions of Japan. Shinto and Buddhism. There is a very strange word in Japanese: *Hotoke*. According to the context, it may stand for the Buddha. It may stand for Jesus Christ, or it may stand for anybody who has died. The thought is really the same, no?

You mentioned this week that you looked very hopefully toward death, as a great adventure.

No, not a great adventure, I should say as a liberation. My father said, I want to die all together. I want to die body and soul. I'm looking forward to death as a kind of sleep. My grandfather, in a sense, committed suicide. He got himself killed on purpose. One of those small battles in the civil wars. That was in 1874. Yes, Colonel Borges. And his death was more or less famous, because he rode a white horse, wore a white poncho, he rode very slowly toward the enemy lines, and he got two shots fired into him. The first time the Winchester rifle was used in my country. Of course it was used in the War between the States, the Civil War. The first time the Winchester rifle was used. The Remington came afterwards I think.

Do you have something you consider your greatest weakness as a writer?

I don't know. Maybe I'm impatient. I'm very clumsy. I take many pains with my writing. Usually it seems to be, well, spontaneous and it isn't. I worry carefully over it. Every page of mine stands for at least a half a dozen rough drafts. They are mental, of course. I have to dictate, I can't write. If I tried to write, it would overlap, the writing would overlap, it couldn't be read by anybody. I've read but few novels, but I've read many short stories. In the beginning, of course, I read Grimm's fairy stories, I read the *The Arabian Nights*. And then to Stevenson, to Chesterton, to Edgar Allan Poe, to Jack London also. The first novel I ever read through in my life was Mark Twain's *Huckleberry Finn*. Then I went on to *Life on the Mississippi* and to *Roughing It*, and *Flush Days in California*, those books few folks seem now to have read. Enjoyable books. He was a man of genius, of course, Mark Twain. He was unaware of the fact that he was a man of genius.

Why do you consider Borges a "minor" writer?

Well, because I have read him, but not only read him, I have written him, I know all about him. Still there may be something in all that stuff for all I know, since so many people have taken it seriously, taken it in earnest. There should be something there.

There are many people who are very grateful for your having devoted yourself to your stories.

They're very generous. Very mistaken, I should say. Generous mistakes.

What does literature have to offer us?

I should say everything, eh? The universe at least. Literature, of course. I am tone deaf, I am blind. I never greatly enjoyed architecture. Painting, yes, perhaps—Turner, Velasquez. And that's that. Words have meant much to me, and languages. I am very fond of words, etymologies.

So, literature is like an aleph, a little window onto the universe?

Well, thank you for remembering that story. It's quite a good story, I should say, even though I wrote it.

I can tell you a story that may please you. I worked with a program where poets went into school classrooms and taught poetry to children. And one of the games we played with them was to give them invisible alephs. And they could hold them up to the light, we told them, and they would see the universe pass in front of them. And they would write down what they saw.

O good for you. Far better than the story I wrote.

I think it's the same story. And the children wrote wonderful poetry by looking through the invisible alephs.

It was a prism, no? Of course, it had to be a prism.

For the children, we said it was an invisible prism and gave each one his own.

That's far better than what I wrote.

We learned from you.

What's good for me, was good for you. Good for me especially.

And good for the children.

A man in Spain asked me whether the aleph actually existed. Of course it doesn't. He thought the whole thing was true. I gave him the name of the street and the number of the house. He was taken in very easily.

But perhaps, as you say, if literature gives us everything, then the aleph is the short story and the poem. Because through it we see everything as through that small prism.

Yes. That piece gave me great trouble, yes. I mean, I had to give a sensation of endless things in a single paragraph. Somehow, I got away with it.

Yes, it's a beautiful catalogue.
Yes. But a lot of trouble.

Is that an invention, the aleph, or did you find it in some reference?
No. I'll tell you, I was reading about time and eternity. Now eternity is supposed to be timeless. I mean, God or a mystic perceives in one moment all of our yesterdays, Shakespeare says, all the past, all the present, all the future. And I said, why not apply that, well, that invention to another category, not to time, but to space? Why not imagine a point in space wherein the observer may find all the rest. I mean, who invented space? And that was the central idea. Then I had to invent all the other things, to make it into a funny story, to make it into a pathetic story, that came afterwards. My first aim was this: in the same way that many mystics have talked of eternity . . . that's a big word, an eternity, an everness. And also neverness; that's an awful word. Since we have an idea of eternity, of foreverness in time, why not apply the same idea to space, and think of a single point in space wherein the whole of space may be found? I began with that abstract idea, and then, somehow, I came to that quite enjoyable story.

Physicists came up with the same idea, when they thought of the big bang theory, that the universe might be moving toward a single point, which would condense and then explode into a universe again. Perhaps they, too, learned from you.
Well, I don't think so. I don't think they would trouble about a minor South American writer, no?□

Jorge Luis Borges
Alastair Reid / 1983

From "Kafka: The Writer's Writer: Conversations with a Writer," introduction by Alastair Reid, *Kafka Society of America*, 28 December 1983, pp. 20–27. Reprinted by permission.

Excerpts of the recorded conversation. Transcribed by Peter Beicken. Centennial Meeting of the Modern Language Association, New York City. Wednesday, December 28, 1983, 7:15–8:30 p.m. Grand Ballroom East, New York Hilton.

Beicken: It is with special pleasure that I welcome you to this workshop *Kafka: The Writer's Writer* with which we celebrate the centenary of Kafka's birth in 1883, and I am particularly pleased to be able to present to you on this occasion the distinguished Argentine author and living legend of modern world literature, Jorge Luis Borges . . . Borges, born into the Kafka generation of the 1880's and 1890's, is probably one of the few early contemporary readers of Kafka still with us today. Living in Switzerland during World War I and having taught himself German with the poetry of Heine, Borges followed the literary scene in Germany at that time, notably the rise of German Expressionist literature. Keenly observing the development of Expressionist poetry, above all the works of Johannes R. Becher, Alfred Mombert, Wilhelm Klemm, August Stramm and others, Borges came across some of the small prose pieces of Kafka published in literary magazines, few pieces indeed which yielded only glimpses of an oeuvre which was saved from oblivion by Max Brod after Kafka's untimely death in 1924. Borges remained faithful to his early reception of and fascination with Kafka. In 1938 he edited a volume of Kafka's stories including his own translation of *The Metamorphosis*, and he added a famous preface which tells us as much about Kafka as it does about Borges, the exceptional reader and translator. Borges' biographer, Emir Rodriguez Monegal, has observed that Borges studied and discussed Kafka when he, himself, was about to begin a new career as a story teller in 1938. Borges continued his conversations with Kafka, and it is today that we have the wonderful opportunity to engage in our conversation with Borges about Kafka.

Alastair Reid: I want to briefly say one or two things at the beginning. It is always an honor to have Borges with us, but much more than that it is always a pleasure. We have been very blessed in this city in recent years with Borges' appearances. People have been reading Borges extensively, in fact, as I said in a similar regard not long ago, not to have read Borges has become the literary equivalent of being a virgin. We have read Borges, we read Borges all the time, and two or three times a year we are lucky enough on these occasions to have Borges with us to talk to us, and the presence of Borges is a very affecting one as is the reading of Borges. For instance, I discovered after one reads a story of Borges, perfectly ordinary events take on an odd significance. One cannot, say, miss a train with impunity without it becoming ominous. Now, one of Borges' most famous essays, much celebrated and much used by critics, I think for wrongful ends, is an essay that he wrote, "Kafka and his Precursors." And he suggests an idea that is very extraordinary there, that, in fact, each writer creates his own precursors and that because we have Kafka we look on the paradox of Zeno, on the manuscript of Han Yu, a poem of Browning, a poem of Lord Dunsany, and see foreshadowings of what Kafka is. Thus Kafka created his own precursors, and so we talk of things as 'Kafkaesque' that long preceded Kafka. This has been seized on. And we can say that things become 'Borgean.' In many ways, Borges has created his own precursors, one of whom is Kafka. [laughter]

Borges is going to talk about Kafka, and then we'll have a conversation followed by your questions.

I remember that Camus wrote of Kafka that the whole art of Kafka consisted in making his reader re-read and sending him back to re-read what he thought he had read. So is Borges. Borges has said once that there are only five or six metaphors and that one rewrites them all the time. Borges, would you like to speak of Kafka?

Borges: I said in a paper that I recorded more or less this way:

All things are given to all men, all things, the sun, the moon, the common stars, the earth, oblivion, memory, friendship, books, that long dream we call the history of mankind, bereavement, betrayals, the kingdom, the power and the glory are given to the writer. And his curious task is to weave those things into dreams, into words, into *cadences*, sometimes into metaphors, and also into fables.

Now, the writer, I think, is not allowed to speak outright. He should return things in a different way. Because if he speaks outright, then he is merely a journalist or a spokesman or a politician which would be very sad, of course;

but what would be quite good, is a *historian*. Now, in the case of any major writer we have to make allowances all the time . . . In many cases you have to take the periods into account: for example, Sir Thomas Browne, a writer of the seventeenth century; then, when we talk about Walt Whitman we have to remember the American dream of democracy and so on.

But in the case of Kafka we find a very strange and a very beautiful difference: we know that Kafka was an Austrian Jew. He thought of himself as German born in America, of course. We know that he lived through that very awful experience of the First World War. And we know that he wrote in the heyday of the Expressionists when people were attempting all sorts of experiments with language, for example, Johannes R. Becher who has just been mentioned. Other examples, not German, are William Butler Yeats and James Joyce.

Well, in the case of any writer you have to make allowances, you have to think this was written in such and such a period. But in the case of classic writers and that goes for all classic writers, you are allowed to forget the period. Of course, Kafka was to suffer greatly, unhappiness which he turned into poetry.

Now, many writers today write hinting of a history of literature, I mean, they write rather to be analyzed than to be read. The reader follows the history of literature. I suppose that was James Joyce's great mistake. He did not write in order to be read or judged, he wrote in order to be famous, to be analyzed. I mean, he wanted his readers, here I quote a very fine line and metaphor from John Keats, "to unweave the rainbow." I suppose when John Keats said, "a thing of beauty is a joy forever," he did not mean that the thing of beauty should wear out; he thought of beauty as timeless.

Now, in the case of Kafka, I think we may safely prophesy that he will be famous let's say when a hundred years are over, because we don't have to think of the circumstances. I suppose, when I read—I prefer the stories to the novels—when I read the story about the building of the great wall of China, when I read that story Odradek ("Troubles of a Householder," "Cares of a Family Man"), then those things are accepted by my imagination as easily as very famous texts, such as the Arabian Nights which were invented in India, rewritten in Persia, originally compiled in Egypt, one reads and accepts them.

Now, in the case of Grimm's fairy tales, I think they are accepted by the imagination, the imagination of children. In the case of Kafka, I think that we accept all his work. His opinions hardly concern us. Well, if I may speak for myself, I try not to meddle with what I write. I want my opinions to be left outside. A dream is a unity ...

In the case of Kafka, if we read him we are dreaming with him; his dreams, of course, are nightmares. They are not nightmares to be found in a single sentence or a single page; they are spread all over the book so to say. I remember, the first thing I read was a short piece of Kafka's in the magazine *Die Aktion*; the editor was Franz Pfemfert, I remember. Well, all the rest of the names, Wilhelm Klemm, Johannes R. Becher, and so on, had been doing adventures in language; well, Kafka wrote in his own quiet style. And I said, how on earth did one publish this, I could faintly understand him, of course. And then afterwards I found out that he was in the right, that Kafka was in the right. But the fact that we think of Kafka as being timeless, is a good omen. We hardly know what the future will think of us. But when people will mention twentieth century writers, they will mention a few names only. We hardly know who will be famous. But it is quite safe to say, especially since I am here at this time, that Kafka will be famous. ...

As to the opinions of Kafka, I suppose he thought the universe a secret cosmos, a cosmos indifferent and hostile to man and he wanted to find a place in that cosmos. Now, personally, I never felt that way. I mean, whether there is a cosmos or not, there is a yearning. I decided to be an ethical man; I tried to be Kafka. And there, of course, I failed. I went on being Borges.

Reid: Borges, you, after all, translated Kafka. You translated *The Metamorphosis*. What was the experience of translating Kafka like?

Borges: I was full of envy. I would have liked to have written the text. I was chuck full of envy. Yes. [laughter]

Reid: Did he prove difficult to translate?

Borges: No, I don't think so, because, after all, he writes in a crystal clear style and does not weave metaphors, I mean, he avoids purple patches quite easily. Of course, Spanish is a different language. In German and in English you can coin words. Not in Spanish, it seems very artificial ...

I was sent to the German language by Carlyle. Carlyle fell in love with Germany and he wrote a number of very fine essays on Richter (Jean Paul), on the *Nibelungenlied*, on Schiller, on Goethe, and above all that wonderful essay on Novalis. I wanted to read Schopenhauer's *Die Welt als Wille und Vorstellung*—the English translation *The World as Will and Idea* is not quite right, idea is not the same as "Vorstellung," maybe appearance is better—and I learned German by reading Heine's *Buch der Lieder* ...

All things have changed since Kafka. Things are read in a different way
. . . I think that anybody who writes now stands in debt to Kafka. I do my
best to keep on being a wordly reader of our common master Franz Kafka.

Reid: Borges, did you feel akin to Kafka when you read him first?

Borges: No, it took me some time, very sensibly, quite some time, but
then I wrote two stories and there I played with being close to Kafka, minor
stories, "The Library of Babel" and "The Lottery in Babylon"; but I went
on being Borges, I couldn't do it. But now and then, when a page of mine
comes out as it should, then I imitate Kafka, really.

Reid: You also wrote parables.

Borges: Yes, I suppose, I owe that to Kafka and also to a quite forgotten
book, to the fables posthumously published, of Robert Louis Stevenson.

Reid: How is Kafka in Spanish? Do you think the Spanish language fits
Kafka or Kafka fits the Spanish language?

Borges: I think that, very happily for us, all languages fit Kafka. That's
the reason for my being here. Let's see, for a classic the words of a language
are not a cold thing. In *Amerika* you have the idea of a factory heaven . . . In
the case of Kafka, you think of heaven being such a factory, of happiness as
being such a factory, that is different. Then you have the other two novels
with the same plot; of course, that kind of book should be endless, see; the
whole scheme of events or postponing events. Somehow Kafka has to work
in an end to feel satisfied with the results. But I think the best things Kafka
ever wrote were his tales. There's a wonderful English translation by Edwin
Muir. I have read the German text and the English text and they seem to go
together insofar as language can replace another language; of course, it can't
really . . .

Reid: Borges, coming back to Kafka for a moment.

Borges: For quite a moment, for all time.

Reid: In your celebrated essay on "Kafka and His Precursors." . . .

Borges: I wonder what I said there, I have forgotten about it. . . .

Reid: I think you'll recall. . . .

Borges: Something about forerunners, and a reception. . . .

Reid: Did this notion that a writer that we read now creates his own forerunners, did that occur to you when you were reading Kafka? Or had it always
been around?

Borges: No, I think it was given to me like so many things, like all things by Kafka.

Reid: And it is the notion that Kafka gives us a certain focus, an eye or a way of looking at things with which one looks back on things one had previously read without that focus. This is what a lot of people have written about your work, however.

Borges: Well, there is a reason to enrich what I wrote. It wasn't all that much. I suppose all readers enrich what they read. For example, Shakespeare is a greater writer now after Coleridge, etc. after the time when he wrote. We enrich him all the time. A writer should be enriched. We read more into him, more than the writer intended. I see that my critics are always inventing new stories of mine far better than the original ones that I wrote . . .

QUESTIONS FROM THE AUDIENCE

Reid: Here is a question. Do you think Kafka has affected the detective novel? Would you comment on that? Who are your favorite detective writers?

Borges: No, I think they came before Kafka, they were forerunners. I think of Edgar Allan Poe, Chesterton, Wilkie Collins, and then quite a known writer, Eden Phillpotts.

I wrote a detective story, in a sense out of Kafka; it was called "Death and the Compass." When it was finished, I felt it was like Kafka, I hope so.

Reid: Here is a question that is very practical. Which poem by Browning makes him a precursor of Kafka?

Borges: When I wrote that, I was thinking of a poem "How it Strikes a Contemporary."

Reid: Here is a question. Oh, I think I am not quite sure that I understand it. Here is another question: Do you think a quiet style is essential to greatness in this century?

Borges: No, because so many fine writers are horribly quiet writers, William Butler Yeats, for example, Carl Sandburg, a very loud poet and quite a good poet, I should say. Of course, I do my best to be quiet, I am not a loud man by any means. Kafka was quiet all the time, quiet and kind and terrifying.

Reid: Apropos, here is a question. Considering how important Kafka is today, why do you think he did not wish for us to see his work?

Borges: Yes, he asked Brod to destroy it. But he knew he wouldn't destroy it. I think Kafka wanted it to be known, that he knew that the work was imperfect, he wanted it to be published, not out of concern for himself; he left his great poem to his friends and said to destroy it. But he knew they wouldn't. A man must destroy his own work or he doesn't . . . He knew that his work would be published. He knew Max Brod, and Max Brod understood. They were friends.

Reid: Do you think he was sure that it would be kept and preserved?
Borges: I met Kafka's ghost last night and he said so.

Reid: What do you think about Kafka's *Metamorphosis*?
Borges: I don't think it is his best story. The title is "The Change." In German it is "Die Verwandlung." And that means "The Change."

Beicken: The transformation.
Borges: Transformation, of course.

Reid: Here is quite a rude question: Did you ever, like Kafka, want to burn your manuscripts?
Borges: I should have done so, but I am afraid I printed them, of course. No, I destroyed many books of mine. Before I published my first book I destroyed three manuscripts. My first book came out in 1923, I was twenty-four at that time. I destroyed three books before that one. Because my father told me: 'Only write when you feel an inner need to do so. Re-write as often as you can.' And one more: 'Don't rush into print.' And yet I rushed into print at the age of twenty-four with that first book. One or two poems can be found in there, the rest is sheer stuff of nonsense, I should say.

Reid: Have you continued to be interested in translation?
Borges: I translated Faulkner's *The Wild Palms*, and then a piece of André Gide. I and my mother translated together. She did Virginia Woolf's *A Room of One's Own*. She also translated a very fine story by a writer called Vincent Benét from a book called *Tales Before Midnight*, a very fine book. I wonder what became of him, whether he still lives or not. Vincent Benét, *Tales Before Midnight*. "Before" makes it more uncanny than Tales at Midnight or Tales After Midnight. "Before" is better.

Reid: Borges, you learned German in Switzerland.
Borges: Yes, in Geneva. Yes, I taught myself German. Not Schweizer-deutsch, I am afraid to say.

Reid: You wrote a poem in *La Rosa Profunda* to the German language.
Borges: Yes.

Reid: What is your connection to the German language?
Borges: I think it is one of the most beautiful of languages except when spoken by Germans, somehow I can't stand it. A beautiful language, like all languages perhaps, when spoken by foreigners.

Reid: How about your connection to the English language?
Borges: The English language is essential to me. [After a long explanation, Borges, digressing into Icelandic, concludes with the Lord's Prayer in Anglo-Saxon.]

Reid: Borges, we thank you and we honor you.

Jorge Luis Borges: An Interview

Clark M. Zlotchew / 1984

From *Voices of the River Plate*, 1984, pp. 23–39. Reprinted by permission. Originally published in *American Poetry Review*.

Zlotchew: What happened to you a long time ago on the Uruguay/Brazil border, in Sant'Ana do Livramento?

Borges: It was the time I saw a man killed, the only time in my life I saw a man killed. It didn't impress me at the time; it impressed me later. The thing grew larger in my memory. Imagine: seeing a man killed.

Zlotchew: Did you actually *see* it?

Borges: Well, maybe I didn't (laughter). We are liars.

Zlotchew: No, no. I didn't mean to imply. . . . I just wanted to know if you were close enough to see it with your own eyes, or if you were only in the same room, or close, when it happened.

Borges: I think so. In any event, that morning. . . . It was in a bar, just a few feet away. And there was this black man, who was the bodyguard of the Governor's son. . . . And this cattle drover came in, a Uruguayan. . . . I think he was drunk, really drunk. He had no reason to kill him, but he killed him. He fired twice.

Zlotchew: I hadn't ever heard those details before.

Borges: Well, that's because time passes and I've embellished it so that I wouldn't be boring. (laughter).

Zlotchew: And the other people. . . .

Borges: Well, the other people have luckily all died and cannot contradict me. They were Enrique Amorim, who was married to a cousin of mine, and Márquez Miranda, an archaeologist. . . . An archeologist in the Argentine Republic has absolutely nothing to investigate. Well, it's an easy job, isn't it?

Zlotchew: Has that experience influenced your fiction?

Borges: I would have to think so. That and what I've read. I believe it was Emerson who said, "Poetry springs from poetry" or "Poetry is born of poetry." I don't remember exactly. . . . Reading is very important. And Alonso Quixano, who became Don Quixote, knew something about that.

Because if one reads *Don Quixote*, the only thing that happened to him was that he read *Amadis of Gaul*, *Tirant lo Blanc*, *Palmerin of England*, and other "books of chivalry," about knights in shining armor. . . .

Zlotchew: The comic books of the time.
Borges: Right. Of course.

Zlotchew: I have another question that. . . .
Borges: Only one?

Zlotchew: Well, one at a time. Last year I read in an Argentine newspaper that you mentioned you had once been in love with Cecilia Ingenieros. . . .
Borges: Yes, that's true.

Zlotchew: But the reporter didn't pursue it. Would you like to talk about that?
Borges: Well, she just became bored and left me. And with good reason, I'm sure. I haven't seen her for a long time. I mean now. . . . Now she's married, she has her children. Why not say that at one time we were sweethearts, why not? And that I remember her with great affection. I think it's all right to say this, isn't it? The better man won. Yes, I can say it now, but at that time, no. She broke off the relationship in a very honorable way. She asked me to meet her at a tearoom that's on Maipú and Córdoba [The St. James]. I hadn't spoken to her for some time and I thought "how strange that she called me," and I was feeling very happy, and then she said to me, "I want to tell you something you're going to hear anyway, but I want you to hear it first from my lips: I've become engaged and I'm going to be married." So I congratulated her, and that was that. A charming woman. She had been a student of. . . . She could have been a dancer with Martha Graham, an American. Well, she studied under Martha Graham in New York for a year. I think it was in the Village. Well, let's be indiscreet and talk about this. Bygones.

Zlotchew: You've said that Greta Garbo had a certain something that was very attractive. Exactly what was it about Garbo that was so attractive?
Borges: Ah, Greta Garbo: the only person in the world, Greta Garbo. Unique. I was in love with Katharine Hepburn too, and with an actress who has been forgotten, Miriam Hopkins. We all were in love with her, all those in my generation. She was really beautiful. And with Evelyn Brent, who worked with George Bancroft in *Prince of Gangsters*. And in *Dragnet*, *Show-*

down, etc. We were all in love with Miriam Hopkins, with Greta Garbo, with Katharine Hepburn, and a few others.

Zlotchew: The BBC made a film about your life. . . .
Borges: It was very good. Very good. Here [in Argentina] they wouldn't have. . . . I wasn't very well-liked. It couldn't have been made here. But the film was made in Paris in the hotel "L'Hôtel," which is the hotel that used to be called the Hôtel D'Alsace, in which Oscar Wilde died in the last year of the last century. . . . in 1900. I was going to say it was one year earlier, 1899, but it was in 1900. Part of it was filmed in the basement—very strange—the circular basement of the hotel. It was a cylinder, quite large, and the walls were lined with mirrors. So, in some way or other, the basement was infinite. And later it was filmed on some ranch in Uruguay, near the town of Colonia, with Uruguayan actors, with other scenes in Montevideo, on that huge hill across from the city itself, Montevideo Heights. The film is the story of my life and I took part in it. María Kodama appears in it too. And there are several scenes taken from my short stories. For example, in the movie I speak with a boy of twelve or thirteen who wears glasses—he represents my childhood, and this scene comes from my short story, "The Other"—and then I converse with an even younger child, like in my story. Well, it's a very serious film, a very good film.

Zlotchew: Can this film be seen?
Borges: You mean here in Buenos Aires?

Zlotchew: Anywhere.
Borges: Probably. Maybe at the municipality you can check it. . . . There was this Mr. David. . . . I don't remember the last name. Well, anyway. . . .

Zlotchew: At various times, you've showed some antipathy to the central region of Spain, to Castile. Why?
Borges: Well, yes, Castile specifically, not Spain in general. I'm not talking about Galicia, about Catalonia, about Andalusia, which are admirable lands—almost countries—but Castile. In general, the average Spaniard is a good man, the best in the world, ethically, but Spanish literature has not impressed me particularly, with certain exceptions: Cervantes's *Don Quixote*, Fray Luis de Léon. . . . But Castile. . . . Castile is where those *conquistadores* came from, as well as all those military men, idiotic military men, fanatic Catholics, all of whom have put their mark on our countries [Hispanic

America]. Militarism, fanaticism in religion, intransigence. . . . All from Castile. It's the source of all our militarism, dictatorships. . . .

Zlotchew: Speaking of militarism, when the military junta overthrew Perón's widow and took over the government of Argentina in 1976, you were glad. . . .

Borges: Well, yes. But, how was I to know what they were going to do later before they did it? And even afterward. . . . We didn't know about the disappearances, torture, murder here because there was total censorship. But, yes, I was mistaken.

Zlotchew: The Chilean dictator, General Pinochet, presented you with a decoration. . . .

Borges: No, no, no. There was no decoration. I had gone to the University of Chile where I was awarded the title of *doctor honoris causa*, and while I was in Santiago to receive that honorary doctorate, the President invited me to come for dinner. Nothing more than to come for dinner. And, well, since I was there in Santiago, I couldn't refuse, could I?

Zlotchew: Is anarchism a viable form of society?

Borges: I think we'd have to wait some 200 years—a very short time, right?—of having no government, having no police force, of being a kind of people different from what we are now. But for the moment—this is not the Soviet Union—government is a necessary evil. And now, I think that in this country we have a certain right to hope, nothing more than to hope. But, I believe that after five years or so. . . . Well, after a long convalescence, shall we say, after so many evils. . . . Perónism, terrorism, the military junta, the ones referred to as the "disappeared," kidnappings, torture, death, and then. . . . This "shortens the meaning of this world," doesn't it? But, I hope and expect that. . . . Anyway, it's a real joy to have Alfonsín [as president], even though I'm not a member of the Radical Party [of Alfonsín].

Zlotchew: Might there be any mutual influences between your early poetry and the tango lyrics that appear in the same era?

Borges: Let's hope not, eh? Because they're so bad (laughter). I don't think so, not the tango. The milonga, yes. I have written a book of milonga lyrics. The milonga is of the people; the tango never was. You know, the instruments used in the tango were the piano, the flute and the violin. If the tango were of the people, the instrument would have been the guitar, as it is in the milonga. Speaking of the guitar, let's get into etymological territory a bit. The origin of the word *guitar* is the word *zyther*. It's almost the same word. Whether you say [in Spanish] *guitarra* or *cítara*, the vowels are exactly the same, aren't they? It seems that string instruments were invented somewhere in Central Asia, and from these string instruments developed the harp, the violin, the zyther, the guitar. But, the guitar has its origins in the word *zyther*, that is, *kithara* in Greek. Just a little etymological curiosity for you. And you, where are you from?

Zlotchew: I was born in New Jersey, but I teach in the State of New York, near Buffalo.

Borges: I'm acquainted with Buffalo. I've been to Niagara Falls. And New Jersey. It's the west side of New York City, isn't it?

Zlotchew: It's west of the city of New York, across the Hudson River.

Borges: Ah, yes, of course. The Hudson. . . . You know, Mississippi means "Father of Waters," something like our great water falls, Iguazú, which means "The Big Water."

Zlotchew: Well, to get back to the tango and the milonga: apart from the musical instruments, what is the difference in the music itself between the tango and the milonga?

Borges: The milonga is a kind of brave, wild music. It's a merry music, while the tango is very sentimental, "respectable" (in the worst sense of the word) music. Yes, and the milonga [Borges means to say *tango*] was never the music of the people. One proof of this is that they never danced the tango in the tenement buildings here. And the tenements were where you could find the representative people of Buenos Aires. They never danced the tango there. Milonga, yes; tango, no. No, the tango would be the music of the bawdy house, of the brothel. And the people rejected it, naturally. But I've seen it danced by men dancing together. Because no woman would be seen dancing the tango, since it was a dance associated with prostitution. But the two dances [tango and milonga] are African: milonga, tango, aren't they? All that *ongo, onga, ongo*, as in Congo.

Zlotchew: Your short story, "The Intruder". . . . Why have you said you consider it the best story you've written?

Borges: No, I don't think so. And listen, I want to tell you to . . . to avoid a frightful film that's been made of it. Now, they've injected into the story two elements which were not in my story, which have nothing at all to do with me. These elements are: incest and homosexuality. Oh, yes. And sodomy. Well now, this gentleman [the director], Christensen, I think his name is, an unworthy descendant of his Viking ancestors, has introduced homosexuality, incest and sodomy into my story. And ridiculous scenes. . . . For example, in my story I say that these two brothers share the same woman, but it's understood that I meant *successively*, not simultaneously. But Christensen has this scene—for comic effect—in which there is an actress standing there, undressed, and then one gentleman advances toward her from the left, while another advances from the right, and they perform a pretty uncomfortable form of coitus, I'd say. But this is done, I imagine, for comic effect.

Zlotchew: You really think it's for comic effect?

Borges: I suppose so. If not, what kind of effect could it have? Two gentleman who are naked, a naked lady, and these gentlemen advancing from both sides. . . . It's madness. And it's not my story. It's something they've added. But what makes me angry is that what it says is "The Intruder, by Jorge Luis Borges." Look, if you were to tell me, "I'm going to respect the original text," I would say, "No, a film is not going to respect the text. The text is just a point of departure for a film. If you want. . . . Do whatever you wish with the film, but if a great many new things occur to you, don't mention my name. Change the title." But there it is with the title of my story, and with my name. And with incest, homosexuality, and sodomy. Charming.

Zlotchew: What do you remember of Rafael Cansinos-Assens?

Borges: As far as I am concerned, he is one of the people who have impressed me most in my life. I don't know if, simply by reading his books, you would feel the same way. But conversation with him was an extraordinary experience. That man once said, for example, . . . Instead of saying, "I'm acquainted with. . . . I know fourteen languages," he said, "I am able to salute the stars in fourteen languages, classical and modern." He translated an entire work of Galsworthy's and he translated part of De Quincey. Then he translated the novel *L'Affaire* by Henri Barbusse, as well as others from French. And then he made a direct translation of the book *The Thousand and One Nights* from Arabic. He was of Jewish origin, as I am, and he made an anthology of the Talmud. And then he had translated from the Greek the work of Julian the Apostate. And he knew Latin. And the first time I met him, we spoke all night long of Thomas De Quincey. Cansinos-Assens had been born in Seville but was living in Madrid. He wrote a very beautiful poem about the sea, and I congratulated him on it. "Yes," he said, "It's a

beautiful poem on the sea. I hope to have a look at the sea some day." He
had never laid eyes on the sea!

Zlotchew: You just mentioned that you are of Jewish origin, and I've seen
you refer to the fact that your mother's maiden name, Acevedo, is a Portuguese-Jewish name. How do you know this?

Borges: Well, it's curious. . . . You know, one day Cansinos-Assens came
across his family's name while looking through the archives of the Inquisi-
tion. He found the name Cansinos, that is. And from that time on, he decided
he was a Jew, descended from those forcibly converted to Catholicism. All
this led him to the study of Hebrew. And he wrote a book of what might be
called erotic psalms called *El candelabro de los siete brazos* [*The Seven-
Branched Candelabrum*], referring, of course, to the menorah. Well, anyway,
in my case, there is a very good book called *Rosas y su tiempo* [*Rosas and
His Times*]. And in that book there is a list of family names referring to the
Buenos Aires of the period. And they were Portuguese Jews. Well, I believe
the first one is Ocampo. And that's why some people in Buenos Aires high
society refer to Victoria Ocampo as a "Jewish upstart" [laughter], right? Well
these Portuguese-Jewish families had names like Ocampo; Pineiro—a name
in my family—; Acevedo, my mother's maiden name; Sanz-Valente and, let's
see. . . . What other names are there? Well, quite a few old names of the old
families of Buenos Aires: Portuguese Jews. Now, the name Borges itself it
not Jewish. Borges is the same as Burgess in English; it means "bourgeois,"
man of the *burg*, the town, as in Edinburgh, Hamburg, Rothenburg, Burgos
in Spain, so that. . . . How strange, my first name means "country man,"
because Jorge ["George" in English] means "man of the soil," you know,
Virgil's *Georgics*, and geography is the study of the earth. Geology, the
stones of the earth. Well. . . . Geometry, measuring the earth. . . . So that my
first name comes out to be something like "farmer," doesn't it? Of course.
And my last name means the opposite; it means "townsman," bourgeois. . . .

Zlotchew: A paradox.

Borges: Yes. When the Communists say that I am bourgeois, I say, "No, I
am not bourgeois [*burgués* in Spanish]; I am Borges." One day on Viamonte
[Street]. . . . I don't know if you know this, but Viamonte used to be the red-
light district at one time. But that was Viamonte out toward El Bajo, for
example, between. . . . Well, between San Martin and what used to be called
the Paseo de Julio, which is now called Alem. Anyway, it was an area of
brothels. And later, the red-light district was at Lavalle and Junín, and it is

there that the tango is supposed to have been invented. Except that it was invented in [the city of] Rosario, and in Montevideo too. It's a matter of dispute as to where the tango was invented. But, what's the difference, right? Speaking about neighborhoods of crime and prostitution, I once asked a police chief, "Which is the most dangerous district of Buenos Aires?", and he said, "I think it's the corner of Florida and Corrientes" [laughter]. You see, because that's where most crimes are committed, because of all those high-priced stores. And he said, "I think the most dangerous district is at Florida and Corrientes." It's really terrible, the high-priced luxury items sold there, when you think of the poverty of people here nowadays. It's terrible. Years of mismanagement, the military men. . . . They may say that [President] Alfonsín is mediocre, but at least he's honest, even though it may seem a contradiction in terms to call someone an honest politician.

Zlotchew: You wrote an essay concerning Shih Huang Ti, the so-called "first Emperor of China". . . .

Borges: Yes, "The Wall and the Books." And Silvina Ocampo told me I had created a new genre with that essay, but the idea came from Herbert Allen Giles' *History of China* which he translated from Chuang Tzu. And Oscar Wilde once commented on that first translation of Chuang Tzu. Now, Chuang Tzu dates back, I believe, to the fifth or sixth century before Christ. So, Wilde was talking about the book and said, "I believe that this translation, published 2,600 years after the writing of the original book, is decidedly premature."

Zlotchew: Premature?

Borges: Yes, premature. You see, Oscar Wilde was a very profound man. I think he was embarrassed by his own profundity. And he had quite an original sense of humor. He was a homosexual, you know. Now, there are many people who pretend to be homosexual. Well, he was advising an acquaintance of his, and he said, "It is not necessary to say that one is homosexual; it is necessary to say that one is *not* homosexual, in order to call attention to oneself." [laughter]. You could take it for granted. [laughter].

Zlotchew: Well, to come back to your essay, "The Wall and the Books". . . .

Borges: I wish I could recall it. I don't re-read my own work. You will not find a single book of mine in this house. And there is no book written about me here, because I try to keep the library free of those things. There are books on Emerson, Bernard Shaw, or Coleridge, or Wordsworth. . . .

Zlotchew: In that essay, the Emperor of China destroys history, destroys all the books written before he became Emperor. . . .

Borges: Well, because he wanted to destroy the past. In this way, history begins with him.

Zlotchew: . . . and, at the same time, orders the construction of the Great Wall.

Borges: In order to create a sort of magical space, right?

Zlotchew: It seems to me that all that has some similarity with what you have done, because you destroy certain works that you had written previously, like *Inquisiciones*. . . .

Borges: And with good reason. I believe that. . . . William Butler Yeats says, "It is myself that I remake." When he corrects the past, he is correcting himself, since the past is so, . . . well, so plastic.

Zlotchew: When you wrote that essay, you didn't think there was any resemblance between you and Shih Huang Ti?

Borges: Certainly not, good heavens. I haven't burned any books, except my own, which don't count, nor have I built any walls either. No, no.

Zlotchew: You have built the rest of your literary work, which would be equivalent to the wall, wouldn't it? In the sense that your later work, like the wall, is what brings you glory, while what you burn, as you point out, would be what accuses you. . . .

Borges: That's not the way it is at all. What I write is not as important as that Wall. It's nothing, rough drafts. . . .

Zlotchew: Others don't agree with you on that.

Borges: Yes, but I do. Besides, there are a great many Swedish people who do agree with me: those who belong to the admirable Swedish Academy. And very sensible men they are. Very sensible, yes. Tell me, where are you from?

Zlotchew: From New Jersey, but I live in Fredonia, south of Buffalo.

Borges: I've taught several courses of Argentine literature in the United States. The first was at Harvard, "English Masters." I received the honorary doctorate at Harvard. Then I taught another course in a small town called East Lansing, Michigan. Then another one in Bloomington, in Indiana. And. . . . There's another place. . . .

Zlotchew: Austin, Texas.

Borges: Of course, the first and most memorable! And that was with my mother. I discovered that America in 1961. And my mother made a terrible *faux pas* there. There were two statues there. And they told my mother, "This is the statue of Washington. . . ." "Yes," said my mother, "and the other one is of Lincoln." And everyone looked at her in horror, because speaking of Lincoln in Texas. . . . Well, the Civil War, the Confederacy. . . . And how my mother must have felt. . . . You know, the American Civil War was the greatest war of the nineteenth century. Many more people died in that war than in the Napoleonic wars, than in the wars of Bismark. . . . Well, than in the Wars of Independence down here. Gettysburg lasted for three days. The battles down here were skirmishes [in comparison]. Now, the battle of Junín, in which my grandfather took part, lasted three quarters of an hour. It was fought with saber and lance. Not a shot was fired. They were skirmishes. But Gettysburg lasted three days. Well, and Waterloo, one single day. And fewer people died at Waterloo than at Gettysburg.

Zlotchew: Could it be that the Spaniards had less interest in retaining these territories of South America than the Confederacy had in being independent of the Union, than the Northerners had in keeping the South in the Union?

Borges: Yes. The Spanish were poor soldiers down here, because the Guarani Indians, led by the Jesuits, easily defeated the Spanish in previous wars. Those Indians were better soldiers than the Spanish or the Portuguese.

Zlotchew: In your short story, "The Secret Miracle," Jaroslav Hládik. . . .

Borges: Oh, yes, I remember. . . . Well, it's the idea that. . . . It's a quite ancient idea, the idea of. . . . that time can be shortened, right? Or that it can be lengthened. Then, the time of this story is lengthened, isn't it?

Zlotchew: Yes. You're playing with time, aren't you?

Borges: Yes, that's it.

Zlotchew: But what I wanted to ask you. . . . Hládik had a dream. I don't know if you remember it. . . .

Borges: No.

Zlotchew: In the dream. . . .

Borges: Oh, of course. He dreamed of finding God in a map. Or wasn't that it?

Zlotchew: Yes. That was the second dream in the story.

Borges: Well, I write a story one single time, and you have read it many times, isn't that so? In that way, the story is more yours than it is mine. You've given more time to it than I have. It's curious, I write them and I don't re-read them. That reminds me of a conversation I had with the great Mexican writer, Alfonso Reyes. He was very kind to me. I used to go to the Mexican Embassy every Sunday to have dinner with him [when he was the Mexican Ambassador to Argentina]. And don Alfonso would be there, his wife, his son and I. And we would speak about English literature, actually. Well, he once said to me, "Why do we publish books?" "Yes," I said, "I often ask myself the same question. Why on earth?" He said, "I think I've found the solution." "And what is it?," I asked. "We publish books," he said, "in order to avoid spending our whole lives correcting the errors." And I agree. If one publishes a book, he can then go on to other things.

Zlotchew: That reminds me. . . .

Borges: Since everything I publish is a rough draft, because every text is correctible. Indefinitely.

Zlotchew: Until it's published.

Borges: Now then, when one publishes, he resigns himself to the text in the published form. If a second edition comes out, of course, he'll try to correct it.

Zlotchew: That reminds me. . . . That idea of publishing in order to be able to forget the book, to go on to other things, is parallel, I believe, to something else you said somewhere, about the reason some men make love to a woman: in order to be able to forget her. Do you see the parallel?

Borges: Yes. But, naturally, if the woman doesn't return the man's love, if the man's love is unrequited, he continues to think of her. But if she pays him some attention. . . . Yes, the ideas are parallel, of course.

Zlotchew: To get back to "The Secret Miracle," in the first dream. . . .

Borges: But, there is only one dream. . . .

Zlotchew: No, the first dream isn't the one with the map of India. It's the one in which Hladík is running through "a rainy desert," trying to arrive in time for his move in a chess game.

Borges: Oh, of course. Now I remember. Yes, Yes.

Zlotchew: And you describe the game as being played, not by two individuals, but by two great families. And Hladík, in the dream, has forgotten the rules of chess.

Borges: Ah, yes, yes. Yes, but I'm not sure if it [the chess dream] was in that story ["The Secret Miracle"].

Zlotchew: Yes, "The Secret Miracle" begins with this dream. The very first sentence of the story is the first sentence that describes this dream.

Borges: Yes, you're right. There are different generations, and each individual of a particular generation makes one move. So that. . . . Yes, of course. . . . I put that dream in because it is the opposite of the main plot. First we have one game of chess, and several generations. And then, the writing of a drama which lasts only one minute. That's why I put it in the story. To obtain that contrast between. . . . the whole idea besides a game that lasts longer than many generations. Yes. That's exactly it. But, are you absolutely sure that it's from the same story?

Zlotchew: Oh, yes. "The Secret Miracle" begins with that dream.

Borges: Ah, yes. It has to be from the same story, of course. It has to be from the same one, because if not. . . .

Zlotchew: Hladik is the one who dreams it.

Borges: Yes, yes, yes. It takes place in Prague. I mentioned the German [the fictional Julius Rothe], so he could have read Schopenhauer, Richter, Novalis, Schiller. . . . Yes.

Zlotchew: In addition to the contrast between the handling of time in the dream and its function in the story, is it possible to think of the dream chess game as symbolic of war, nation against nation, rather than individual against individual?

Borges: Yes, if you like. Yes. Perhaps war is less interesting than a game of chess.

Zlotchew: And why do you say they were playing for a prize, but that no one could remember what the prize was, except that it was "enormous and perhaps infinite"?

Borges: Well, because it comes out better if no one any longer knows what it is. It comes out better. You know, people play chess for nothing, usually. I mean, they don't play for money. Like in [the card game of] truco, for example. But in poker, yes, you play for hard cash, don't you?

Zlotchew: Yes.

Borges: Hard cash, yes. But not truco, no. The proof of this is that no one says, "I won so much at truco." People say, "I beat so-and-so." So it's something very personal. Whether one plays for pieces of candy or for money, that doesn't matter, no.

Zlotchew: I know that truco is a card game, but I don't know how it's played.

Borges: Well, there are several ways to play it. There is a very complicated form popular in Montevideo called "truco up to two." And then there is what is called "blind truco," which is a Buenos Aires form of truco, the kind of truco I know how to play. It's played with three cards. Now, in poker, for example, you have to keep playing. But in truco, it's understood that a good player, . . . well, he stops playing, he tells a story, tells some jokes, and tries to irritate his opponent that way. And then, when you have a *flower.* . . . Well, *flower* means three cards of the same suit, right? And you announce that you have a *flower* in verse, actually. And that verse could be, for instance, "In the gardens of Diana, I found a rosebud in the bower./Keep yourself chaste and pure if you want to be called a *flower.*" Or it might be something bawdy. For example, "Because he was involved with a narrow-hipped woman,/His peter became like the spout of a sprinkling can for *flowers.*" Or you put your cards to one side, for example, and you tell a story. So that anything that might hold the game up. . . . Or else you look at your cards and say, "Good heavens! What a terrible hand!" Now, this could mean that you have good cards and you're trying to conceal the fact, or it could mean you really have terrible cards. Yes, but it's a very slow game, a game for people who have very little to do. It's a game made for killing time. Now poker, if I'm not mistaken, is not for killing time. It goes rapidly, and fooling around is not tolerated. Because poker, I think, was invented by adventurers in the American West, by gold miners who wanted to get rich quickly. But truco is more a pastime than anything else. A more unusual form of truco is fifteen-fifteen. Or twenty-something-or-other. And this game, played by good players, can last from five to twelve hours.

Zlotchew: Do people still play the game of truco?

Borges: No doubt they do. There used to be truco championships at the Paloma Tearoom, on the corner of Santa Fé and Juan B. Justo.

Zlotchew: Are there still championship competitions?

Borges: No. I don't think so. I used to attend with three fellows from the Uruguayan provinces. And [we attended] the chess championships at that café, the Tortoni.

Zlotchew: The detective story, which has labyrinths in time and space, and myths. . . . What is the purpose of all this? Is there a purpose?

Borges: No. I'm a great reader of detective novels, that's all. I met one of them, the one who used to sign himself. . . . Ellery Queen. The other one died, I think.

Zlotchew: Dashiell Hammett?

Borges: No, no. Dashiell Hammett. . . . He was rather a writer of novels of violent action, not of what you might call intellectual detective novels. It was. . . . I know Ellery Queen, but. . . . There were two persons who wrote the Ellery Queen mysteries, but I don't remember their names. One of them died, and I met the other one. It was at a dinner for mystery writers.

Zlotchew: Is it possible that part of the detective narrative's appeal is that the reader receives the impression of being a co-author, in the sense that he solves the mystery himself by the time the author does, and consequently feels a sense of accomplishment? A sense of superiority?

Borges: Superiority. . . . With respect to Dr. Watson, yes, but to Sherlock Holmes, perhaps not, eh? Superior to Father Brown, unlikely, right? Yes. I remember my sister was re-reading *The Moonstone*, a novel by Wilkie Collins, a friend of Dickens. . . . My grandmother heard Dickens in person, because he traveled throughout England, reading two chapters of his novels. And those chapters were "The Trial Scene" from *The Pickwick Papers* and the one about the murder of this girl by Bill Sikes. Well, according to my grandmother, Dickens used to change, not only his accent, the dialect, but his face even looked different when he read the dialogue. When he read the trial scene from Pickwick, in which, I don't know, about from ten to fifteen characters appear, he was our Pickwick, and he was our Topman, and he was. . . . Well, all of them. And he played them admirably. And he would read those two chapters. First, "That Very Grim Murder of Nancy by Bill Sikes." And then the other chapter, "Trial Scene," from Pickwick.

Zlotchew: Are you familiar with the work of [French novelist] Alain Robbe-Grillet?

Borges: Robbe-Grillet . . . ? No, I haven't read him.

Zlotchew: I ask because I think he has been influenced by you.

Borges: You see, I lost my sight, for reading purposes. It was in 1955. But I have done a great deal of re-reading. Someone comes to visit me, and I ask him or her to read to me. Right now I've begun a re-reading in that way of a biography of Emerson by [Van Wyck] Brooks.

Zlotchew: And people read to you?
Borges: And what else can I do? If I can't read, I can't write. The letters overlap. There's no other way. One has to resign oneself. It's easy to become resigned. I'd been losing my sight gradually from the time I was born, so that it has been a slow twilight, a long summer twilight. There was no single dramatic moment when I lost my sight. It's been happening little by little that things have been disappearing from my sight. Like the people in my stories whom I've forgotten. What luck that that has occurred to me!

Zlotchew: What purpose does internal duplication, the story-within-the-story, have in your work?
Borges: I think. . . . Well, since the story is fantastic, the fact that there is another poet present accentuates the fantastic. The poet creating the poet who creates another work. . . . It's an ancient tradition. *The Thousand and One Nights*, for example. Well, the *Quixote*, too. These books with stories inside . . . The Chinese novel. . . . In the Chinese novel there are many dreams and in those dreams there are others. It's an artifice, a device. It's natural, isn't it? Dreams within dreams.

Zlotchew: In what way have you applied the ideas contained in your essay, "El arte narrativo y la magia" ("Narrative Art and Magic")?
Borges: I don't try to apply them. I don't remember the essay very well. Now, I can tell you something that may interest you. The way I write. . . . I receive a very modest revelation, you know? A mild revelation? Yes. But, then, in that mild revelation I receive the beginning and the end of a short story, right? The starting point and the goal. But, what I don't know is what happens in the middle, in between. I have to invent that part. Sometimes I make mistakes, of course. But I always know the beginning and the end. But afterward I go along discovering if this should be written, or if that should be written. Whether it should be in the first person, the third person, in what country, in what era. . . . That is my work. That is my work, and I can make mistakes. So, I try to interfere as little as possible with the revelation, I believe, no? I believe the author is actually one who receives. The idea of the muse. . . . Of course, I'm not saying anything new.

Zlotchew: The way that Coleridge received in a dream the poem, "Kubla Khan," isn't that so?

Borges: Of course, yes. (Here Borges recites dramatically the beginning verses of "Kubla Khan"):

> In Xanadu did Kubla Khan
> A stately pleasure-dome decree:
> Where Alph, the sacred river, ran
> Through caverns measureless to man
> Down to a sunless sea.

(Then he skips to the end):

> His flashing eyes, his floating hair!
> Weave a circle round him thrice,
> And close your eyes with holy dread,
> For he on honey-dew hath fed,
> And drunk the milk of Paradise.

Beautiful. I wish I could write like that. My work is mere shavings. I am just an international superstition, which is something, but I don't exist. I'm a pretext, a prop. A mere prop.

Zlotchew: No one agrees with you.

Borges: Borges agrees, said the god [laughter].

Zlotchew: Which Borges: the one who writes or the one who is speaking now?

Borges: Yes, Borges or Borges? Yes, of course. My family names are Portuguese; Borges and Acevedo. And why not. When I was in Brazil—I've been in Sant'Ana do Livramento, in Sao Paulo—I would speak Spanish, and they would speak Portuguese, and we understood each other perfectly. Spanish, Portuguese. . . . A dog latin, nothing more. *Le latin de cuisine.* . . .

Zlotchew: You have said that *El sueño de los héroes* is Adolfo Bioy Casares' best work. Why?

Borges: Absolutely.

Zlotchew: Yes, but why? Can you explain what makes it his best?

Borges: Well, because I've read it.

Zlotchew: But, you've read other works of his too, haven't you?

Borges: When I read Bioy Casares. . . . His stories dealing with love, or with the pursuit of love, come out badly, but his fantastic stories come out well. He told me that one must write every day. And my sister, who recently celebrated her eighty-second birthday, devotes two hours a day to painting or to drawing. And she used to say that one has to versify continually in order to be worthy of a visit from the muse. So that the muse will deign to come, isn't that so? Writing has to become a habit. But since I can't write. . . . Well, I try to fool the secretary, but I can't write personally, because of my vision. So I write off and on when people come to see me, and can write while I dictate.

Zlotchew: What are you writing these days?

Borges: There is a book [I'm working on] with María Kodama, which are notes on travels, and it is generously illustrated with collages of her photographs. I've traveled a great deal, because I've been in Austin, Texas. I've been to the New York Hilton. I've been to East Lansing, and then to Iceland, Japan, England, Scotland, Israel, Switzerland. . . . I was educated in Geneva. I lived for a long time in Geneva, you know. Every time I go to Europe, I make it a point to visit Switzerland. And I've been in France, then in London, and then they awarded me the doctorate at Cambridge, *doctor honoris causa.*

Zlotchew: Are you planning to write more fiction at this time?

Borges: Yes, yes, yes. A book of short stories which will be entitled, *La memoria de Shakespeare [Shakespeare's Memory].* And it refers, not to his memory, but to his fame, yes. The memory he has left us of him. Yes, *Le memoria de Shakespeare.* I'm working on that, and on a book of poetry too. And besides all that, I have to write—good Lord!—I have to write ninety-four prologues for ninety-four books. That would take me at least a hundred years to write, wouldn't it? I'm a very slow writer. There's one on Bernard Shaw, for example, whom I love very much.

Zlotchew: In "Hombre de la esquina rosada" [translated into English as "Streetcorner Man"]. . . .

Borges: A terrible story. Let's not talk about that.

Zlotchew: No, no. . . .

Borges: It's phony. . . .

Zlotchew: There's something about it I'd like to know.

Borges: No, no. It doesn't interest me in the least. I'm ashamed of it, thoroughly ashamed of it. [Norman Thomas] Di Giovanni told me it seemed like an opera, and he was right.

Zlotchew: There's a character in it named "La Lujanera," and, of course, the most obvious reason for the nickname is that she simply comes from the town of Luján in the Province of Buenos Aires. But, is that the reason you called her that, or was there some other reason?

Borges: No, no. Because she's from Luján, which is not far from here. I don't see any other reason there could be.

Zlotchew: Someone has suggested that it is because "la lujanera" is a name for an unlucky card.

Borges: Ah, yes, possibly. I believe I read that in Ascásubi. But I wasn't thinking about that when I gave her the name. It's just that, since everyone had names, this one came along with a nickname. So, instead of So-and-So. . . . Put away Jane or Mary, and she was "La Lujanera." It seems right, doesn't it? I'm just suggesting Luján, which is the name of a town.

Zlotchew: You once said, ". . . I think Conrad and Kipling have demonstrated that a short story—not too short, what we could call, using the English term, a "long short story"—is able to contain everything a novel contains, with less strain on the reader."

Borges: Absolutely!

Zlotchew: You still feel that way?

Borges: Yes. Even though I may not be the one who said it, I agree [laughter]. Yes, I think so. I think I've chosen good examples, so?

Zlotchew: Well, [Enrique] Cadicamo has said that the lyrics of a tango, which has a duration of about three minutes in its performance, can express perfectly well everything that can be expressed in a ninety-minute motion picture. Would you say that this is basically the same idea you express with regard to the short story and the novel?

Borges: Yes. Cadicamo is so bad that anything he says is usually an error, right? Then this is the only thing he's ever done right. Cadicamo is so bad. Everything he has written is so phony. . . . No one uses Lunfardo [Buenos Aires slang], for one thing. It's an entirely artificial dialect, Lunfardo is. Everyone used to tell him, "Don't write, my friend," but he goes on writing. All his friends advised him.

Zlotchew: Why was the Argentine tango so popular in Paris between the two World Wars? Why Paris?

Borges: I don't know. I can't answer that. And if someone asks me to explain my own country, I can't. I don't understand it. Or if I'm asked to explain my own work, even less so. I myself don't know who I am.

Zlotchew: You are the instrument of an archetype that is trying to enter the material world, aren't you?

Borges: Well, yes. That's a good explanation. Walt Whitman said, "I don't know who I am." And Victor Hugo, more prettily:

Je suis un homme voilé par moi même; Dieu seul sait mon vrai nom; I am a man hidden by myself; God alone knows my real name.

Borges on Life and Death
Amelia Barili / 1985

From *The New York Times Book Review*, 13 July 1986, pp. 1, 27–29.
Reprinted by permission.

I met Jorge Luis Borges in 1981, when I returned to Buenos Airés from a job
at the BBC in London and began working for *La Prensa*. He received me
very kindly, remembering that during the 1920's, when he was not well
known, *La Prensa* had been the first newspaper to publish him. Later I returned to see him frequently. Sometimes he would dictate a poem that he had
been composing during a long night of insomnia. After typing it, I would put
it in his desk near his collection of Icelandic sagas, a precious gift from his
father.

Sometimes we would walk to a nearby restaurant, where he would eat
something very simple. Or we would go to a bookstore, searching for yet
another book by Kipling or Conrad in an English edition for friends to read
to him. People would stop to greet him, and he would jokingly tell me they
must have mistaken him for someone else. His fame as a writer seemed to
burden him, and he often regretted that he had to go on living so that Borges
the writer could weave his literary fantasies.

One morning shortly before he left Argentina in November, we spoke
about his recent work, his beliefs, his doubts. I did not know it would be our
last conversation before his death last month in Geneva. We started by discussing one of his latest books, "Los Conjurados" ("The Conspirators"), in
which he calls Geneva "one of my homelands."

Where does your love for Geneva come from?

In a certain manner, I am Swiss; I spent my adolescence in Geneva. We
went to Europe in 1914. We were so ignorant that we did not know that was
the year of the First World War. We were trapped in Geneva. The rest of
Europe was at war. From my Genevan adolescence I still have a very good
friend, Dr. Simon Ishvinski. The Swiss are very reserved people. I had three
friends: Simon Ishvinski, Slatkin, and Maurice Abramowicz, a poet who is
now dead.

You remember him in "Los Conjurados."

Yes. It was a beautiful night. María Kodama [Borges's secretary, traveling companion and, during his final weeks, wife], Maurice Abramowicz's widow and I were at a Greek tavern in Paris, listening to Greek music, which is so full of courage. I remembered the lyrics: "While this music lasts, we will deserve Helen of Troy's love. While the music lasts, we will know that Ulysses will come back to Ithaca." And I felt that Maurice was not dead, that he was there with us, that nobody really dies, for they all still project their shadow.

In "Los Conjurados" you also speak about one of your nightmares. Do some repeat themselves?

Yes. I dream of a mirror. I see myself with a mask, or I see in the mirror somebody who is me but whom I do not recognize as myself. I arrive at a place, and I have the sense of being lost and that all is horrible. The place itself is like any other. It is a room, with furniture, and its appearance is not horrible. What is atrocious is the feeling, not the images. Another frequent nightmare is of being attacked by beings who are children; there are many of them, very little but strong. I try to defend myself, but the blows I give are weak.

In "Los Conjurados," as in all your work, there is a permanent search for meaning. What is the sense of life?

If life's meaning were explained to us, we probably wouldn't understand it. To think that a man can find it is absurd. We can live without understanding what the world is or who we are. The important things are the ethical instinct and the intellectual instinct, are they not? The intellectual instinct is the one that makes us search while knowing that we are never going to find the answer. I think Lessing said that if God were to declare that in His right hand He had the truth and in his left hand He had the investigation of the truth, Lessing would ask God to open His left hand—he would want God to give him the investigation of the truth, not the truth itself. Of course he would want that, because the investigation permits infinite hypotheses, and the truth is only one, and that does not suit the intellect, because the intellect needs curiosity. In the past, I tried to believe in a personal God, but I do not think I try anymore. I remember in that respect an admirable expression of Bernard Shaw: "God is in the making."

Even though you present yourself as a nonbeliever, there are in your work some references to mystical experiences that have always puzzled me. In the story "The God's Script" you say: "From the tireless labyrinth of dreams I

*returned as if to my home, to the harsh prison. I blessed its dampness, I
blessed its tiger, I blessed the crevice of light, I blessed my old, suffering
body, I blessed the darkness and the stone. Then there occurred what I cannot
forget nor communicate. There occurred the union with the divinity, with the
universe." It seems that when you accept your circumstances and you bless
them, then you come back to your center, and clarity dawns upon you. In the
story "El Aleph" too, only when you accept your circumstances do you get
to see the point where every act in the whole history of the cosmos comes
together.*

This is true. It is the same idea. Since I do not think often about what I
have written, I had not realized that. Nevertheless, it is better that it should
be instinctive and not intellectual, don't you think? The instinctive is what
counts in a story. What the writer wants to say is the least important thing;
the most important is said through him or in spite of him.

*Another idea that appears in many of your stories is that of the union of all
creatures. In "The God's Script" the pagan priest realizes that he is one of
the threads of the whole fabric and that Pedro de Alvarado, who tortured
him, is another one. In "The Theologians," Aureliano and Juan de Panonia,
his rival, are the same; and in "The End" Martin Fierro and El Negro have
one and the same destiny.*

That is true. But I do not think about what I have already written; I think
about what I am going to write—which is usually what I have already written,
lightly disguised. Let's see. These days I am writing a short story about
Segismund, one of the characters of "La Vida Es Sueño." We will see how
it turns out. I am going to read "La Vida Es Sueño" again, before writing
the story. I thought of it some nights ago. I woke up; it was about 4 o'clock
and I could not get back to sleep. I thought, let's use this sleeplessness. And
suddenly I remembered that tragedy by Calderón, which I must have read 50
years ago, and I told myself, "There is a story here." It should resemble (but
not too much) "La Vida Es Sueño." To make that clear, it is going to be
titled "Monologue of Segismund." Of course, it will be quite a different
soliloquy than the one in that play. I think it is going to be a good story. I
told it to María Kodama, and she approved of it. It has been some time since
I wrote a story. But that is the source of this one.

*What is the source of "The God's Script"? When the priest says the fact that
a prison surrounded him was not an obstacle to his finding the clue to the
hidden language, I thought that was similar to what happened with you and
your blindness.*

I lost my sight some years later. But in a certain way there is a purification in the blindness. It purifies one of visual circumstances. Circumstances are lost, and the external world, which is always trying to grab us becomes fainter. But "The God's Script" is autobiographical in another sense. I united there two experiences. Looking at the jaguar in the zoo, I thought the spots on the jaguar's skin seemed to be a writing; that is not true of the leopard's spots or the tiger's stripes. The other experience was the one I had when, after an operation, I was forced to lie on my back. I could only move my head to the right or left. Then I put together the idea that occurred to me, that the jaguar's spots suggest a secret writing, and the fact that I was virtually imprisoned. It would have been more appropriate to the story for the main character not to have been a priest from a barbarian religion but a Hindu or a Jew. However, the jaguar had to be placed in Latin America. That impelled me toward the pyramid and the Aztecs. The jaguar could not appear in other scenery. Although Victor Hugo describes the Roman circus and says that among the animals there are *"jaguars enlacés,"* that is impossible in Rome. Maybe he mistook leopards for jaguars, or maybe he did not mind that sort of mistake, just as Shakespeare didn't.

Like the kabbalists, you try to find in that story the sense of God's writing. You consider that the whole cosmos could be present in one word. How do you personally conceive the beginning of the universe?

I am naturally idealistic. Almost everyone, thinking about reality, thinks of space, and their cosmogonies start with space. I think about time. I think everything happens in time. I feel we could easily do without space but not without time. I have a poem called "Cosmogony" in which I say it is absurd to think the universe began with astronomical space, which presupposes, for example, sight, which came much later. It is more natural to think that in the beginning there was an emotion. Well, it is the same as saying, "In the beginning was the Word." It is a variation on the same theme.

Can we find a relationship among the various conceptions about the origin of the universe among the Greeks, the Pythagoreans, the Jews?

Strangely enough, they all start with astronomical space. There is also the idea of the Spirit; that would come prior to space, of course. But in general they think of space. The Hebrews believe that the world was created from a word of God. But then that word should exist prior to the world. Saint Augustine gave the solution to that problem. Let's see, my Latin is poor, but I remember the phrase: *"non in tempore sed cum tempore Deus creavit . . .* I do not know what . . . *ordinem mundi.*" That means, "Not in time but with time God created the world." To create the world is to create time. If not, people would ask, what did God do before creating the world? But with this explanation they are told that there was a first instant without a before. This is inconceivable, of course, because if I think of an instant I think of the time before that instant. But they tell us that, and we rest content with the inconceivable. An infinite time? A time with a beginning? Both ideas are impossible. To think that time began is impossible. And to think that it doesn't have a start, which means that we are going, in Shakespeare's words, to "the dark backward and abysm of time," is also not possible.

I would like to come back to the idea of the word as origin of the world. For example, in the Hebrew tradition there is a search through cryptographic and hermeneutic methods for that exact word.
   Yes, that is the kabbala.

Not long ago Haaretz, a newspaper in Israel, reported that computer experiments on the Bible had discovered in Genesis a secret clue that had remained hidden up to then and that is too complicated to have been thought of by human beings. The letters that form the word "Torah" appear all through Genesis, one by one, in strict order, at regular intervals of 49 letters, perfectly integrated into the words that compose the text.
   How strange that the computer would be applied to the kabbala! I did not know that they were making those experiments. It is beautiful, all that.

Is it necessary to prove that the Scriptures are the revealed word of God in order to believe in the existence of God, or is that something that is felt regardless of proofs?
   I cannot believe in the existence of God, despite all the statistics in the world.

But you said you believed some time ago.
   No, not in a personal God. To search for the truth, yes; but to think that there is somebody or something we call God, no. It is better that He should not exist; if He did he would be responsible for everything. And this world is often atrocious, besides being splendid. I feel more happy now than when I was young. I am looking forward. Even I don't know what forward is left, because at 86 years of age, there will be, no doubt, more past than future.

When you say you are looking forward, do you mean looking forward in continuing to create as a writer?

Yes. What else is left for me? Well, no. Friendship remains. Somehow, love remains—and the most precious gift, doubt.

If we did not think of God as a personal God but as concepts of truth and ethics, would you accept Him?

Yes, as ethics. There is a book by [Robert Louis] Stevenson in which we find the idea that a moral law exists even if we don't believe in God. I feel that we all know when we act well or badly. I feel ethics is beyond discussion. For example, I have acted badly many times, but when I do it, I know that it is wrong. It is not because of the consequences. In the long run, consequences even up, don't you think? It is the fact itself of doing good or doing bad. Stevenson said that in the same way a ruffian knows there are things he should not do, so a tiger or an ant knows there are things they should not do. The moral law pervades everything. Again the idea is "God is in the making."

What about truth?

I don't know. It would be very strange for us to be able to understand it. In one of my short stories I speak about that. I was rereading "The Divine Comedy," and, as you will remember, in the first canto, Dante has two or three animals, and one of them is a leopard. The editor points out that a leopard was brought to Florence in Dante's time and that Dante, like any citizen of Florence, must have seen that leopard, and so he put a leopard into the first canto of the "Inferno." In my story, "Inferno, I, 32." I imagine that in a dream the leopard is told it has been created so Dante can see it and use it in his poem. The leopard understands that in the dream, but when he awakens, naturally, how could he understand that he exists only so a man could write a poem and use him in it? And I said that if the reason he wrote "The Divine Comedy" had been revealed to Dante, he could have understood it in a dream but not when he awoke. That reason would be as complex for Dante as the other one was for the leopard.

In "The Mirror of Enigmas," you say, quoting Thomas De Quincey, that everything is a secret mirror of something else. That idea of the search for a hidden sense is in all your work.

Yes, I think so. It is a very common human ambition—is it not?—to suppose everything has an explanation and to think we could understand it. Let's take as an example the various conceptions about the origin of the world, of which we spoke a while ago. I cannot imagine an infinite time, nor a beginning of time, so any reasoning about that is barren, since I can't conceive of it. I haven't arrived at anything. I am just a man of letters. I am not sure I have thought anything in my life. I am a weaver of dreams.

Since we have spoken about the kabbala, that is, about the studies to decipher the word of God, let's speak about the Bible. What do you think about the inspiration of the Bible?

What I find very strange is the fact that the Hebrews did not take into account the various authors or the different epochs when the books were written. It is strange to see everything in the Bible as a creation of the Spirit, which inspires those who write it, through different epochs. It is never thought, for example, that the works of Emerson, Whitman and Bernard Shaw have the same author. But the Hebrews took writers that were many miles and centuries apart and attributed their work to the same Spirit. It is a strange idea, is it not? Nowadays we think of authors, even of entire literatures, as consecutive. But they didn't. They saw everything as written by one author, and that author was the Spirit. Maybe they thought the circumstances of the writing do not matter, that the circumstances are trivial, that history is trivial. "The Bible"—the name is plural—comes from "the books" in Greek. It is a library, really, and a very heterogeneous one too. It is evident that the author of the Book of Job cannot be the author of Genesis, nor can the Song of Songs or Ecclesiastes and the Book of Kings have the same author. It is as if the individuals did not matter, nor the epochs, nor the chronological order. All is attributed to only one author, the Spirit.

One of the fundamental books of the kabbala, the "Sefer Yezirah" ("Book of Creation"), deals with the 10 Sefirot. That term means "numbers," and they are taken to be an emanation from God, the Ein-Sof. Should we think, then, that the First Being is a cipher, that He is abstract?

I feel that the First Being, the Ein-Sof, cannot be defined. It cannot even be said that He exists. Even that is too concrete. Then you cannot say that He is wise or that He knows. Because if He knows, then there are two things— the known and the One who knows. And that is too detailed for God. He should be an indefinite divinity. And then from there spring forth the "10 emanations," or Sefirot, and one of them creates this world. It is the same idea as, the Gnostics had, that this world was created by a subaltern god.

[H. G.] Wells had that idea also. That way you explain imperfections such as evil, diseases, physical pains, so many things. Because if an absolute God had made the world, he would have done it better, no? Instead, He has made our bodies, which are very liable to err, decompose and become diseased; the mind also decomposes, and it fails with age, and, well, there are so many other objections.

In the "Zohar" ("The Book of Splendor"), which Gershom Scholem considers the most important literary work of the kabbala, there are many speculations about life after death. Swedenborg describes in detail hells and paradises. Dante's poem is also about hell, purgatory, paradise. Where does this tendency of man come from, to try to imagine and describe something that he cannot possibly know?

In spite of oneself, one thinks. I am almost sure to be blotted out by death, but sometimes I think it is not impossible that I may continue to live in some other manner after my physical death. I feel every suicide has that doubt: Is what I am going to do worthwhile? Will I be blotted out, or will I continue to live on another world? Or as Hamlet wonders, what dreams will come when we leave this body? It could be a nightmare. And then we would be in hell. Christians believe that one continues after death to be who he has been and that he is punished or rewarded forever, according to what he has done in this brief time that was given to him. I would prefer to continue living after death if I have to but to forget the life I lived.

Index

Hardy, Thomas, 116; "Hap," 87
Harte, Bret, 45
Hawthorne, Nathaniel, 45, 84, 131–32; *The Scarlet Letter,* 132; *Twice-told Tales,* 132; "Wakefield," 40, 132
Hegel, Georg, 80
Heine, Heinrich, 190, 203, 213; "Abroad," 202–03; *Book of Songs (Buch der Lieder),* 202, 216
Hemingway, Ernest, 106
Hepburn, Katharine, 223
Hernández, José, 48, 49, 56; *Martín Fierro,* 48, 98
Herrera y Reissig, Julio, 67
Hidalgo, Bartolomé, 48
High Noon, 64
Hiroshima Mon Amour, 64
Hitchcock, Alfred, 64
Hitler, Adolph, 21, 27, 52, 113
Hládik, Jaromir, 25
Hoffmann, E. T. A., 78
Hölderlin, Friedrich, 146
Homer, 5, 206; *The Iliad,* 25, 73
Hopkins, Gerard Manley, 98
Hopkins, Miriam, 223
Hudson, William Henry, *The Purple Land that England Lost,* 98
Hugo, Victor, 47, 102, 115, 168, 206, 239, 243; "Boaz Endormi," 102
Hume, David, 80, 85, 130; *Treatise Concerning Natural Religion,* 125

Ibsen, Henrik, 65, 154
Ingenieros, Cecilia, 222
Innis, Michael, 24
Ishvinski, Doctor Simon, 240

James, Henry, 4, 8, 34–35, 37–38, 45, 84, 132, 194; "The Abasement of the Northmores," 37; "The Turn of the Screw," 37; *What Maisy Knew,* 39
James, William, 85
Johnson, Dr. Samuel, 118, 209; *Dictionary,* 93, 127, 142
Jonson, Ben, "Childe Roland to the Dark Tower Came," 1
Joyce, James, 10, 192, 215; *Finnegan's Wake,* 157–58, 159; *Ulysses,* 35–36, 39, 100–01, 166
Julian the Apostate, 226

Kafka, Franz, 37, 132, 142, 159–60, 193, 213–20; *Amerika,* 217; "Cares of a Family Man," 215; "The Metamorphosis," 213,

216, 219; *The Trial,* 37; "Troubles of a Householder," 215
Kant, Immanuel, 160
Keats, John, 215; "Chapman's Homer," 110
Kipling, Rudyard, 10, 41, 98, 151, 155, 156, 172, 203, 206, 238, 240; "The Ballad of East and West," 204; "Beyond the Pale," 115; "Children of Antioch," 159; "Harp Song of the Dane Women," 116; *The Jungle Book,* 160–70; *Kim,* 10, 109; *Plain Tales from the Hills,* 3, 83, 114, 194; *Second Jungle Book,* 169–70; "Wireless," 111
Klee, Paul, 173
Klemm, Wilhelm, 213, 216
Kodoma, María, 112, 209, 223, 237, 241, 242
Kunitz, Stanley, "After Pastor Bonhoeffer," 108

Lafinur, Luis Melián, 56
Láinez, Manuel Mujica, 67
Lang, Andrew, *Modern Egyptians,* 29
Lanusse, González, 167, 168
Larco, 33
Last Year in Marienbad, 64
Lawrence, D. H., 116
Lebrun, Rico, 96
Lessing, Gotthold, 150, 241
Levingston, President Roberto, 109
Lewis, Sinclair, 108
Light, Nora, 168
London, Jack, 45, 210
Longfellow, Henry, 84; "The Grave," 101
Longinus, 5
Lovecraft, H. P., 40, 41, 182
Lugones, Leopoldo, 47, 48–49, 58, 66, 67, 70, 98, 141, 146, 167–68, 191, 203, 207, 209; *Lunario sentimental,* 49; *El Payador,* 167–68; *Strange Forces,* 49; "Yzur," 49
Luther, Martin, 128

Machado, Antonio, 69, 173
Machado, Manuel, 69, 173
Mallarmé, Stéphane, 128
Mallea, Eduardo, 67
Man for All Seasons, A, 64
Marchand, Paul, 169
Marlowe, Christopher, 82, 142, 209
Mastronardi, Carlos, 48, 49, 104; "Light of the Province," 49
Melville, Herman, 45, 84, 131, 194, 203; "Bartleby the Scrivener," 40; *Moby Dick,* 39, 187
Meredith, George, 108
Meyrink, Gustav, 202–03; *The Angel of the Western Window,* 203; *Bats,* 203; *The Golem,* 203; *The Green Face,* 203